P9-DUT-435

STRATEGY AND STRUCTURE OF BIG BUSINESS

The International Conference on Business History 1

STRATEGY AND STRUCTURE OF BIG BUSINESS

Proceedings of the First Fuji Conference

edited by
KEIICHIRO NAKAGAWA

UNIVERSITY OF TOKYO PRESS

Published by
University of Tokyo Press
UTP 3334-47060-5149
Printed in Japan

ISBN 0–86008–170–2

COMMITTEE FOR THE CONFERENCE

Moriaki Tsuchiya
(University of Tokyo)
Tadakatsu Inoue
(University of Kobe)
Kesaji Kobayashi
(Ryukoku University)
Hidemasa Morikawa
(Hosei University)
Keiichiro Nakagawa
(University of Tokyo)
Akio Okochi
(University of Tokyo)
Yoshitaro Wakimura
(University of Tokyo)
Shigeaki Yasuoka
(Doshisha University)
Shin-ichi Yonekawa
(Hitotsubashi University)

Participants

Raymond Benish
(University of Tokyo)
Alfred D. Chandler, Jr.
(Harvard University)
Toshiaki Chokki
(Hosei University)
Richard Dyck
(Harvard University)
Johannes Hirschmeier
(Nanzan University)
Yoshio Hon-iden
(Dokkyo University)
Tadakatsu Inoue
(University of Kobe)
Ryushi Iwata
(Musashi University)
Yoshio Katsura
(University of Kobe)
Nobuo Kawabe
(Waseda University)
Yosuke Kinukasa
(Yokohama Municipal University)
Kesaji Kobayashi
(Ryukoku University)
Yasuo Mishima
(Konan University)
Mataji Miyamoto
(Kwansei Gakuin University)
Hidemasa Morikawa
(Hosei University)
Keiichiro Nakagawa
(University of Tokyo)
Tsutomu Nakamura
(Nanzan University)
Hisaichi Nakase
(Osaka Industrial College)
Junko Nishikawa (Tokyo Metropolitan College of Commerce)
Akio Okochi
(University of Tokyo)
Yotaro Sakudo
(University of Osaka)
Koichi Shimokawa
(Hosei University)
Tsuneo Shinozaki
(Otaru Commercial College)
Mitsuzo Tamura
(Meiji University)

Kin-ichiro Toba
(Waseda University)
Yoshio Togai
(Senshu University)
Moriaki Tsuchiya
(University of Tokyo)
Yoshitaro Wakimura
(University of Tokyo)
Charles Wilson
(Cambridge University)
William Wray
(Harvard University)

Yukio Yamashita
(Chuo University)
Norio Yanagihara
(Kyoto Industrial College)
Kenichi Yasumuro
(Kurume University)
Shigeaki Yasuoka
(Doshisha University)
Shin-ichi Yonekawa
(Hitotsubashi University)
Tsunehiko Yui
(Meiji University)

CONTENTS

PREFACE

In modern society, because of the internationalization of business activities, it is becoming urgently necessary to have an understanding of the differences and similarities among the business enterprises of various countries. It is true that in terms of business technique or business practice many common concepts have been formed and used, but the peculiar characteristics of business behavior based upon the nationals social, or cultural heritage still appear to strongly persist, despite the growing trend of internationalization in business activities. Take Japanese business, for example, without a knowledge of such peculiarities in the employment system as lifetime commitment and seniority, Japanese business cannot be understood nor the direction of its future development predicted.

As far as academic studies in Japan are concerned, it was the Business History Society of Japan, founded in 1964, that first took up these problems and promoted intensive studies. In fact, for the past few years the society has organized its annual meetings around such topics as the international comparison of business enterprise and the characteristics of business management in Japan.

In addition to our growing concern, foreign business historians have become increasingly interested in the traditional aspects of Japanese business. Foreign business historians could make valuable contributions in many respects, especially by throwing light on aspects which, partly because of being native born, we Japanese business historians too easily overlook. We have much to contribute to the knowledge of foreign scholars as well. Foreign scholars often do not have full access to information concerning the tradition of business enterprise in Japan; nor have they often been able to enjoy the insight which only personal observations gained through the experience of living in Japan can provide. The same is true with respect to foreign studies by Japanese.

Under these circumstances, it seemed it would be most effective to have joint meetings of foreign and Japanese business historians to discuss problems relating to the different characteristics of business among the nations. We believe that through such joint meetings we shall be able to gain clues to understanding what should be accepted as internationally common features, and what should be maintained as peculiarities of each country.

Thanks to the Taniguchi Industrial Foundation, the Japan Business History Society has had the good fortune to be funded for the convening of such international meetings once a year for five years. The first meeting was held on January 5th through 8th, 1974, at the Fuji Education Center, Susono, Shizuoka, with the topic of international comparison of strategy and structure of big business as its central theme. Two pioneering experts on this topic, Professor Alfred D. Chandler, Jr. (Harvard University) and Charles Wilson (Cambridge University) were invited to participate in the meeting. Names of all participants are listed on page v of this book.

The meeting was a very exciting one for all participants and was successful from many points of view. This book is a record of the proceedings of the meeting. Reading through these pages, one can perhaps imagine the lively exchange of ideas that took place during the conference.

I gratefully acknowledge all contributions to the meeting, and must say a special word of thanks to the members of the organization committee for their devoted efforts in organizing and managing the conference. Miss Jacqueline Kaminski helped us with English corrections and typing. This book could not have been published without her hard work.

Keiichiro Nakagawa
Editor

PART I

STRATEGY AND STRUCTURE IN JAPANESE BUSINESS

I–1

Business Strategy and Industrial Structure in Pre-World-War-II Japan

Keiichiro Nakagawa
University of Tokyo

1. Industrialization Led by the Government: Investment into External Economies

Japan just after the Meiji Restoration was basically a country with a peasant economy, and in order to industrialize quickly she had to create not only various Western styles of manufacturing industries but also almost all of the modern economic institutions and business organizations which were to form the external economies for industrial enterprises. In other words, entrepreneurial opportunities were opened widely in Japan in the varied fields of national economy, but, on the other hand, the accumulation of capital resources and entrepreneurial abilities were very much limited. Therefore, the central government had to take the lead for industrialization, and only a limited number of entrepreneurs, who had accumulated initial capital through economic activities closely related with government initiative, could seize and venture into various entrepreneurial opportunities. As a matter of course, diversification became a dominant feature of the Japanese entrepreneurship from the very start of industrialization in this country.

A) Investment in Modern Systems of Communication and Transportation

The Meiji government leaders who visited the developed countries of the West were most impressed by the railway and telegraph, and the steamship had been a symbol of Western power ever since Commodore Perry's visit to Japan. It seems quite natural that the Meiji government pushed the construction of such means of communication and transportation. By 1880 almost all the major cities of Japan had been linked by a government-owned telegraph network. The government had to take the lead also in railway construction since in mountainous Japan it was more difficult and expensive than the construction of a telegraph network. The eighteen-mile Tokyo-Yokohama line, the first railway in Japan, was opened in 1872, and the forty-seven-mile Kyoto-Kobe line was also completed in 1877.

The unexpected success of the government-owned Tokyo-Yokohama line, the profit rate of which in 1886 was 20% on its capital investment, encouraged private entrepreneurs. In 1881, a group of aristocrats, mostly former feudal lords, led in the establishment of the Nippon Railway Company to construct the 529-mile line between Tokyo and Aomori. With a guarantee by the central government of an 8% annual net return, and carrying raw silk and silks, the largest items of Japan's export in those days, the first private railway enterprise also proved a success, and by 1885 had grown into the largest joint-stock company in Japan, leading to the subsequent railway mania. By 1890, 1,368 miles of private lines, nearly three times the length of the total government lines, had been established by ten joint-stock companies, the four largest of which were the Nippon, Sanyo, Kyushu, and Hokkaido-Tanko railway companies. From the fact that in each of these larger lines the number of freight cars was 2.4 to 14 times greater than the number of passenger cars, it is evident that these lines were of great industrial use.

The government itself did not invest in the shipping industry as aggressively as in railways. By 1868 the shogunate, or central government, and the local lords already owned 138 modern ships, including warships, and the new government had to be satisfied with these for the time being. But the Formosa Expedition, the growing hostility with Korea, and the Satsuma Rebellion in the 1870s made the government seriously conscious of the shortage of shipping tonnage. Conspicuously generous subsidies were then afforded to the Mitsubishi Company of Yataro Iwasaki, an ex-samurai who had started in 1870 a coastal shipping service using the ships of his lord. The company was lent, or given for nothing, about forty steamers the government had bought abroad or inherited from the shogunate, and the Mitsubishi Company itself bought fourteen large steamers with a low-interest government loan. With this fleet of ships, the company undertook military transportation in the successive wars, prevailing over the Pacific Mail and P. & O. on the Yokohama–Shanghai line. At the end of 1877, the Mitsubishi Company owned 73% of the total tonnage of modern steamers in Japan.

Many shippers and local shipowners became critical of such a monopoly, and in 1882 the Kyodo Unyu Company was organized by Eiichi Shibuzawa and other leading businessmen through the integration of smaller-scale shipowners. This company was also generously subsidized by the government, and the two major companies, Mitsubishi and Kyodo, competed with each other by reducing freight rates drastically. The government took the initiative in 1885 for the merger of the two, resulting in the formation of the Nippon Yusen Kaisha (NYK), to which the government guaranteed an 8% net return for fifteen years. As the Mitsubishi Company had already acquired more than 50% of the shares of Kyodo, they could continue to control the new NYK, although it was formally separated from the Mitsubishi Company.

B) The Promotion of Financial and Trading Organizations

The establishment of the modern monetary system or banking organizations was the most urgent task for the new Meiji government which had been forced to use the wealthiest traditional merchants such as the Mitsui and the Ono as the temporary government financial agents. Although the National Bank Act of 1872, which copied the American national banking system, authorized the issue of national bank notes, the wealthy merchant class was not responsive to it. The government was able to force only four national banks to be established, one by the Mitsui and the Ono, who had accumulated resources by the lucrative dealings with government funds, and others by a group of raw silk dealers in Yokohama, a group of wealthy rural landlords in a prosperous rice-producing area, and a group of ex-samurai leaders in Satsuma Prefecture.

In 1876, the government revised the National Bank Act, releasing the national banks from the obligation of converting bank notes into specie and allowing 80% of their capital to be subscribed in the form of government bonds. The response to this new act surpassed government expectations, and by the end of 1879, 153 national banks had been established, and of their total capital of ¥40.62 million over 29 million was in samurai pension bonds.

But wealthy merchants also did not stay away from the bank mania. Some of the major national banks were promoted by the Konoike family, the greatest money-changer in the Tokugawa era, and other rich local merchants closely connected with traditional tea manufacturing and raw silk reeling. In addition, the merchant class became more enthusiastic in the promotion of private banks. Already in 1876, the Mitsui family was allowed to use the term *bank* for its monetary transactions, and thus the Mitsui Bank became the first and largest private bank in Japan. The house of Mitsui had developed over two centuries and, with the wealth amassed and the financial acumen acquired, became the financial agent for the new Meiji regime, underwriting the government bonds and new currency, in exchange for the privilege of availing themselves of government funds at no interest. Even after the formation of the Mitsui Bank, nearly half of the bank deposits continued to be government money.

The Meiji government also earnestly promoted the establishment of powerful trading companies. In Western countries, the merchant class had been actively engaged in extensive foreign trade for a long time before the industrial revolution. But Japan had been secluded from foreign countries for two and a half centuries and on the eve of urgent industrialization there was neither any experience nor any organization for foreign trade. To break through the import and export monopoly of the foreign merchants at the Yokohama and Kobe settlements and to compete successfully with the overseas foreign trade network of the advanced countries, organization of mighty trading firms was an imperative task in the investment in external economies. Again the Mitsui family responded quickly to this overwhelming need by promoting in 1876 Mitsui Bussan, which became the sole agent for the government-owned Miike Coal Mine, and, for the export of Miike coal, established an overseas marketing network which covered several Asian ports, such as Tientsin, Shanghai, Hong Kong, and Singapore. Within ten years, the coal exported by this first bona fide foreign trader increased to almost 200,000 tons a year, yielding a handsome profit to the company.

C) Sales of Government Enterprises as an Opportunity for Diversification

The Meiji government had established public enterprises as "pilot plants" to demonstrate to private entrepreneurs essential features of western industrial civilization. These included mines, cotton-spinning mills, a silk-reeling mill, cement works, glass works, and several shipbuilding yards. But to cover the shortage of national funds, the government decided in 1880 to sell out the pilot plants to private entrepreneurs. But capital accumulation and entrepreneurial abilities in the private sector were still limited, and there were few spontaneous undertakers of the pilot plants, even though the government reduced gradually the prices of the government enterprises.

The government enterprises themselves had generally been equipped with the newest technology from the Western countries, but most of them had not yet yielded a profit, probably on account of the bureaucratic management and limited domestic market. Eventually the people who had acquired the monetary resources and entrepreneurial experiences through economic activities closely related with the government had to appear again as the buyers of government enterprises.

The house of Mitsui purchased a silk filature and a cotton spinning mill in addition to the highly prosperous Miike Coal Mine, for which Mitsui Bussan had been a sole agent. Mitsubishi acquired another rich coal mine, the Takashima mine, and also the Nagasaki shipbuilding yard as well as the Sado gold and Ikuno silver mines. The Takashima mine had been modernized by 1874 by Thomas Glover, an English merchant, in cooperation with the lord of Saga, introducing English mining technology, and it was sold first to Shojiro Goto, a government leader who was a friend of Yataro Iwasaki. But Goto could not maintain the operation of the mine and it was finally acquired by the Mitsubishi Company. Anyhow, it is noteworthy that

Mitsui and Mitsubishi diversified themselves into mining through purchases of government enterprises.

The mining business in those days can be considered to some extent an investment in external economy. The gold, silver, and copper mines were closely connected with the government mint and other systems of modern currency. Even coal was not primarily used as the source of energy for domestic industries, but a major part of it was exported to the Asian coaling stations for earning foreign currency.

The sales of government enterprises also afforded new economic opportunities for pioneering entrepreneurs other than Mitsui and Mitsubishi. Ichibei Furukawa, a manager of the silk export branch of the Ono family, had operated the Ashio Copper Mine since 1877, and in 1885 he purchased two government copper mines, the Ani and Innai, together with the newest foreign-made equipment and educated engineers. He transferred the machines, equipment, and engineers to the Ashio mine to modernize it, and within ten years the output of Ashio increased tenfold. With the increasing profit Furukawa continued to purchase new mines, and around 1890 produced 40% of the national output of copper.

Soichiro Asano, a coal dealer, earned windfall profits by selling unused coke, the by-products of the Yokohama Gasworks, to the Fukagawa government cement works. In 1883 Asano purchased the Fukagawa Works, and from 1884 to 1889 the output of the Asano Cement Works increased fivefold. Shozo Kawasaki, who purchased the Hyogo Shipbuilding Yard, was once a pioneering shipowner, and after trials and failures in the establishment of a modern shipbuilding yard at Tokyo Bay, the government offered to sell him the Hyogo Shipbuilding Yard. It seems that the government highly appreciated Kawasaki's experience and avoided the double sale of the government yards to the Mitsubishi Company, which had already purchased the Nagasaki yard.

Generally speaking, unprofitable government enterprises turned profitable under the management of private entrepreneurs, for the domestic market had just started to grow and the initial risk of new business had already been undertaken by the government. At any rate, we should keep in mind that the sales of government enterprises not only gave rise to several prosperous pioneering entrepreneurs but also provided opportunities for further diversification of already diversified enterprises.

D) Business Organizations of the Banks, Railways, and Diversified Enterprises

One aspect of Western civilization the Meiji government tried most earnestly to introduce into Japan was the system of the joint-stock company. But at the beginning the traditional merchant class could not understand, and even hated, working by joining stock with other people, in spite of the Ministry of Finance's effort at education by publishing books and pamphlets on the joint-stock system.

The National Bank Act issued in 1872 declared that the national bank should be established as a chartered joint-stock company on the principle of limited liability, and the revised National Bank Act of 1876 attracted the ex-samurai who had been trained in functional activities in the feudal bureaucracy of the lords' governments. They could understand the functional authority based on limited holding. The national banking mania from 1876 to 1879 was thus really the first stage in popularizing the joint-stock company system in Japan. Although the general law of incorporation was not yet issued, the people were in actuality free to promote joint-stock companies under the supervision of prefectural authorities, and since the late 1870s a limited number of joint-stock companies started to be promoted in the railway, insurance, shipping, spinning, and other fields.

The following table shows the joint-stock companies with capital of more than 200,000 at the end of 1885:

Company Name	Year of Foundation	Amount of Capital	Notes
Nippon Railway	1881	20,000,000	
Nippon Yusen	1885	11,000,000	shipping
Osaka Merchant Marine	1884	1,800,000	
Kosaka Mining	1884	601,168	copper
Tokyo Marine Insurance	1879	600,000	
Osaka Cotton Spinning	1883	600,000	
Oji Paper Mills	1873	500,000	
Ani Mining	1885	337,766	copper

Komaki Mining	1884	300,000	
Kuwabara Cotton Spinning	1882	250,000	
Copper Manufacturing	1881	250,000	(copper rolling plant in Osaka)
Choseikan	1875	257,000	copper smelting
Cotton Spinning	1883	201,420	(former government mills at Hiroshima)
Osaka Warehousing	1883	200,000	
Tokyo Stock Exchange	1878	200,000	
Osaka Stock Exchange	1878	200,000	
Fujita	1869	200,000	copper mining
Innai Mining	1885	200,000	copper

Almost all the above companies capitalized at more than 500,000 yen were owned by a number of subscribers beyond the kinship and local communities. For example, there were 9,520 stockholders for Nippon Railway at the time of promotion, 590 for Osaka Merchant Marine, 203 for Tokyo Marine Insurance, and 95 for Osaka Cotton Spinning. But the stocks of the mining companies, among which we notice many former government enterprises, were not generally made public in the capital market, but were usually owned by an individual or a kinship group. For example, Ichibei Furukawa owned and operated the Ani and Innai mines as his family fortunes, as he hated to "bow to majority decisions." It was also same with the Fujita Company which owned and operated the Kosaka Mining Company. Even the largest family enterprises such as Mitsui and Mitsubishi did not invite subscribers in the public market in spite of their extensive diversification at this stage.

The total capital of the Mitsui Bank was subscribed by the Mitsui Family Partnership or Omotokata (¥100 million), the eight Mitsui families (¥50 million) and the Mitsui employees (¥50 million yen). Mitsui Bussan was first organized as a separate partnership of the two young family members, and as it was a partnership without capital, profit earned by the resources loaned by the Mitsui Bank was to be the revenue of the Mitsui Family Partnership. The Miike Coal Mine had been owned and operated by Mitsui Bussan until 1892 when it was combined with the Kamioka Copper Mine, purchased in 1886, to form the Mitsui Mining Limited Partnership, totally owned by the Mitsui Family Partnership. In addition to the above three lines of business—banking, trading, and mining—the Mitsui family controlled the cloth retailing enterprise (*gofuku* store) as a separate business and had already ventured into paper manufacturing as the largest shareholder of the Oji Paper Mills since its establishment in 1873.

The Mitsubishi Company separated its shipping business to form the NYK in 1885, and then poured its resources into the development of the Takashima coal mine, the Yoshioka copper mine, and others, as well as the Nagasaki Shipbuilding Yard. The coal from the Takashima mine was sold at Asian ports as bunker coal for steamers, some of which entered the Nagasaki port to be repaired at the Mitsubishi Shipbuilding Yard. The Mitsubishi Company, totally owned by the Iwasaki family, continued to be a major shareholder of the NYK, and the family itself had owned since 1879 one-third of the total shares of the Tokyo Marine Insurance Company.

In any case, it is remarkable that the diversified enterprises comprising the biggest units in each field of the national economy continued to be entirely family-owned businesses in spite of the aggressive propaganda by the government for the joint-stock company system. To a certain extent this is probably explained by certain traditional factors, as in the case of Mitsui, but in the period of rapid industrialization when new entrepreneurial opportunities were successively opened, the system of "majority decisions" of joint-stock companies was evidently seen as unfit for aggressive entrepreneurship, as we can perceive from the statement by Ichibei Furukawa quoted above. As the best enterprises were thus self-financed by Mitsui and Mitsubishi, and secondary enterprises, such as the Furukawa Mines and Kawasaki Shipbuilding Yard, were owned as family possessions, the stock exchanges, opened in Tokyo and Osaka as early as in 1878, had to remain as speculative markets rather than investment markets. Dealing in a limited number of stocks, including the stocks of the stock exchanges themselves, they could not perform the function of normal price formation until the boom from 1887 to 1889, when many joint-stock companies were promoted in the field of railways and cotton spinning.

The railway mania in this period turned out again to be the chance for further diversification of the diversified zaibatsu enterprises. Especially the Iwasaki family, which had already been a major shareholder of the Nippon Railway Company, invested in the largest of the newly promoted railway companies, such as the Sanyo Railway (Kobe to Shimonoseki), the Kyushu Railway (Moji to Kumamoto), and the Chikuho Railway, which ran through the northern Kyushu coal basin to the port of Wakamatsu. These family investments seem to have been related to the Mitsubishi Company because the top executives of the company joined each railway company as a member of the promoting committee or the board of directors.

2. Entrepreneurial Performance and Business Organization before World War I

Overall development of single-product enterprises in Japan was achieved during the boom from 1887 to 1889 by the promotion of large joint-stock companies in the cotton spinning industry. As we can perceive from Table 1, this industry was to play a leading role in Japan's economic growth and was promoted by nonzaibatsu entrepreneurs (mostly merchants and local landowners) whose relations with the government were not close. In 1896 there were already flourishing more than twenty cotton mills equipped with the newest frames (mostly Ring frames). But on account of the ingrained taste of the Japanese people for sophisticated fabrics and of the dominant existence of a network of middlemen since the Tokugawa period, it was not easy for the large-scale cotton spinning mills to capture the overall domestic market by integrating forward into weaving, not to mention the difficulty of selling their products directly to the consumer market. They became inevitably aggressive in the export of their products to the continental market and, for the export of cloth as well as for the import of raw cotton, they became gradually dependent on general trading companies such as Mitsui Bussan. In other words, without integrating into marketing and/or purchasing, they had to remain single-product and single-function firms. We can perceive the same trend, to some extent, in other consumer-goods industries such as sugar refining and flour milling. On the other

TABLE 1 The Fifty Largest Manufacturing and Mining Companies in 1896.

Company Name	Total Assets (unit: ¥1,000)	Company Name	Total Assets (unit: ¥1,000)
1 Kanegafuchi Cotton Spinning	3,284	26 Senju Paper Mills	642
2 Osaka Cotton Spinning	2,413	27 Kyoto Textile Mills	639
3 Mie Cotton Spinning	2,245	28 Tokyo Woolen Mills	627
4 Hokkaido Flax Spinning	1,506	29 Shimotsuke Flax Spinning	614
5 Settsu Cotton Spinning	1,436	30 Nagoya Cotton Spinning	610
6 Okayama Cotton Spinning	1,397	31 Kurume Cotton Spinning	599
7 Tokyo Cotton Spinning	1,358	32 Meiji Cotton Spinning	587
8 Kanekin Cotton Weaving	1,333	33 Kishiwada Cotton Spinning	547
9 Osaka Alkali Mfg.	1,309	34 Osaka Woolen Spinning	539
10 Amagasaki Cotton Spinning	1,264	35 Osaka Beer Brewery	511
11 Oji Paper Mills	1,230	36 Tokyo Ishikawajima Shipyard	510
12 Naniwa Cotton Spinning	1,204	37 Osaka Copper Mfg.	494
13 Nihon Cotton Spinning	1,151	38 Koriyama Cotton Spinning	492
14 Fuji Paper Mills	1,111	39 Fukuyama Cotton Spinning	460
15 Miike Cotton Spinning	1,019	40 Osaka Sulphic Acid and Soda	457
16 Owari Cotton Spinning	908	41 Nippon Beer Brewery	440
17 Daiichi Silk Spinning	786	42 Osaka Cement Works	438
18 Senshu Cotton Spinning	735	43 Kasaoka Cotton Spinning	437
19 Onagawa Cotton Weaving	726	44 Wakayama Cotton Weaving	426
20 Tamashima Cotton Spinning	704	45 Jukuhi Mfg. (leather)	426
21 Kurashiki Cotton Spinning	703	46 Hokkaido Cement Works	407
22 Asahi Cotton Spinning	673	47 Sakai Cotton Spinning	406
23 Fukushima Cotton Spinning	670	48 Iwaki Coal Mining	401
24 Hosokura Mining	655	49 Tsushima Cotton Spinning	386
25 Sapporo Sugar Mfg.	643	50 Yokohama Shipbuilding Yard	385

hand, the lines of enterprise functions being thus limited, a cartelization movement was to be intensified in the cotton industry as long as individual firms were not controlled by the diversified zaibatsu groups.

After the end of the nineteenth century, the heavy industries, such as the shipbuilding and iron and steel industries, started to grow rapidly by aggressive technological borrowing and/or direct government investment. But because the mechanical engineering and steel industries had not developed ahead as in the English case, the shipbuilding industry in Japan could not develop as an assembly industry, and most of the shipbuilding yards tended to diversify into mechanical engineering and steel industries. In the case of Japanese iron and steel industries, the take-off had to be achieved by large-scale combined iron and steel mills, established by the government itself, and such government mills were forced to produce diversified products for private as well as public markets.

In the course of the industrial development stated above, the joint-stock company system, which had been introduced at the very start of Japan's industrialization, was extensively applied to a number of new industrial firms, and such development gave rise to a new type of specialist corporation manager, who was again to accelerate the development of joint-stock companies in all economic fields in Japan except agriculture and small-scale retailing. On the other hand, the zaibatsu family businesses, such as the Mitsui and Mitsubishi, having developed through the investment in external economies, became increasingly diversified into various kinds of new industries, and on the eve of World War I they had already promoted the organization for controlling their diversified enterprises.

A) The Wholesale Development of Single-Product Firms in the Cotton-Spinning Industry

Although at the end of 1885 there already existed nine cotton-spinning firms, their scale, except for the Osaka Cotton-Spinning Mills, was too small to be competitive with the overseas mills. Osaka Cotton Spinning, established in 1883 with 10,500 spindle mule frames, developed quickly into a competitive firm equipped with more than 40,000 spindles (mostly the newest Ring frames), working twenty-four hours a day on the two-shift system, facilitated by the pioneering adoption of the incandescent electric light in their factory. The success of this mill, which yielded from 16 to 18% dividends on its stocks, stimulated the promotion of cotton spinning firms in the period between 1887 and 1889 when the rate of interest had been reduced through the financial reorganization by the finance minister, Masayoshi Matsukata.

Among the twenty pioneering new mills, the larger were the Kanagafuchi, Tokyo, Settsu, Hirano, Naniwa, Kanekin, Temma, Owari, and Miike spinning companies. Most of them were promoted by the merchants and landlords in and around the cities of Osaka, Tokyo, and Nagoya, who had been more or less connected with traditional cotton trade. In addition to the fact that none of them alone had the resources to promote a modern cotton mill, we should also notice that the educated engineers did not like to be employed by family businesses. In fact, some engineers worked for several joint-stock company mills on account of the scarcity of trained and educated engineers in those days, and we may say that the new mills introduced Western business organization, that is, the joint-stock company, together with Western industrial technologies. In addition, many of the major shareholders invested in the stocks of several mills, just as in the case of American cotton spinning mills on the Merrimack established by the Boston Associates, and such relations among the leading mills were evidently to accelerate the subsequent cartelization and merger movement in the Japanese cotton-spinning industry.

By 1897 when the total value of the export of cotton yarn exceeded for the first time that of import, the number of spindles increased to 970,000, thirteen times greater than ten years before. But the cotton-spinning mills in Japan could not cultivate the total domestic textile market. The modern Japanese continued in general to dress in kimono made of silk, cotton, or linen, fabricated by the traditional producers. They preferred cloth with delicate striped patterns, which the power looms in large-scale mills could not produce. Some of the leading cotton-spinning mills integrated forward into weaving broadcloth on the power looms introduced from England and America. But the traditional pattern of consumption as well as the network of middlemen, established between producers and consumers since the Tokugawa period to cater to the ingrained traditional taste of the people for fabrics, precluded the establishment of an appropriate market for the mass-produced plain cloth. With such a limited domestic market, the six largest cotton mills, which had established their own power-loom weaving mills at the end of the nineteenth century, consumed even in 1914 only 19% of the cotton yarn they produced.

The rapid development of cotton-spinning mills had already led to overproduction in 1890, when the Japan Cotton Spinners' Association executed the first curtailment of operations, repeated again in 1899 and 1900. The association became the largest and strongest cartel in Japan, and on account of the low domestic demand, it curtailed the operation of cotton-spinning mills for nearly six of the eight years after 1907. Meanwhile merger movements were simultaneously accelerated. Kanegafuchi merged with Miike and seven other mills to become the largest cotton mill in Japan. Osaka, which had absorbed Kanekin, merged in 1914 with Mie, which had already integrated with Owari, Nagoya, and five other mills in the Nagoya district, and the resulting Toyo Cotton-Spinning Mill became the second largest. Settsu first merged with Hirano, integrated later with Amagasaki, which had absorbed Tokyo, and thus developed into the third largest, the Dainihon Spinning Mill. In this way the number of cotton-spinning mills among the top fifty public manufacturing joint-stock companies was reduced from twenty-nine in 1896 to nine in 1919, as is shown in Table 2.

In the course of this struggle for survival, the cotton-spinning mills became aggressive in their search for overseas markets, and for both overseas marketing and purchasing raw cotton, Japanese cotton mills became precipitatedly dependent on the general trading firms (*sogoshosha*) owned by the diversified zaibatsu combines. For example, Osaka, Kanekin, and Mie formed, in 1906, the Sanei Export Association for exporting their products to the Korean market, making Mitsui Bussan the sole agent of the association. In the same year, Osaka, Kanekin, Mie, Okayama, and Temma organized the Japan Cotton Cloth Export Association to capture the Manchurian market, and again Mitsui Bussan was entrusted the role of organizer in this market. We may thus say that Mitsui Bussan played a role similar to that of the Manchester shippers in the English cotton industry.

But in addition, they also had to perform the function of the Liverpool Cotton Exchange. Japan had imported raw cotton from various sources in China, India, America, and so on, and the skillful mixing of various kinds of raw cotton, acquired at low cost, for spinning good yarn of standard quality became the vital factor for the rapid development of the Japanese cotton industry. But an extensive raw cotton market such as the Liverpool Cotton Exchange could not develop

TABLE 2 The Fifty Largest Manufacturing and Mining Companies in 1919.

Company Name	Total Assets (unit: ¥1,000)	Company Name	Total Assets (unit: ¥1,000)
1 Kawasaki Shipbuilding Yard	171,448	26 Asano Cement Works	30,123
2 Mitsubishi Shipbuilding Yard	133,002	27 Tokyo Iron and Steel	29,995
3 Kuhara Copper Mining	101,531	28 Meiji Sugar Refing	29,529
4 Kanegafuchi Cotton Spinning	84,316	29 Uraga Shipbuilding Yard	29,524
5 Toyo Cotton Spinning	72,940	30 Tokyo Gas Electric Mfg.	28,183
6 Dainihon Cotton Spinning	69,738	31 Teikoku Sugar Mfg.	26,237
7 Mitsubishi Mining	67,980	32 Tainan Sugar Mfg.	23,432
8 Hokkaido Coal Mining and Shipping	61,973	33 Dainihon Chemical Fertizers	22,917
9 Taiwan Sugar Mfg.	53,519	34 Teikoku Flax Spinning	22,411
10 Fuji Cotton Spinning	48,525	35 Shibaura Electric Works	22,134
11 Dainihon Sugar Refining	47,012	36 Dainihon Beer Brewery	21,998
12 Mitsubishi Iron and Steel	46,942	37 Ishikawajima Shipbuilding	21,562
13 Oji Paper Mills	46,673	38 Fukushima Cotton Spinning	20,452
14 Nihon Oil Refining	43,999	39 Kobe Steel Works	20,059
15 Osaka Ironworks (shipbuilding)	43,009	40 Tokyo Rope Mfg.	19,063
		41 Naigai Cotton Spinning	18,752
16 Fuji Paper Mills	42,138	42 Nihon Nitrogen Fertizers	18,586
17 Nihon Steelworks	41,057	43 Kishiwada Cotton Spinning	18,046
18 Nihon Steel Tube Mfg.	38,213		
19 Nihon Woolen Mills	36,212	44 Kurashiki Cotton Spinning	18,016
20 Yokohama Shipbuilding Yard	34,750	45 Saghalien Mfg. (paper)	16,347
21 Ensuiko Sugar Mfg.	32,804	46 Kawakita Electric Works	15,814
22 Tokyo Woolen Mills	32,302	47 Dainihon Celluloid Mfg.	15,368
23 Osaka Godo Cotton Spinning	31,184	48 Niitaka Sugar Mfg.	15,113
24 Toyo Sugar Mfg.	30,947	49 Osaka Alkali Mfg.	14,941
25 Hoden Oil Refining	30,350	50 Muslin Spinning and Weaving	14,769

in Japan, and therefore the general merchants, who had established worldwide trading networks, served again as an organization for securing enough raw cotton of appropriate quality at the lowest price. The Kanegafuchi mills, of which the Mitsui family had been the largest shareholder since its beginning, had contracted a "special contract" with Mitsui Bussan for an advantageous discount on the price of raw cotton on the condition that Kanegafuchi guarantee to purchase a fixed amount of raw cotton over a long period.

Anyhow, the Japanese cotton mills had thus to depend, on the one hand, entirely on the established chains of middlemen for marketing their products in the domestic market and, on the other hand, on the general merchants (*sogoshosha*) for overseas marketing and the purchasing of raw cotton. They could integrate neither forward nor backward and had to stay as single-product and single-function firms, until they started to be diversified in the 1920s and 1930s into man-made silk, woolen, and other textile industries. But the Japanese cotton industry could cultivate the vast and profitable Asian market, and most of the cotton mills were allowed to develop rather independently from the government and zaibatsu control. In the case of the sugar industry, another big consumer-goods industry before World War II, major mills were far more tightly controlled by the zaibatsu combines and were more seriously influenced by the government economic policy.

B) Development of Heavy Industries: Shipbuilding and Iron and Steel

As far as technology was concerned, the Japanese shipbuilding industry could catch up rather easily to the European level. The technological innovation in the European shipbuilding industry was very rapid in the latter half of the nineteenth century—from wooden to iron and steel ships, from paddle to screw steamers, from reciprocating to compound, triple compound, and turbine engines. Therefore, the shipbuilding industry in Japan could develop rapidly by borrowing, mostly from England, the newest technologies, and in 1907 the Nagasaki Shipbuilding Yard of Mitsubishi launched two oceangoing steamers driven by turbine engines, which were the largest in the world (13,000 tons each).

In addition, the growing market for shipbuilding yards was created by the Shipbuilding Subsidies and Shipping Subsidies Acts, issued in 1896. Especially after 1899, when the latter act was revised to reduce the amount of subsidy given to a ship ordered from an overseas yard to half that given to a ship ordered from a domestic yard, the orders to the Japanese shipbuilding yards grew rapidly, and in 1901 the total value of steel ships built at the domestic yards became larger than that of the imported steel ships. Out of the total 310,000 tons of ships built through the Meiji period on the shipbuilding subsidies, 200,000 tons were built by the Mitsubishi yards, 77,000 tons by the Kawasaki yard, 30,000 tons by Osaka Ironworks, and 25,000 tons by the Ishikawajima yard. The Japanese Navy also appreciated the technological progress at the Japanese shipyards and started in 1911 to order capital warships from the domestic yards. Subsequently, the scale of the yards was further enlarged, and Kawasaki and Mitsubishi became the top two of fifty public manufacturing joint-stock companies in 1919.

But the Japanese shipbuilding companies could not develop as single-product firms. Because in Japan the shipbuilding industry developed ahead of the mechanical engineering industry, all the shipbuilding yards had to build their own engines as well as hulls from the beginning, in sharp contrast to the English shipbuilding firms who could purchase engines built by developed engineering firms. Some yards started also to produce their own steel products. In addition, since government subsidies were allowed only to ships larger than 1,000 tons, the smaller-scale yards could not be maintained without diversifying themselves into other lines of products. For example, the Ishikawajima Shipbuilding Company was extensively employed in the manufacturing of mining machines, rolling stocks, bridges, structurals, cranes, etc.

Whereas the Japanese shipbuilding firms were favored with considerable demand by the navy and growing mercantile marines, they found it difficult to export ships, primarily because of the shortage and high cost of raw materials, iron and steel, in Japan. The application of chemical science to industry, skillful plant engineering, and above all the huge amount of capital to be invested in iron and steel mills seem still to have been unsurmountable barriers for the Japanese entrepreneurs before World War I. In this industry, investment was also restrained on account of the lack of rich iron ore mines in Japan. In 1896, primarily for the purpose of furnishing steel to arsenals and naval shipyards, the government decided to establish themselves an epoch-making iron and steel mill, the Yawata Iron and Steel Mills. The plan to produce 90,000 tons of steel per year was formulated on the German model of combined iron and steel mills, and, securing iron ore from the Ta Yeh mines in China, they started the operation of the first furnace in 1901. But it was not until 1910 that the mills could overcome various initial barriers and yield a profit. These barriers included the structural defects of the furnace and coke oven and the unskillful operation of the melting furnace.

At the end of the nineteenth century, the iron and steel mills in Europe and America were highly developed, already applying the devices for a fuel economy. In 1896 60% of the iron and 95% of the steel consumed in Japan was imported from advanced countries. It is little wonder that no one but the government could promote modern iron and steel mills that were competitive in scale and technology with the European and American mills. On the other hand, the government Yawata works could not be devoted to the production of steel only for the arsenals and naval shipyards. The large amount of iron required by open-hearth furnaces of competitive scale could not be produced for such a limited public market, and the Yawata works was rapidly diversified into the production of rails, structurals, and other products for the private market.

It may also sound strange to say that Japanese private steel mills started from the fabrication of steel goods for the arsenals and naval shipyards. The Sumitomo family, who had operated the Beshi Copper Mine since the early Tokugawa period and had established a copper rolling plant in Osaka, diversified into the steel industry at the turn of century. In 1901 they established the Sumitomo Steel Works for casting steel products for naval use and steel wheels and shafts for rolling stocks, and in 1912 started to roll jointless steel tubes for naval use. Sumitomo, since 1901, had already been operating the first open hearth in Japan.

The Suzuki Company in Kobe, which was to become the second largest general merchant (*sogoshosha*) during the boom of World War I, had already established the Kobe Steel Works in 1905, which developed primarily as the designated plant of the naval shipyards until they discovered a wider market in the booming private shipbuilding yards during the First World War.

The Kawasaki Shipbuilding Yard also started in 1906 to produce cast, forged, and rolled steel goods at their Hyogo plant, and the Nippon Steel Tube Company was established in 1912 by Soichiro

Asano, Eiichi Shibusawa, and others to manufacture steel tubes by the Mannesman type of drilling machines, from the raw steel produced by their own open hearth from the Indian pig iron which was soon to be imported in growing volume. At any rate, on account of such private steel mill development, the share of domestic steel production in the total domestic steel consumption grew from 0.5% in 1896 to 44% in 1914.

One of the questions left unanswered is why usually resourceful Mitsui and Mitsubishi did not move aggressively into the iron industry. In addition to the expected difficulties of private iron mills, suggested above, the failure of the governmental Kamaishi Iron Works during the early Meiji period and the prolonged hardship at the Tanaka Iron Mill, which succeeded the Kamaishi works in 1885, can be considered reasons why Mitsui and Mitsubishi declined to enter the iron industry. The Tanaka works could not work on a continuing basis until the Sino-Japanese War (1894–95) in spite of persevering efforts by educated engineers, and even in 1912 the works could not produce more than 50,000 tons of pig iron and 10,000 tons of steel.

C) Development of the Joint-Stock Companies and the Establishment of Zaibatsu Control

The joint-stock company system, which had been introduced in Japan through the two promotion booms, that is, the national bank mania from 1876 to 1879 and the railway and cotton mills mania from 1887 to 1889, was more widely applied to other industrial enterprises after the issue of the General Incorporation Act in 1893 and through the industrial booms during and after the Sino-Japanese War (1894–95) and Russo-Japanese War (1904–05) as is seen in Table 2. (Almost all the companies in Table 2 had been established before World War I although they expanded markedly during the war.) In short, the joint-stock company system had within forty years after its introduction spread into all the major fields of the Japanese economy except agriculture and retailing. It may be said that this rate of expansion was several times greater than that of England.

There are several reasons for such a rapid development of the joint-stock company system. First, new industries in Japan had to start as large-scale competitive firms by absorbing resources from the public money market. Second, the newest Western industrial technologies introduced were accompanied by the newest business organization. Third, the educated sons of ex-samurai preferred to be employed by joint-stock enterprises rather than by traditional family businesses. Fourth, members of family enterprises that expanded through investment in external economies at the early stage of industrialization turned to investment in new industries in the form of joint-stock companies.

With such development of joint-stock enterprises in various industries, a new class of specialist corporation managers emerged, especially after the middle 1890s when the Mitsui combine was reorganized by Hikojiro Nakamigawa, a president of the Mitsui Bank. Being enthusiastic for the industrialization and modernization of the Mitsui family business, he recruited many able college graduates, mainly from Keio University, and put them in charge of the various sections of the reorganized Mitsui combine, paying them exceptionally high salaries. These policies attracted an increasing number of able and reliable young men to the business world, and the joint-stock companies, staffed with such specialist managers, grew more prosperous and started to attract public investors.

The rise of the new class of corporation managers gave rise to another type of diversified investment in various product lines. In addition to high salaries, corporation managers were usually given a substantial executive bonus, and with the sum thus amassed, most of them gradually became major shareholders of their companies. Some of them also invested their own recources in the stocks of various kinds of other prospective companies, usually becoming the directors of these industrial firms and thus earning more executive bonuses. It was not uncommon for a leading businessman to serve as a member of the board of directors in more than thirty joint-stock companies. Needless to say, such practices often led to unreliable management and business failures.

But such irresponsible entrepreneurship could not prevail in the enterprises controlled by the zaibatsu combines. The head offices of Mitsui and Mitsubishi were already well organized, as elucidated by Professor Morikawa, and their individual industrial enterprises were closely supervised by the zaibatsu banks and their markets shrewdly organized by their general merchants (*sogoshosha*). For example, through the reorganization of the Mitsui family business by H. Nakamigawa, referred to before, each of their four main enterprises, banking, trading, mining, and cloth retailing, was formalized into a legal partnership (*gomeikaisha*) in 1893, and the industrial department established the following year was authorized to control all the subsidiary manufacturing firms, such as the Kanagafuchi Cotton Mills, Oji Paper Mills, and Shibaura Electric Works.

Bolstered by such organization, Mitsui became more active in diversification, utilizing their bank and trading company as channels for development. Kanegafuchi and Oji had already come into the combine through an active loan by the Mitsui Bank. The Mitsui Mining Company, the most prosperous at this period with its rich Miike coal mine, provided the combine sufficient resources to acquire several new mines in fierce competition with Mitsubishi and Sumitomo, and Mitsui succeeded in 1913 in gaining control of the Hokkaido Coal Mining and Shipping Company with its newly created Nihon Steel Mill, again through a daring bank loan to rescue it from bankruptcy.

On the other hand, Mitsui Bussan extended its network as a sole agent in close cooperation with the Mitsui Bank. Mitsui Bussan, first establishing its trading network at the Asian port cities for the export of Miike coal, later rapidly extended its network to Paris, New York, London, Bombay, Yingkou, Taipei, San Fransisco, Hankow, and Sydney, primarily for exporting coal, raw silk and silks, cotton yarns, and cotton cloths, and for importing raw cotton, raw sugar, wheat, wool, and machines. By 1907 it was already trading in more than 100 articles, and in 1913 it handled 25.8% of the national foreign trade. As a matter of course, more and more industrial firms had to depend on such *sogoshosha* for their marketing and purchasing activities, and several first-rate industrial firms, such as Taiwan Sugar Refining and Onoda Cement, came into Mitsui Bussan's network, which acted as their sole agent.

Mitsui Bussan extended its control over industrial firms by the active introduction of foreign technology. The company had imported, mainly from England, various machines for textile industries and the materials and equipment for the railway industry. For the products of the Pratt Brothers in particular, the company had been a sole agent in the Asian market. With such transactions, its staff accumulated knowledge and information about Western industrial technology. An industrial firm which was going to venture into a new industry or to replace old equipment had to rely on Mitsui Bussan's staff located in London, New York, and Hamburg to decide what kind of technology should be introduced. The industrial firms, which thus imported machines and equipment through Mitsui, usually appointed it as their sole agent, and some of them eventually became new members of the Mitsui combine.

To solidify and to mobilize this diversified enterprise, three major partnerships, the Bank, Bussan, and Mining, were reorganized in the period between 1907 and 1911 into joint-stock companies, and the administrative department (*kanribu*) of the Mitsui Family Partnership was also incorporated into a legal partnership, the Mitsui Company (*Mitsui Gomei*) to hold the stocks of the three newly established joint-stock companies.

The course of the development of Mitsubishi in this period was to some extent the same as that of Mitsui, although the trading activites of the former were fairly backward compared with those of the latter, and all the lines of Mitsubishi business were organized just as departments in the Mitsubishi Limited Partnership. The combined effort of the banking and trading department proved to be a powerful means for acquiring and controlling new mines in the Kyushu and Hokkaido areas. But the Mitsubishi Company in its early stage of development can be considered primarily a mining enterprise combined with shipbuilding. In addition to the Takashima Coal Mine, which produced coal of the best quality, it owned and operated the Yoshioka, Osaruzawa, Makimine, and many other high-yield copper mines as well as the Sado gold and Ikuno silver mines. Some of these mines had a high profit return, as copper was one of the most important of Japan's exports throughout the nineteenth century. Furthermore, we should remember that the stock dividend from the Nippon Yusen Kaisha (NYK) was the largest item in the company's revenue.

In the initial stage of Mitsubishi Limited Partnership, the general manager of the central office, Heigoro Shoda, himself controlled directly about fifteen operating units (*jigyosho*), composed of nine mines, four trading branch offices, and the Nagasaki shipyard. But in the following years three departments were soon organized in the central office: the banking department in 1895, the coal sales department in 1896, and the mining department in 1897, and a vice-general manager was appointed in charge of each department. The 119th Bank, in which the Iwasaki family was the major shareholder, was disorganized in 1896 and was absorbed into the banking department. Basically this line of organization did not change until the World War I era, except that the coal sales department was reorganized into the trading department to deal in copper as well as coal, and the shipbuilding department was created in 1907 to administer the newly established Kobe shipyard together with the Nagasaki yard. Then the mining department was divided in 1912 into two departments, coal mining and metal mining.

The trading department was concerned mainly with dealing in products from within the combine, and the diversification of the Mitsubishi Company at this period was not so extensive as that of the Mitsui combine. Since 1890 they had been operating a real estate business in order to develop the business center of Tokyo, and since 1899 they had owned the Tokyo Warehousing Company. But it must be kept in mind that the Iwasaki family itself had ventured into various fields of enterprise. In 1898 the family organized the Kobe Paper Mills as a limited partnership, taking over the paper mills which had been a joint venture of the family with the Walsh Brothers, a prosperous American enterprise in the Yokohama settlement. They had also promoted the pioneering Asahi Glass works in 1907 and since 1899 had owned the extensive Koiwai Farm for breeding the best stock of horses and cows. Further, the Iwasaki family, together with NYK and Mitsubishi executives, became the major shareholder in 1907 of the Kirin Beer Brewery and in 1911 of the Inawashiro Electric Power Company, not to mention the three major railway companies which were nationalized in 1907.

3. Entrepreneurship and its Organization in the Course of "Heavy Industrialization" Since World War I

Investment in heavy industries in Japan was promoted first during World War I by the stoppage of the import of iron, steel, and chemical products, and secondly by the development of the electric power industry during and after World War I. But the aggressive leadership in this heavy industrialization was taken mainly by nonzaibatsu entrepreneurs, some of whom later developed into the "new zaibatsu" entrepreneurs. Through the long and severe economic stagnation and depressions after the First World War, many of the inefficient firms created during the boom of the war went bankrupt, and as a result of the failures and difficulties of the smaller local banks, the zaibatsu banks fortified their monetary control over the national economy. With such consolidated monetary powers, the "old zaibatsu" combines, such as Mitsui and Mitsubishi, led the second stage of heavy industrialization, especially in the course of the militarization of the Japanese economy after the Manchurian Incident in 1931. Under the influence of these general factors in the interlude between wars, the total output of light and heavy industries was ¥7,224 and ¥10,102 million respectively in 1937, whereas it had been ¥626 and ¥168 million in 1909. In Table 3, we notice the dominant existence of heavy industrial firms among the top fifty industrial and mining companies.

A) The Development of Heavy Industries Accelerated by the Rising Electric Power Industry

The incandescent electric light was introduced into Japan at the very start of Japan's industrialization, as mentioned above in connection with the Osaka Cotton-Spinning Mills. The Tokyo Electric Light Company, with steam power stations, was established in 1883, and in 1892 the Kyoto City Authority constructed a water power station to supply electricity for its tramways as well as for household light. Local water power stations emerged in many areas, utilizing abundant water resouces in Japan, and the construction of water

TABLE 3 The Fifty Largest Manufacturing and Mining Companies in 1940.

Company Name	Total Assets (unit: ¥1,000)	Company Name	Total Assets (unit: ¥1,000)
1 Nihon Iron and Steel	1,242,321	26 Mitsubishi Electric Mfg.	164,994
2 Mitsubishi Heavy Industries	969,491	27 Furukawa Electric Industries	159,964
3 Oji Paper Mills	562,088	28 Dainihon High-Frequency Industries	159,956
4 Hitachi Electric Works	552,515	29 Dainihon Sugar Refining	158,706
5 Nihon Mining	547,892	30 Taiwan Sugar Refining	158,186
6 Nihon Nitrogen Fertizers	540,344	31 Nihon Steel Works	143,143
7 Kanegafuchi Cotton Spinning	434,716	32 Meiji Sugar Refining	140,906
8 Tokyo Shibaura Electric Works	414,761	33 Diesel Automobile Mfg.	138,595
		34 Nihon Light Metals	136,880
9 Mitsubishi Mining	407,555	35 Dainihon Beer Brewery	134,133
10 Sumitomo Metal Mfg.	380,200	36 Katakura Silk Spinning	132,809
11 Showa Steel Mills	378,961	37 Ensuiko Sugar Mfg.	127,908
12 Nihon Steel Tube Mfg.	324,017	38 Asano Cement Works	123,742
13 Kawasaki Heavy Industries	306,616	39 Nippon Oil and Fats	122,940
14 Toyo Cotton Spinning	284,444	40 Kureha Cotton Spinning	122,124
15 Mitsui Mining	283,604	41 Nihon Electric Mfg.	121,831
16 Honkeiko Iron Mills	280,201	42 Asahi Glass Works	120,020
17 Dainihon Cotton Spinning	235,839	43 Rasa Mfg.	114,125
18 Nihon Soda Mfg.	234,754	44 Osaka Ironworks	106,032
19 Kobe Steel Works	222,219	45 Manchurian Light Metals	105,277
20 Nissan Chemical Industries	212,353	46 Nihon Woolen Mills	105,187
21 Showa Electric Chemicals	209,917	47 Sumitomo Mining	103,064
22 Korean Nitrogen Fertilizers	206,873	48 Sumitomo Electric Industries	101,484
23 Nihon Fisheries	199,028		
24 Hokkaido Coal Mining and Shipping	190,487	49 Naigai Cotton Spinning	101,315
		50 Asahi Bemberg Silk Spinning	100,153
25 Nihon Oil Refining	170,791		

power stations by large joint-stock companies was accelerated, especially after 1907 when Tokyo Electric Light succeeded in transmitting power over eighty kilometers to Tokyo. By the end of the Meiji period about twenty joint-stock companies had been established in this industry, and most of the stocks of these companies were subscribed by local landlords and businessmen. The zaibatsu combines, however, were rather indifferent to this new industry since they had monopolized the alternative source of energy, the rich coal mines.

During the 1910s and 1920s the supply of power increased at the annual rate of 30%, and, as the demand for power for the lamp business was almost satisfied, the price of electric power relative to steam power declined. This trend stimulated, first, the development of electric chemical industries, such as the carbide, ammonium sulphate, and electrolysis soda industries, which had already started during the war in response to the decline in imports of chemical goods. Secondly, it gave a boost to the construction of electric railways and in turn activated a rolling stock industry and the building of traction engines in electric manufacturing firms.

Jun Noguchi, a sales engineer of a German firm, Siemens, established, in 1908, the Nihon Nitrogen Fertilizers Company to produce calcic nitrogen fertilizer, utilizing the unused water power generated by the station he himself established in southern Kyushu. Before long he turned to the production of sulphic ammonium from calcic nitrogen, and, helped by the reduction in imports of this fertilizer during the war, his firm expanded rapidly, appearing in 1919 among the top fifty manufacturing and mining firms. Immediately after the war, Noguchi established a new plant to produce synthetic ammonium sulphate by the Italian method, and his company diversified also into the production of man-made silk, establishing the Asahi Bemberg in 1931. Building huge water power stations and chemical fertilizer plants in Korea as well, Noguchi's enterprise developed as a leading new zaibatsu combine, controlling more than twenty joint-stock companies by the end of the 1930s.

For manufacturing soda the Japanese firms had long relied on the traditional Lebrun method, probably because the Solvey Company had insisted on 100% shareholding for the export of their patent. But, during the war, when the import of Brunner & Mond soda was suspended, Arinori Nakano started to produce electrolysis soda, and his Nihon Soda Company gradually diversified into mining, iron and steel, man-made silk, and pulps. The development of the electric power industry gave rise also to the metal chemical industry, and the leading entrepreneur in this field was Nobuteru Mori, who had also diversified his enterprise organically into the manufacturing of various products such as aluminum, electric copper, kali, soda, explosives, and synthetic ammonium sulphate, leading eventually to the formation of the Showa Electric Manufacturing Company, which controlled his various chemical industrial enterprises as well as several electric power stations.

Whereas the above three new zaibatsu started from the electric chemical industry, the largest new zaibatsu, Nissan, originated in mining. Fusanosuke Kuhara developed and modernized the Hitachi Copper Mine by employing trained and educated engineers, and in 1912 incorporated the Kuhara Mining Company which earned a windfall profit during World War I so that by 1919 it had become the third largest industrial firm. During the war boom period, Kuhara Mining diversified into two lines: first into electric manufacturing, and secondly into various other noncopper businesses, such as shipping and trading. The electric works in the Hitachi Copper Mine, established originally for repairing apparatus for the company's own use, was incorporated into an independent Hitachi Electric Works in 1920 and, relying mainly on its own technological innovation, developed by 1940 into the largest electric manufacturing firm. But the second line of diversification, shipping and trading, was simply speculative and was a complete failure. In addition, the international price of copper fell precipitously during the postwar depression, and the management of Kuhara Mining, which was on the verge of bankruptcy, was taken over in 1926 by Yoshisuke Ayukawa, who reorganized and developed it into the Nissan combine.

Ayukawa had operated the Tobata Cast Steel Works and succeeded in the postwar period in producing, by the electric furnace, malleable cast iron for the use of naval shipyards and the national railway authority. Ayukawa reorganized Kuhara Mining into a new holding company, Nihon Sangyo (shortened to Nissan), all stocks of which were sold in the public stock market. It seems that, like all the new zaibatsu, handicapped by the lack of his own "agent bank," Ayukawa tried to appeal to public investors. On the other hand, the mining department and power stations of the company were incorporated respectively into the Nihon Mining and the Hitachi Electric Power companies, and in the course of rapid diversification, Nihon Fishery, Nissan Chemical Industries, Nihon Oil and Fats, and Nissan Motors were also incorporated to be controlled, together with Hitachi Electric Works, as the subsidiaries of Nihon Sangyo. Ayukawa had studied in America in his youth, and it seems that he applied the method of stratified holding companies which was invented by Samuel Insull. At any rate, the Nissan group thus grew into the largest new zaibatsu and controlled more than eighty firms by the middle of the 1930s.

B) Diversification of the Diversified Old Zaibatsu Combines

As already stated, before World War I Mitsui and Mitsubishi had purchased and controlled many independent industrial firms through two channels for their diversification, that is, their own banking and trading activities. Because those industrial firms had passed the unprofitable gestation stage, and, furthermore, were furnished with adequate resources by the zaibatsu banks, they quickly became highly profitable. They could now expand by ploughing back their own profits, without offering their stocks for public subscription. In proportion to the ability of zaibatsu subsidiaries to be thus self-financed, the role of zaibatsu banks as "agent banks" decreased after the beginning of this century. On the other hand, since many nonzaibatsu banks went into bankruptcy through frequent crises after the Russo-Japanese War and World War I, the deposits of the Japanese people as a whole became increasingly concentrated in the major zaibatsu banks. It is no wonder that the zaibatsu banks ventured into financing the development of new industries during and after World War I. For example, the development of the electric light and power industries and the electric railway industry was financed in the 1920s by the flotation of debentures which were aggressively underwritten by zaibatsu banks. But simultaneously the zaibatsu combines themselves ventured into various new industries, especially into heavy industries.

a) *The Case of Mitsubishi*

Mitsubishi incorporated several divisions of the Mitsubishi Limited Partnership and established the Mitsubishi Shipbuilding Company in 1917, the Mitsubishi Warehousing Company, Mitsubishi Trading

Company, and Mitsubishi Mining Company, all in 1918, and the Mitsubishi Bank Limited in 1919. The fourth president of Mitsubishi, Koyata Iwasaki, primarily an industrialist, was aggressive in investing in heavy industries. In 1917 he established the Mitsubishi Iron and Steel Mills and began operating three melting furnaces and two open hearths on the Daido River in Korea to supply steel for building warships. He also established Mitsubishi Combustion Engines in 1920 and started to build the engines for aircraft at the Kobe Shipbuilding Yard. This company established a large aircraft building plant at Nagoya and, in 1929, absorbing the above combustion engine department, developed into the Mitsubishi Aircraft Company. The electric manufacturing department at the Kobe Shipbuilding Yard was also incorporated into the Mitsubishi Electric Manufacturing Company in 1921 to build generators, steam turbines, and other apparatus, and in 1923 it succeeded in introducing American technology from Westinghouse in exchange for 10% of its total shares. The Mitsubishi Trading Company had been the sole agent in Japan of the Associated Oil Company of America since 1923, and in 1931 a joint venture, Mitsubishi Oil Refining, was established by Associated Oil (50%), Mitsubishi Limited Partnership (30%), Mitsubishi Trading (10%), and Mitsubishi Mining (10%) to improve the domestic technology of oil refining. Finally, in 1934 the Mitsubishi Shipbuilding Company, composed of four shipyards, was merged with the Mitsubishi Aircraft Company, and by absorbing also the Yokohama Shipbuilding Yard, the newly formed Mitsubishi Heavy Industries became the largest industrial firm in the combine.

Generally speaking, the old zaibatsu which had owned rich coal mines were not enthusiastic about diversifying into electric chemical industries. But in the 1930s the price of electric power began to rise owing to the limited water resources combined with the growing demand from rapid heavy industrialization, and thus the opportunities were now open for coal chemical industries. The Mitsubishi Mining Company joined in 1934 with the Asahi Glass Works of the Mitsubishi combine to establish an integrated chemical industrial firm to produce from coal synthetic dyestuff, fertilizers, and other products, introducing the newest German technology of synthethic ammonium from the I. G. Farben Company.

In the meantime, Mitsubishi also incorporated Mitsubishi Warehousing, Mitsubishi Marine and Fire Insurance, Mitsubishi Trust Company, and Mitsubishi Real Estate, and maintained its major share holdings in the NYK, Tokyo Marine Insurance, and other companies. The diversification of Mitsubishi in the 1920s, it may be said, occurred because the profit rate from its coal mining was declining, owing to the increasing output of electric power, and also because its shipbuilding yards were idle on account of the worldwide disarmament movement at that time. Therefore it seems quite natural that Mitsubishi, which had been far less diversified than Mitsui, now became quite aggressive in promoting various new enterprises, mainly in the field of heavy industries. These newly promoted enterprises were mostly from within the Mitsubishi combine itself. It can be argued also that Mitsubishi incorporated its banking, mining, trading, and shipbuilding departments simply in order to raise the resources necessary for such diversification from the public money market, but in fact the number of shares made public was rather limited. We should also keep in mind that Mitsubishi had secured enormous resources through the nationalization of some trunk-line railways in which it was a major shareholder.

b) The Case of Mitsui

The development of the Mitsui combine since World War I was due mainly to the growing prosperity of its major subsidiaries, Bussan, Mining, Bank, Oji Paper Mills, Shibaura Electric Works, and Hokkaido Mining and Shipping. In addition, the prime mover for diversification was not the Mitsui Company (*Mitsui Gomei*) itself, but these prosperous subsidiaries.

Mitsui Bussan, which had already established its shipping department in 1896, created a shipbuilding department in 1917 primarily to repair the increasing tonnage of its own ships. The next year, to insure the growing number of ships and cargos, Mitsui Bussan established Taisho Marine Insurance as a subsidiary, and in 1920 separated its raw cotton division, incorporating it as the Toyo Raw Cotton Trading Company to deal in the growing import of raw cotton. But the most aggressive venture of Mutsui Bussan in this period was the establishment of the Toyo Rayon Company in 1926. Though raw silk had been the largest item among Japan's exports before World War I, Bussan became conscious of the early development of the rayon and nylon industries in the United States and recognized in these new industries the most promising objective for investment of its resources accumulated in the boom during the war. Bussan, which by 1919 already controlled over eighty firms under its sole agency network, extended its network further by becoming the sole agent for Nippon Flour Milling, Dainihon Celluloid, and other promising firms which had been controlled by the Suzuki Company, another large *sogoshosha*, which went bankrupt in 1927.

In 1923 Mitsui Mining acquired the Taiheiyo Coal Mine, one of the richest in Hokkaido, and in addition diversified into the iron industry in 1924 by gaining control of 90% of the stock of Kamaishi Iron Mines. This mine was once the government iron mill, and since 1885 had been operated by Chobei Tanaka, a pioneering iron master who produced over half of the national output of pig iron in 1894.

Mitsui Mining had started manufacturing synthetic dyestuff at the Miike mine in 1918, but with the stagnant demand for coal as the source of steam power, the company had to explore other industrial uses for it and thus took control of the Toyo Nitrogen Industries of the Suzuki Company, when the latter went bankrupt. This chemical firm later became the Toyo High Pressure Company, the largest producer of sulphic anmonium in Japan.

Through the long depression after World War I, three major paper mills, Oji, Fuji, and Saghalien Industries, competed with one another, organizing a cartel and immediately violating it, and in the process leading the minor mills to bankruptcies. Heizaburo Okawa, the president of Saghalien, who was once dismissed from Oji by Mitsui, tried to control Fuji in order to compete with the larger Oji. But instead, Oji secretly succeeded in purchasing a majority of Fuji's shares and by 1930 controlled 65% of the national output of modern paper. Furthermore, in 1933 the three majors finally merged to form the new Oji Paper Mills, which produced over 80% of the national output.

c) The Case of Sumitomo

It might be said that Mitsui was less heavy industrialized than Mitsubishi, but the third largest old zaibatsu, Sumitomo, was more heavy industrialized than Mitsubishi. From the Besshi Copper Mines, Sumitomo diversified into every new line of product closely related with it. The Sumitomo Copper Rolling Mills, established in 1897 to fabricate the copper refined from the Besshi ore, set up one of its divisions as the Sumitomo Cable Works in 1911, and the next year the Rolling Mills started to roll jointless steel tubes. On the other hand, with long experience in metal manufacturing, in 1901 they had already established the Sumitomo Cast Steel Works to produce steel products for the railways and naval shipyards. Furthermore, in 1912, a chemical plant was established at the copper refineries near the Besshi mine for the purpose of producing superphosphorate of lime from the sulfuric acid acquired in the process of copper smelting. This concern grew rapidly in response to the growing demand for chemical fertilizer and the raw material of nitric acid during World War I.

The Sumitomo family, having already incorporated its banking business and its Cast Steel Works in 1912 and in 1915 respectively, next established the Yoshinogawa Electric Power Company in 1919 and incorporated the Sumitomo Electric Cable Works in 1920, when the Cable Works exchanged shares with the Nihon Electric Manufacturing Company to introduce American technology for rolling from the latter's parent company, Western Electric. To hold the shares of these joint-stock companies, the head office of the family business was formalized in 1921 as the Sumitomo Limited Partnership with the five unlimited partners composed of two family members and three nonfamily directors.

As high-purity copper was gradually being exhausted, the Besshi mines introduced electric furnaces in 1919 to improve the quality of copper and to compete in the depressed world market after the war. In addition, Sumitomo became more aggressive in forward integration by expanding their Steel Works and Cable Works to supply steel wheels, shafts, and cables to the developing electric railways. The mining, refining, and fabricating were thus closely integrated in this combine, and Sumitomo Electric Cables, together with the associated Fujikura Cables, produced 39.2% of the total national output in 1925. Further, Sumitomo, which had owned and operated coal mines in the Kyushu district, acquired new coal mines in the 1920s in the Hokkaido area and incorporated the Sumitomo Coal Mining Company. In 1937 Sumitomo Coal Mining merged with the Besshi Copper Mines to form the Sumitomo Mining Company. The steel business of Sumitomo also developed rapidly in the 1930s, and the Sumitomo Metal Manufacturing Company, established in 1935 through the combination of Sumitomo Steel Works and Sumitomo Copper Rolling and Steel Tube, became the largest industrial firm in the combine.

The chemical fertilizer plant was also incorporated in 1926, and later ventured into the production of synthetic sulphic ammonium from coal, leading to the formation of Sumitomo Chemical Industries, the second largest producer of sulphic ammonium in Japan. In addition, the Sumitomo Company controlled the Nihon Dyestuff Manufacturing Company and the Nihon Plate Glass Works, a joint venture with Libby Owens of America. The Sumitomo Company was also a major shareholder in the Nihon Electric Manufacturing Company and in Osaka Merchant Marine, while it owned and operated Sumitomo Warehousing and the Sumitomo Trust Company. Although the total capital of the Sumitomo combine was about one-third that of Mitsui and Mitsubishi, the combine was the most organically developed and most heavy industrialized among the three largest old zaibatsu.

d) The Lesser Old Zaibatsu

Unlike the above three major zaibatsu, the lesser scale old zaibatsu, such as Furukawa, Asano, and Okura, did not have their own "agent bank," and not being able to profit from the opportunities in the World-War-I boom they stagnated through the long postwar depression. For example, Furukawa, originating from the Ashio Copper Mine, had specialized in copper mining and smelting until World War I, when it suddenly tried to diversify into trading, banking, and shipping, as well as into the chemical and rubber industries. But without trained staff and an extended trading network, Furukawa Trading was unsuccessful in the competition with leading trading companies, such as Mitsui Bussan, and it had to be dissolved in 1921. This failure kept the newly established Furukawa Bank from dynamic financing, and the bank itself was absorbed in 1931 by the Daiichi Bank (the former First National Bank). The only successful company in the Furukawa combine was Furukawa Electric Industries. In 1921 it established Fuji Electric Manufacturing as a joint venture with Siemens, and in 1937 it set up Nihon Light Metals (aluminum), also as a joint venture with the Tokyo Electric Light Company. For promoting both of these joint ventures, Furukawa Electric Industries had to depend on resources from various banks outside the Furukawa combine.

In the case of Asano, the Asano Cement Works continued to be the largest firm in the Japanese cement industry, but other enterprises such as coal mining, shipping, shipbuilding, and steelworks floundered, although Asano utilized the resources of the Yasuda "money combine" that had established a nationwide banking network by combining more than ten large banks. The most valuable fortune left by Asano was probably the vast reclaimed land in Tokyo bay; Nihon Steel Tube, of which Soichiro Asano was one of the founders, became a leading steelworks. The Okura Company, founded by a daring Meiji merchant, Kihachiro Okura, also diversified into mining, the construction industry, hotels, and theatres, but all of these enterprises were of lesser scale except for the Honkeiko Coal Mining and Iron Mills, which he established in 1911 in Manchuria.

C) Combines and Cartels in Japanese Industries

We have seen the process through which the major firms in almost all industries in Japan became gradually controlled by a limited number of combines that had diversified into various fields, although the process of diversification varied from combine to combine. Among the three major zaibatsu, Sumitomo diversified most systematically or organically, while the diversification of Mitsui was the least systematic. In the cases of Sumitomo and Mitsubishi, we can also perceive certain processes of vertical integration within the framework of extensive diversification. The diversification in the new zaibatsu can be considered much more organic or systematic since they developed on the basis of chemical industries, but in the later stage of Nissan's development the process of diversification was rather unsystematic, as in the case of Mitsui. Another notable phenomenon which we can find in the development of both the old and new zaibatsu is that mining could be the basis for systematic integration and diversification. For example, the mining enterprise, which at first had only produced and smelted copper, integrated gradually into refining and rolling, and then diversified into electric manufacturing and further into general mechanical engineering. Such systematic diversification can be recognized in the cases of Mitsubishi, Sumitomo, Furukawa, and Nissan (Kuhara Mining).

At any rate, it was difficult in Japan to organize lasting cartels in industries, because the major firms were already controlled by the combines and such majors were loyal to the headquarters of the combine rather than to the cartel agreements. Therefore, the formation of big business through horizontal combination was not as general as in America except in the case of the cotton industry. Generally speaking, cotton mills could stay out of the zaibatsu controls and could organize exceptionally strong and lasting cartels. This was probably due to the fact that most of the cotton mills were able to develop into large-scale corporate enterprises before the zaibatsu family businesses themselves grew into large industrial combines. In the late Meiji period the Japanese cotton mills also had had to rely on the zaibatsu trading firms for both marketing and purchasing, but after they earned handsome profits during World War I, they no longer needed to be financed by the *sogoshosha.* Major mills could themselves finance the purchasing of raw cotton, giving instead long-term credit to their agents, the *sogoshosha,* which must have been one of the reasons for the development of *sogoshosha* themselves in Japan.

With such accumulated resources, major cotton mills diversified into the production of other kinds of textiles: into rayons in the late 1920s and into woolens in the early 1930s. In 1932 the total amount of Japanese cotton cloth exports surpassed that of England. The Japanese cotton mills could no longer expect to grow without diversifying into other textiles, and in fact only the diversified firm could stay among the top fifty industrial firms. Usually, however, they stayed within the textile industry and should be considered another form of systematic diversification.

Another industry which the zaibatsu combines could not totally control or even develop themselves was the iron and steel industry.

The government mill, the Yawata works, continued to loom large in the Japanese iron and steel industry, producing 63% of the pig iron and 58% of the raw steel produced in Japan in 1929. In particular, the production of pig iron in the private sector was still underdeveloped and in 1932 the national output of pig iron did not exceed 70% of the total domestic demand, whereas the national output of steel had already surpassed the total domestic demand. The lack of rich iron ore mines in Japan had been a fatal handicap for the domestic iron mills, whcih could not compete in price even with the pig iron imported from India. In addition, the Japanese steel mills developed with the open hearth, relying heavily on the scrap imported from America. In other words, the integrated iron and steel mills were seriously underdeveloped, and there had been a rather chronic conflict between the open-hearth mills, which desired the free import of cheap Indian pig iron, and a limited number of integrated mills, which were anxious to secure a wider domestic market by limiting the import of Indian pig iron.

In the search for access to iron ore, Okura had already established the Honkeiko Coal Mine and Iron Mills in Manchuria in 1911, and in 1918 the semipublic Manchurian Railway Company established the Anzan Iron Mills (later reorganized into the Showa Steel Mills). Both of them were to grow and play important roles in the militarized Japan of the later 1930s, but for the time being, in the early 1930s, the government Yawata Works had to integrate the Japanese iron and steel industries by overcoming the conflicts between the open-hearth mills and the integrated firms. In 1933, the Yawata Iron and Steel Mills was made private and it absorbed seven firms: Kamaishi, Wanishi (Mitsui), Mitsubishi, Toyo, Fuji, Kyushu, and Osaka. The last three were open-hearth mills, but the major steel mills, such as Sumitomo Metal Manufacturing, Nihon Steel Tube Manufacturing, Kobe Steel Mills, and Nihon Steel Works, stayed outside. It is little wonder that the iron and steel industry remained so backward throughout the period before World War II. They could not overcome their chronic comparative disadvantage until the postwar period when the iron and steel mills in the United States and European industrial countries also became dependent on imported iron ore.

COMMENTS

1

Alfred D. Chandler, Jr.
Harvard University

I have very little to add to Professor Nakagawa's speech. It's an excellent paper. He was willing to gather a tremendous amount of data, almost all of which was new to me, and I found it fascinating and revealing. I would just like to raise a couple of questions that come out of the major differences between the Japanese experience and the American experience.

One obvious difference, and this one I don't have many questions on, is the role of government. I did learn from the paper a couple of things I hadn't quite realized: the importance, as you stressed, of the impact of the government on developing external economies; and secondly, I guessed that this meant the government's important role was in initiating not only the modern economy but the modern enterprise. After that it doesn't seem to have played a major role outside of the iron and steel industries.

The other basic and most obvious difference between the American experience and the Japanese is certainly the importance of foreign trade. And I have noticed that on those useful lists almost all those companies except the railroads and the utilities would be involved in the foreign market. Here clearly comes the important role of the general merchants and of the trading companies, and I would be interested to know more about these companies. The one we hear the most about is the Mitsui, which, as you pointed out, by 1913 had traded 25 % of the Japanese foreign trade, which is most amazing for one company. I would still be interested in the others. What kinds of companies were the other trading companies? Did they specialize in a certain area or certain sets of products? I noticed that some of them seem to have become the zaibatsu as they moved back into controlling suppliers. This would seem to be the pattern.

The important thing, though, seems to be that here, unlike the United States—maybe more like Britain and Europe, as you suggest,—the middleman, the general merchant, stood between the manufacturer and the market. Since the domestic market was so small and thus in a sense was being handled by the traditional distributors, it meant that all the new industries had to go through middlemen to their market except for those few middlemen who went back into industry, like the Mitsui. This then may be something I had not realized, and I wanted to look at this connection between the middleman and the rise of the other zaibatsu. Here we see the importance of mining, both coal and copper, in the industrializing economy and in the rise of the large enterprise. It seemed as I read this paper and others, that Mitsubishi's main strength, besides the shipbuilding, was its mining. Sumitomo, as you stressed, was built out of the family-based copper mines, and a little later Nissan came out of copper, Furukawa out of copper, and even Mitsui was very much involved in copper. This I had not realized from any of my earlier readings, this great importance of mining: coal, as you pointed out, largely to provide bunker coal for ships throughout the East, and copper as a basic material.

I wondered, then, why other large firms were not general traders like Mitsui in mining? Was this because they bypassed the general merchant and developed their own markets? Clearly, Mitsubishi did. As you pointed out, they had a coal export division very early—a coal marketing department. And I wondered about the other firms—Sumitomo. In a sense was it one of the very first to bypass the general merchants? And by doing so it gained contact with the market and were able to begin to build a much larger organization. The cotton textile industry could only do this after the boom of World War I. They could break with the zaibatsu, could go to the market and go back to the raw materials, and could begin to develop a large, integrated enterprise. But I don't quite see what the relationship between copper and a marketing organization is. I can see that for coal you would develop a marketing organization so you could reach the various ports that were using the coal to supply the ships. But in the case of copper, I am somewhat puzzled. It would seem to me, then, that the new zaibatsu, outside of those that were based on mining, did come out of the new chemical-electrical industry, and the list that you have there shows them. And would they, too, have had their own markets? Maybe they also did not have to rely on the general merchants to buy and sell, the way the cotton textile people did. Therefore, they might have been able to build a larger organization that had a direct contact with the market rather than going through middlemen. This would be something I would be interested in knowing.

I was interested, too, that as the firms further developed it seems that those that came from mining developed their diversification, as you say, in a systematic and organic way, much more so than Mitusi, which came directly from the general merchants' kind of role into industry. Mitsubishi seemed to be half and half, as you say, but still there is quite a logic, it seemed to me, in their diversification. Certainly Sumitomo, as you stressed, went very logically from copper to electric cables. And later on, after the textile firms had developed an integrated organization in the sense of going into marketing, they too diversified into other textiles. What I am suggesting here is that it may not be *so* different from the American experience in the sense that once the firms had developed sets of resources outside of just finance and commercial resources, they could use those to make a kind of systematic diversification, whereas Mitsui diversification was of the essentially conglomerate type based on the fact that they had financial resources and many commercial outlets. So my questions are around the matter, did the other large firms in Japan grow because they could and did bypass the general merchant, or is this relevant to the development? Essentially that was the question that came to mind as I read the paper. Again, I must always go back to the American experience: it is the only one I really know. I find that the enterprises there that moved into marketing first tend to become the large, multifunctional, major diversified firms.

2

Yotaro Sakudo
Osaka University

Professor Nakagawa's paper encompasses the long and eventful stretch of time between the Meiji Restoration and the outbreak of the Second World War. The scope of this paper is further broadened by its references to the traditional institutions of the Tokugawa era, and other elements of premodern society that have influenced Japan's development. The major themes which Professor Nakagawa elucidates in his presentation include the establishment and development of zaibatsu versus nonzaibatsu enterprises, the comparison between the old and new zaibatsu, the transformation of an industrial structure in the Meiji period centered on cotton-spinning industry to the one in the Taisho and Showa periods centered on heavy industry, and the interrelation of these two phases. It can be said that these constitute some of the fundamental themes of our present conference.

I understand Professor Nakagawa's paper to be a response to the most immediate problem we face today in the study of Japanese business history, which is to enrich the content of entrepreneurial history as set forth by Prof. Johannes Hirschmeier in his book *The Origins of Entrepreneurship in Meiji Japan* (1964), and to attempt to develop new approaches to its issues. Furthermore, this paper is notable for having borrowed from Alexander Gerschenkron's model in analyzing the historical nature of Japan's process of modernization. Another noteworthy feature is that Professor Nakagawa offers us the outline of a Japanese model which we may employ in drawing a comparison of Japanese business strategy and industrial structure with American ones as elucidated by Prof. Alfred D. Chandler.

There may remain some questions on the general direction of this approach and Professor Nakagawa's basic framework, but I would like to pose several questions about some specific points which warrant further discussion.

The first issue arises from the first section, entitled "Industrialization Led by the Government: Investment in External Economies," in which Professor Nakagawa emphasizes the central government's role in taking the initiative in the process of industrialization. What underlying historical current enabled this strategy of modernization "from above" to succeed? In what way can the cognitive system and behavior pattern of Japan's nation-centered entrepreneur be linked to the underlying historical current? And how do they compare with Prof. Gustav Ranis's "community-centered entrepreneur"?

The second issue involves the analysis of the sale of government pilot enterprises to the private sector. Professor Nakagawa sees a reason for the success of this policy in government's shouldering initial risks of those new enterprises. However, is it premature to evaluate in this period the merit of family businesses which were organized on the traditional principle in Japanese management?

Turning next to the second section, entitled "Entrepreneurial Performance and Business Organization before World War I," which deals with the development of the joint-stock company system, Professor Nakagawa finds in this development the rudiment for the establishment of a zaibatsu-controlled economy. The creation of the national bank system and its influence on the introduction and growth of the joint-stock company system is fully described in this section, and I find Professor Nakagawa's analysis of the significance of its spread noteworthy. As a related question, I would like to ask how may we view the fate of this typically credit-financed Japanese firm in the Taisho and Showa periods as the dependence on borrowed capital was beginning to outweigh owner's capital?

My fourth question involves the third section, entitled "Entrepreneurship and Its Organization in the Course of 'Heavy Industrialization' since World War I." Professor Nakagawa compares the old and new zaibatsu, and describes their important differences, which were observed during the process of heavy industrialization, explaining that the growth of old zaibatsu was lead by their coal mines while the new zaibatsu forcused on the electric-chemical industry. What factors contributed to this divergence in strategy? In investigating the traditional dualism of the Japanese economy, I feel it is necessary to consider the subcontracting system which existed between big business and small scale firms. What kind of approach can we adopt in examining this topic, and other issues of the small-scale firm?

My final point concerns the penetrating observations that Professor Nakagawa makes on commercial organization in the Tokugawa era and the traditional Japanese consumption patterns as he considers the domestic market in Japan as compared to the American case. In this respect, how does Professor Nakagawa propose to cope with the subject of continuity versus discontinuity in the transition from the Tokugawa era to the Meiji period and beyond?

I have just mentioned several questions which I feel we may profitably reflect upon in greater depth, and look forward to hearing Professor Nakagawa's opinion and approach to these issues.

I–2

Management Structure and Control Devices for Diversified Zaibatsu Business

Hidemasa Morikawa
Hosei University

1. A Characterization of Japanese Business Strategy

Historically, the decisive characteristic of Japanese business strategy has been diversification. This diversification strategy has been relentlessly pursued since the start of Japan's industrialization.

According to Professor Chandler, the strategy of product diversification in American big business became dominant in the twentieth century, especially since the 1920s after a long period in which the dominant strategy had been one of vertical integration, at least since the middle of the nineteenth century.[1] But, by contrast, in Japan, during the earlier stages of industrialization, the effort to integrate industrial processes from procurement of raw materials to consumer marketing into a single corporate management was very limited, except in the case of the oil industry. Japanese big business has continuously tried since its beginning to invest its resources in diversification, that is, parallel management of different kinds of enterprises. Zaibatsu were the typical result of such diversification efforts.[2]

As Alexander Gerschenkron pointed out, the more backward a national economy is, the more diversified the areas are in which it is forced to start industrializing simultaneously.[3]

As Japan was more backward than the backward countries in Gerschenkron's model, it is no wonder that Japanese business was strongly inclined toward diversification, although we should take into account other factors, such as the geographical isolation of Japan from Western countries, the instability of the military in Meiji Japan, the intensive intellectual curiousity of the Japanese people, and the typical "one-set-ism" of Japanese society.

But, of course, entrepreneurial resources in Japan were not adequate for the simultaneous industrialization of the various sectors of the national economy. There were few people who were capable of mobilizing enough monetary resources for establishing modern industrial enterprises or who were capable of managing these new firms once they had been established. Also, the ability to gather and understand the knowledge and information necessary for industrialization was not yet adequately developed. Also lacking was the entrepreneurial spirit of risk-taking. In the course of events, a single entrepreneur was often induced to undertake plural entrepreneurial ventures. The Japanese government encouraged such diversification, and nationalistic Japanese entrepreneurs were also quite willing to venture into new fields of the national economy.

Secondly, the tendency to diversify can be explained by a shortage of natural resources and the existence of a dominant traditional marketing system.

The industrial leaders of Meiji Japan sought not only for autonomy of industrial production but also for an autonomous supply of raw materials. Their ardent desire for such autarky might sound strange if we reconsider it in light of the later stages of development of the Japanese economy—the dependence on the raw material supply from abroad. But as it became gradually evident that Japan was highly dependent on overseas supplies, Japanese industrialists became anxious to secure a stable supply of raw materials.

At the start of Japan's industrialization, all machines and equipment had to be imported from advanced countries. But because of centuries of seclusion, individual manufacturers were not in a position to import directly from abroad their necessary raw materials, machines, and equipment. For raw materials, they had to resort to the *shokan* (foreign merchants in port settlements) and subsequently to the Japanese general merchants (*sogoshosha*) who took the place of the *shokan.* These general merchants gradually monopolized the supply of raw materials from abroad by extending their information networks and by increasing their ability to mobilize monetary resources. And unlike the American case, it was not necessary for

Japanese industrial firms to create marketing channels for their own products. Since the Tokugawa period, there had existed an elaborte system of marketing, composed of various types of middlemen, and it was not until the 1910s that drastic changes in the domestic market forced Japanese industrial firms to establish direct contact with the consumer market. Although the Japanese economy was highly dependent on exports, industrial products were not exported by the industrial firms themselves but were exported by the *shokan* and later by the general merchants.[4]

2. The Strategies of Diversification in Mitsui and Mistubishi

Both Mitsui and Mitsubishi, who were the dominant business groups in pre-World-War-II Japan, developed into zaibatsu through diversification.

A) Mitsui

The business history of the Mitsui family started in 1673 when they opened a *gofuku* (clothes) retail store. In 1683 they diversified into financing (money-changing), and until the Meiji Restoration *gofuku* retailing and financing were the two pillars of Mitsui's enterprise. In 1876 their financing business was reorganized into Mitsui Bank and Mitsui Bussan (a newly established trading company). But the latter was not organized as a part of the formal business of the Mitsui family but rather was established as a separate partnership of two young family members who had no rights of inheritance to the family fortune and were considered as outsiders (*bekke*) of the orthodox Mitsui family. Their traditional *gofuku* retailing business was also handed over to other *bekke*, the Mitsukoshi. In other words, only the banking business constituted the formal business of the Mitsui family.[5] But, in fact, these measures served to further diversify their business interests into foreign trade. In 1888 a governmental enterprise, the Miike coal mine, was sold to the Mitsui family and the Miike Coal Mining Company was founded with fifty-fifty subscriptions by the Mitsui Gumi (a nominal person of the Mitsui Bank) and

Mitsui Bussan. The business of Mitsui became thus even more diversified. The Miike Coal Mine was later merged with the Kamioka Copper Mines and other mines owned by Mitsui Gumi and Mitsui Bussan, to eventually form Mitsui Mining Company. On the other hand, Mitsui Bussan and the Mitsukoshi Kimono Store were reorganized as formal businesses of the Mitsui family in 1891 and 1893 respectively.[6]

In 1893 the General Law of Incorporation was issued by the government and the four Mitsui businesses were formally incorporated as the *gomei kaisha* (a partnership in its substance but registered under the General Law as one corporation). The heads of the eleven Mitsui families were divided into four groups and each group became subscribers to each of the four Mitsui enterprises. Each business was in fact owned by the entire Mitsui family, but to disperse and limit the risk to any one branch of the family, they devised this elaborate type of organization.[7] A managing director and directors were appointed for each firm to formulate policies and manage the day-to-day business. The following were the managing directors of the four Mitsui firms:

Mitsui Bank	Hikojiro Nakamigawa
Mitsui Bussan	Takashi Masuda
Mitsui Mining	Takuma Dan
Mitsui Gofuku-ten	Yoshio Takahashi

The most active managing director, Nakamigawa, who was a nephew of Yukichi Fukuzawa, a famous ideologue of modernization, tried to transform Mitsui into a modern industrial combine, by buying up and/or controlling various independent industrial firms and factories, such as the Kanegafuchi Cotton-Spinning Mills, the Oji Paper Mills, the Shibaura Engineering Works, and silk-reeling mills such as Shinmachi and Tomioka. For controlling Shibaura Works and the six silk-reeling mills, the industrial division was newly formed as a subdivision of the Mitsui, the *motokata* , a special institution which was responsible for the total assets of the Mitsui families. Side by side with the industrial division, the real estate division was also organized.

But Nakamigawa's aggressive policy of industrializing the Mitsui business led to failure: the industrial enterprises Nakamigawa attempted to establish required gestation periods of too great a duration before they could begin to yield profits, and the ambitious industrial division was disbanded. Takashi Masuda grasped the leadership of the Mitsui zaibatsu and suspended the policy of rapid industrialization. He sold the silk filatures, silk reeling mills, the Kanegafuchi Spinning Mill, and the Oji Paper Mill. He also separated the Shibaura Works as an independent joint-stock company. The process of industrializing the Mitsui business was brought to an abrupt halt, and it was not resumed again until the 1910s when Mitsui Mining Company and Mitsui Bussan started to diversify into industrial production. Meanwhile the unprofitable Mitsui Gofuku Company was also detached and organized as the Mitsukoshi Gofuku Company, Limited.[8]

B) Mitsubishi

Although Mitsubishi developed first as a shipping enterprise founded and led by Yataro Iwasaki, we should keep in mind that Mitsubishi had already become a conglomerate of diversified enterprises in the early stages of its development. The motives behind Iwasaki's aggressive diversification were not simple. Because of political changes in 1881, Mitsubishi could no longer rely on government favors and was forced to hand its shipping business over to the newly established Nippon Yusen Kaisha (NYK). Mitsubishi developed the Yoshioka Copper Mine, the Takashima Coal Mine, the Nagasaki Shipbuilding Yard, and the 119th National Bank (a predecessor of the Mitsubishi Bank), all of which were more or less subordinated to the last shipping business.

Immediately after the death of Yataro, his younger brother Yanosuke took over leadership of the reorganization of the combine. In 1885 he founded the Mitsubishi-sha which he used to reconstruct and control the various businesses of the Iwasaki family, being helped by able *kanji* (general managers) such as Koichiro Kawada and Heigoro Shoda.[9]

Although shipping was no longer Mitsubishi's main business, the Mitsubishi-sha still controlled 45% of the stocks of the NYK, and as the NYK was guaranteed a profit and dividend by the government, Mitsubishi continued to secure abundant monetary resources. The Mitsubishi-sha invested the resources thus secured into diversified activities, by purchasing new metal and coal mines, enlarging the banking business, buying up the government-owned Nagasaki Shipbuilding Yard, newly establishing the Kobe Shipbuilding Yard, and starting a real estate business at Marunouchi, now the central business center in Tokyo. In 1888 Mitsubishi was defeated by Mitsui in a tender bid for the Miike Coal Mine because it bid at a sum marginally lower than Mitsui. But whereas Mitsui had to squeeze out a million yen in cash for securing the Miike Mine, Mitsubishi was much more resourceful. And the Iwasaki family gradually became the major stockholder of various large enterprises such as Tokyo Marine Insurance, Meiji Life Insurance, Kobe Paper Mills (later Mitsubishi Paper Mill), Nippon Railway, and Sanyo Railway. Furthermore the Iwasaki family owned and operated the large-scale Koiwai Farm and invested extensively in the Kirin Brewery, the Asahi Glass Works, and so on.[10]

3. Administrative Organizations of Mitsui and Mitsubishi

For the diversification strategy related above, Mitsui and Mitsubishi responded with strikingly different types of organizations. Mitsui organized each enterprise as an independent company and tried to control them by establishing a powerful headquarters. By contrast, Mitsubishi organized its various enterprises as divisions within a single company, first the Mitsubishi-sha and at the end of 1893 the Mitsubishi Limited Partnership. Mitsubishi was interested in keeping each business independent as a unit but under control of a single management.

This contrasting difference of administrative organizations between Mitsui and Mitsubishi is astonishingly similar to the difference in organizational development between General Motors and Du Pont in the 1920s. One suffered from excessive decentralization and endeavored to establish a powerful headquarters, while the other moved toward decentralization, realizing the inefficiency of its centralized organization for administering its diversified enterprises.[11]

a) The Case of Mitsui

All Mitsui enterprises, that is, Mitsui Bank, Bussan, and Mining, and Gofuku-ten, had been independent companies from their beginnings. In addition, all of them had experienced a long process of development and were the largest enterprise in their field of business. The managers and other employees of the companies desired to maintain their identity and independence and naturally were reluctant to be integrated under the single authority of the Mitsui families.

A striking example was the remarkable development of Mitsui Bank under the leadership of Nakamigawa. He made up his mind to industrialize the Mitsui combine through the Mitsui Bank and was apt to ignore the interests of other Mitsui companies. Nakamigawa supplied enough money to Mitsui Mining, which was going to modernize its operation and purchase other mines, and therefore no serious conflicts arose between Mitsui Bank and Mitsui Mining. But Nakamigawa disregarded the interests of Mitsui Bussan, and, as a result, personal conflicts with Masuda, the leader of Bussan, developed. Nakamigawa firmly believed that Mitsui should develop through industrial expansion and disliked the fact that Bussan put stress on commerce, especially small lots of dealings in the domestic market.

In fact, Nakamigawa disregarded Masuda's demand for financial aid to Bussan's Osaka branch, which had lost an enormous sum of money because of a rise in the price of raw cotton in the depression following Sino-Japanese War. On the other hand, he continued to loan considerable funds to independent mines in the Kyushu district. When the Hyogo plant of Kanegafuchi Cotton Spinning, of which Mitsui Bank was a major shareholder and Nakamigawa himself the president, became involved in a conflict with competitive mills in the Kansai district over the problem of the female labor force, the Mitsui Bank supported Kanegafuchi by suspending loans to the competitive mills who were all regular customers of Mitsui Bussan.[12]

On account of growing frictions between the Bank, Bussan, and Mining, it became an urgent task for Mitsui to mediate between these operating companies and to integrate their activities under a single administrative organ of the Mitsui family.

Already in 1891, the *karihyogikai* (temporary council) of the Mitsui family had been established as an organ for supervising the activities of its diversified business enterprises. But its relation with the *omotokata yoriai* (the formal meeting for discussing household affairs) remained ambiguous. Two years later the *dozokukai* (family council) was organized by integrating the *karihyogikai* with the *omotokata yoriai*, but naturally its functions became too diversified and it could not devote its energies to the task of coordinating and integrating all of the Mitsui business activities. Being pressed by the conflict between the operating companies stated above, the Mitsui *shoten rijikai* (board of directors of the Mitsui Company) was established in 1896 to coordinate the business activities of the four operating companies and of the industrial and real estate departments.[13]

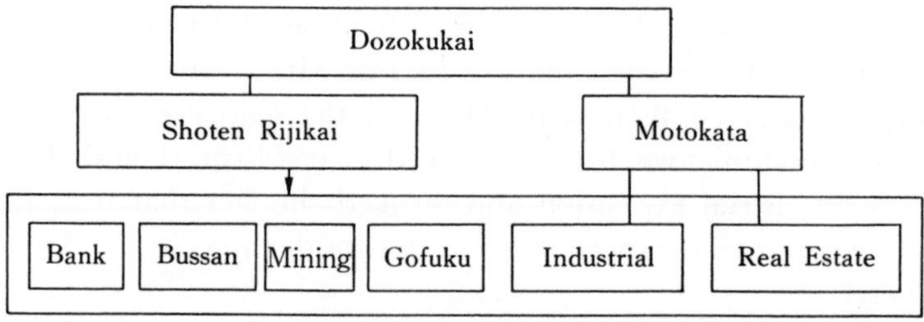

But the *shoten rijikai* was not simply a coordinating committee. It was given the authority to inspect and approve the policies presented by the four companies and the two departments. And the *shoten rijikai* took over some parts of the decision making of each operating unit. For example, Mitsui Bussan had been authorized by its articles of incorporation to engage only in the commission business; in the case of dealings other than commission business, each operating unit had to seek approval from the president. After the establishment of *shoten rijikai*, the president of Bussan had to present to *shoten rijikai* the requests of operating units to be allowed to deal on their own accounts and to get approval of the latter. Bussan's top management could no longer make decisions themselves unless authorized transactions were excuted within the limits approved by the *shoten rijikai*. The Mitsui *shoten rijikai* was thus the head office of the centralized organization.[14]

But, on the other hand, in reality, the *shoten rijikai* was no more than a coordinating committee. The persistent desire for autonomy of operating companies and departments did not allow for the existence of an all-powerful control center, and in fact the *shoten rijikai* was composed of the heads of the Mitsui families and the representatives of all operating units: Torashiro Nishimura and Hikojiro Nakamigawa of Mitsui Bank, Takashi Masuda and Yasusaburo Ueda of Mitsui Bussan, Takuma Dan of Mitsui Mining, Yoshio Takahashi of Gofuku, and Eiji Asabuki of the industrial department. It is no surprising that the *shoten rijikai*, where the interests of each operating company came into conflict with others', could not play the role of an effective controller for the widely diversified business enterprises. In 1900 the *shoten rijikai* was renamed the *Mitsui eigyoten juyakukai* (board of directors of Mitsui firms). In the following year the *kanribu* (administrative department) was created in the bureau of the *dozokukai* (family council) to supervise the *eigyoten juyakukai* and it was anticipated to function successfully as the general controller of the diversified enterprises. The preamble of the law of the *kanribu* reads: "The *eigyoten juyakukai* could not fulfill its duties. The members, who were directors of each of the operating companies, were mainly interested in the management of their own companies. Being naturally prejudiced in favor of their own companies, they lacked the sprit of mutual cooperation and failed in their coordination efforts. Each company, acting as an isolated unit separate from others, could not conceive of itself as being under a single unified management. For overcoming such drawbacks and for controlling all units we are going to establish the *kanribu*."[15]

The *kanribu* was given authority for revising the articles of the operating companies, formulating policies, staffing director positions, controlling reserved funds, supervising operations, and planning the rationalization of each company. Takashi Masuda, who was appointed managing director of the *kanribu*, grasped this extensive authority, and, in addition, he could, when necessary, rely upon the support of Kaoru Inoue, who was an advisor to the Mitsui families while one of the dominant figures in Meiji Japan's politics. It seemed that at last an effective centralized administrative organization for the Mitsui zaibatsu had been established.

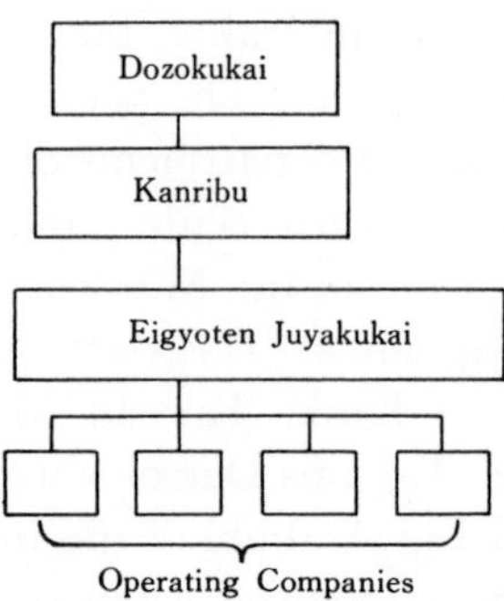

But there still remained some weaknesses in Mitsui's new administrative organization, now established on the basis of the newly created *kanribu*. First, the authority of administrative control was divided between the *kanribu* and the *eigyoten juyakukai*. The decisions made by the operating companies had to be approved by the *kanribu* as well as by the *eigyoten juyakukai* and consequently decision making by Mitsui's top management lost the merits of quickness and dynamism. Therefore, it was natural that the *eigyoten juyakukai* was abolished in 1904 in order to overcome this dual structure of administrative control[16]

Second, on account of the stubborn demand for atonomy in each operating company, even the newly created *kanribu* could not play the clear-cut role of general headquarters, just as the *shoten rijikai* and *eigyoten rijikai* could not. The *kanribu* was headed by its managing director, Masuda, but it still acted as an organ for coordination and agreement by the representatives of the operating companies, Mitsui Bussan (Masuda), Mitsui Bank (Senkichiro Hayakawa, a successor to Nakamigawa), Mitsui Mining (Dan), Mitsui Gofuku (Asabuki), and the Mitsui family council (Nagafumi Ariga). There continued to exist organizational weaknesses: "the representative of each company promoted the interests of his own company and could not perform as a rational negotiator."

There were various motives for the establishment of Mitsui Gomei as a holding company in 1909 and the simultaneous reorganization of Mitsui Bank and Mitsui Bussan into joint-stock companies. (Mitsui Mining was transformed in the same way in 1911.) It is evident that it was guided also by the ardent desire for complete control over all the Mitsui enterprises. However, the conflict between centralized control and operational autonomy continued to exist even in the new organization. The newly created holding company Mitsui Gomei could not centralize enough authority to control the diversified enterprises, again because of the extreme desire for autonomy in each operating company, and the Mitsui Gomei remained a place for coordination and agreement by the representatives of the operating companies. Takuma Dan, who was the chairman of the board of directors of Mitsui Gomei from 1914 to 1932, suffered seriously from the difficulties of coordinating the interests of the three operating companies and of the eleven Mitsui families. He could not make decisions quickly on proposals from the operating units and was nicknamed *Kimezu no Dan* (Indecisive Dan).[17]

b) *The Case of Mitsubishi*

For a time after the establishment of the Mitsubishi-sha in 1885, Mitsubishi did not give much consideration to the organizational need for effective control of its diversified enterprises. According to a statement published in 1888, the central office was divided into three departments: mining, accounting, and general affairs. A *shihainin* (manager) was responsible for the activities of each department, and they were under the over all control of the *kanji* (general manager). But this control device, following the line of authority which came down from the president to the general manager and then to the manager, was only applied to production, marketing, and procurement in the metal and coal mines administered by the mining department. The activities of the Nagasaki Shipbuilding Yard were administered by its vice-manager, Rokuro Mizutani, and the 119th National Bank was an entirely separate organization.

After the formation of the Mitsubishi Limited Partnership, the first major reorganization was carried out in 1895. Banking was added to the lines of business in the articles, and the newly created banking department became responsible for the 119th National Bank. This dual system in the banking department and the 119th National Bank continued to work until 1898 when the latter's term of business expired. The establishment of the banking department was the beginning of divisionalization among the enterprises in Mitsubishi. Thereafter, the trading department (*baitanbu* and later *eigyobu*), the mining department, the shipbuilding department, and the real estate department were in turn organized. Further, in 1899 the general affairs department (*shomubu*) and the inspection department (*kensabu*) were established. The former was responsible for accounting, personnel, letters, and other services to the operating departments and for the real estate business. The latter seems to have undertaken research and planning as well as inspection. Each of these operating departments, banking, mining, and trading, and each of two staff departments, general affairs and inspection, was headed by a manager (*shihainin*) who reported to the general manager (*kanji*). Throughout the period of these reorganizations, Heigoro Shoda dominated Mitsubishi as the *kanji* because the authority of the *kanji* was extensive and the family head, Hisaya Iwasaki, was still young and of gentle personality.

Though Mitsubishi was divisionalized among the diversified enterprises as stated above, lines of authority and communication remained centralized as before. For example, the mining division controlled more than ten mines, but offices of these mines reported directly to the general manager in the central office. As each of the diversified enterprises grew, the lack of mobility in such a centralized structure gradually gave rise to administrative strains which had to be resolved by a second reorganization.[18]

In 1908 extensive authority was delegated by the following procedures to the mining, banking, and shipbuilding divisions for making these divisions independent profit centers:

1) The amount of capital was fixed for each division:

Mining Division	¥15,000,000
Banking Division	¥ 1,000,000
Shipbuilding Division	¥10,000,000

As the amount of capital of the Mitsubishi Limited Partnership was ¥15,000,000, each division can be said to have been allocated extensive monetary resources.

2) It was decided that a part of the profit of each division would be paid into the treasury of the Mitsubishi Limited Partnership. The banking division had already been paying this assessment on profits since 1897.

3) The investment, within the limits of the amount of capital allocated to each division, was free to be invested as decided by the divisions themselves. But for investments larger than their capital, divisions had to borrow money from outside sources with the approval of the president.

4) The rules and procedure governing activities within each division were decided on the authority of each division itself except in some special cases for which the president's approval was necessary.

5) Personnel affairs of each division's employees were primarily the item of decision in each division, and the division sent reports of their decisions to the president together with the division manager's comments. But college graduates and white collar workers continued to be employed through the central office.

6) Each division was responsible for its operating costs, entertainment expenses, personnel costs (including allowances and bonuses), and donations. The central office became responsible only for pensions, annuities, and special bonuses.

7) Communication channels were established between the central office and the divisions and between the divisions and operating units.

Direct communication between the central office and operating units was prohibited.

8) The real estate business within each division was to be excuted on the authority of the division itself. It had no obligation to report to the head office.

9) The general affairs department belonged to the central office as before and was to offer staff services to the top management and the divisions.[19]

As stated above, management decentralization in Mitsubishi was carried out extensively and smoothly. During the same period, the enterprises in Mitsui were strictly controlled by the central office. Although each firm in Mitsui could employ white collar workers on its own authority, all affairs—such as purchasing, construction, reconstruction and sales of real estate, contracts with other firms, holding other company's stock, delegation of directors, and non-business expenditures (donations, condolence money given to employees, etc.)—had to be decided by the *kanribu*, the central office of *dozokukai*, the Mitsui family council bureau. Most of the enterprises in Mitsui started as independent firms, and they continued to keep management autonomy. The more persistent the desire for autonomy of the operating units was, the more drastic the measures applied for the Mitsui's reorganization. On the other hand, because Mitsubishi's operating units had been within a single company and had been under central office ever since their beginnings, Mitsubishi could develop management decentralization smoothly and gradually in proportion to the growth and changes in the units which had been under the central office ever since their beginnings. Later new divisions were added, and in 1913 the Mitsubishi combine was composed of six divisions, banking, metal mining, coal mining, trading, shipbuilding, and real estate.

The reorganization of Mitsubishi in 1908 can be considered the beginning of the modern decentralized, product-defined, divisional structure, going ahead of the model followed later by Du Pont and GM in the 1920s. In the case of the decentralization of American management, marketing was closely integrated with other functions in the product division, but Mitsubishi organized marketing or distribution as a separate division. Mitsubishi did not develop a system of budget control, and personnel management of white collar workers was still under the auspices of their central office. In that sense, we must admit that the decentralized organization of Mitsubishi was far less developed than the organizations of Du Pont and GM in the 1920s. But on the other hand we cannot conclude that Mitsubishi's reorganization in 1908 was entirely different from those of the Du Pont and GM in substance.

For example, in Mitsubishi, in addition to the delegation of operational authority to division managers, there developed a top managerial level responsible for overall policy making, supervision, and coordination, and it was staffed with able executives, like President Hisaya Iwasaki, Vice-President Koyata Iwasaki, General Manager Heigoro Shoda, and Kyugo Nanbu. Secondly, the staff organization in the central office was enlarged and fortified: a research section was established in 1911 in the general affairs department, and the planning department (*sagyobu*) was organized as a part of the central office in 1917 by combining the research and oriental sections of the general affairs department with the research sections of the metal mining and coal mining departments. Thirdly, the rules and procedures for consultation and coordination between the divisions were firmly established. In other words, we can find in Mitsubishi at this period management decentralization that is imperfect but nonetheless quite similar to the development which took place in American big business after 1921.

Furthermore, a third major reorganization was carried out by a nephew of Yataro, Koyata Iwasaki, who became the president of the Mitsubishi Limited Partnership in 1916. After 1917 the divisions were reorganized one by one into independent joint-stock companies. And the Mitsubishi (Limited Partnership) Company became a holding company, controlling almost 100% of the stocks of the newly created operating companies. In short, management decentralization, similar to the American organizational model which was used by Mitsubishi, and quite unique in Japanese business history, failed to become a permanent feature of modern Japan's industrial landscape.

It is not clear why the divisional structure was transformed into a *konzern*. As the levels of authority and responsibility in the new joint-stock companies were not so different from those in the old divisions, organizational efficiency cannot be considered as a major reason. The need to have access to the public money market seems to have been a contributing factor because some stocks of Mitsubishi Mining Company were in fact sold in 1920 in the public market. But it was not more than a nominal publication, and the Mitsubishi zaibatsu continued to develop until 1945 on the basis of self-financing. Therefore we cannot emphasize the monetary reason either.

To the author's understanding, personnel problems seem to have been the major reason. For the employees of Mitsubishi it was, of course, more desirable that the end of the ladder of promotion was not the division manager but was the president. By reorganizing divisions into joint-stock companies, the number of presidents in Mitsubishi was increased from one to a group. Otherwise, the head of the Iwasaki families might have monopolized the position of president. As the promotion of white collar employees to president was the usual practice in Japanese business, Mitsubishi was not been able to neglect personnel problems which affected the morale of their executives. It may have been due to Japanese culture that personnel problems were given priority over such other factors as efficiency and resources.

References

1. Alfred D. Chandler, *Strategy and Structure: Chapters in the History of the Industrial Enterprise* (Cambridge, Mass.: MIT Press, 1962).
2. Hidemasa Morikawa, *Original Stream of Japanese-type Business Enterprise* (Tokyo: Toyokeizai, 1973), Chap. 3.
3. Alexander Gerschenkron, "Economic Backwardness in Historical Perspective," in *The Progress of Underdeveloped Countries,* ed. B. Hoselitz (Chicago: The University of Chicago Press, 1952).
4. Morikawa, *Business Enterprise,* Chap. 3.
5. Shigeaki Yasuoka, *A Study on the Development of Zaibatsu in Japan* (Kyoto: Minelva, 1970).
6. *Ibid.*
7. *Ibid.*
8. "Mitsui honsha shi" [A history of the Mitsui head office], (unpublished).
9. *The Life of Yataro Iwasaki,* 2 vols. (Tokyo, 1967); *The Life of Yanosuke Iwasaki,* 2 vols. (Tokyo, 1972).
10. *The Life of Hisaya Iwasaki* (Tokyo, 1961).
11. Hidemasa Morikawa, "The Organizational Structure of Mitsubishi and Mitsui Zaibatsu, 1868–1922: A Comparative Study," *B.H.R.* (Spring 1970).
12. *Nakamigawa Hikojiro-kun denkishiryo* [Biographical materials on Hikojirō Nakamigawa] (Tokyo, 1927).
13. Hidemasa Morikawa, "The Organizational Structure of Mitsui Zaibatsu," *Hosei Keiei Shirin* 6, no. 1–2 (1969).
14. *Ibid.*
15. "Mitsui honsha shi."
16. Morikawa, "Organizational Structure."
17. *Ibid.*
18. Morikawa, "Mitsubishi and Mitsui Zaibatsu."
19. *Ibid.*

COMMENTS

Yasuo Mishima
Kohnan University

Professor Morikawa reported on the contrasting business structure and strategy of Mitsui and Mitsubishi. The most important point, I think, is the fact that Mitsubishi Goshi (Limited Partnership) delegated many authorized powers to its nonindependent *jigyobu* (divisions) and executed the decentralized management. We must estimate justly the decentralization of Mitsubishi Goshi compared with the modern "operating division system."

Professor Morikawa pointed out that the decentralization of Mitsubishi Goshi was different from the modern operating division system in the adoption of whitecollar workers (university graduates) in the general office. But can we consider that the adoption of high-class management candidates belongs to the task of a general office even nowadays?

Next, Professor Morikawa pointed out that the lack of distributing divisions in 1908, and the establishment of *eigyobu* (distributing division) in 1913 as one of the six divisions (banking, mineral mining, coal mining, shipbuilding, land holding, and distributing) were other different points. But the *kogyobu* (mining and distributing division) in 1908 contained the distributing division in it as shown in Fig. 1.

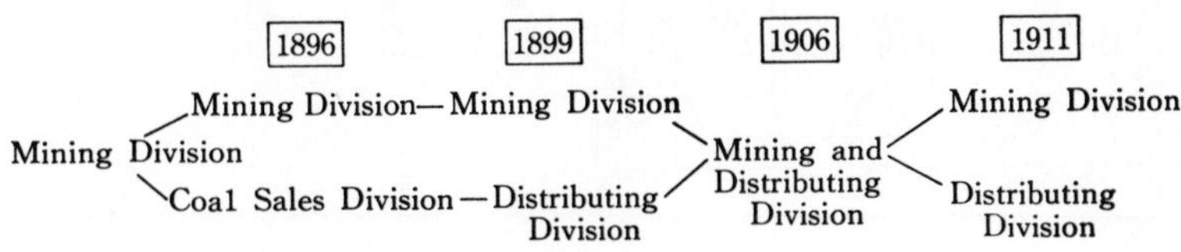

Fig. 1.

Out of the six divisions above mentioned, neither the banking division nor the land holding division needed sales function. The shipbuilding division had its own sales function. So the *eigyobu* dealt only in the products of the mineral mining division (mainly copper) and the coal mining division. The most important matter was the process of price formation with the coal mining division as well as with the mineral mining division and distributing division. Then I want to know whether there existed the independent profit system based on market price basis or intradepartment transfer price between the two divisions. If there were such systems, can we call them primitive manufacturing divisions?

Next, Professor Morikawa suggests that the reason for changing each division in Mitsubishi Goshi into a joint-stock company was to realize the executives' desires of becoming presidents. Of course, it may be true.

According to the list of stockholders of Mitsubishi Shoji Comapny (Mitsubishi Trading Company) in 1923, for instance, Mitsubishi Goshi had 285,500 shares; Koyata Iwasaki had 3,000 shares; Mitsubishi Shipbuilding, Mitsubishi Steel Manufacturing, Mitsubishi Mining, Mitsubishi Warehouse, and Mitsubishi Bank each had 1,000 shares; and thirteen chief exectives (K. Kimura, S. Eguchi, M. Ku-

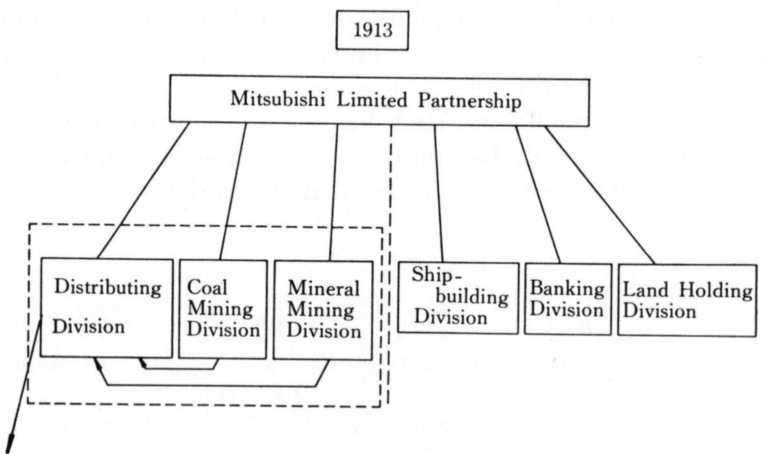

Fig. 2.

shida, K. Aoki, M. Miyagawa, M. Sakamoto, K. Kato, and so on) had 500 shares each.

So another reason for establishing joint-stock companies was, I think, that the mutual holding of stock among companies was better for the Mitsubishi Limited Partnership than directly controlling its operating divisions for the stabilization of the Mitsubishi zaibatsu. And I hope to know whether allowing the executives to hold stock was desirable for improving executive loyalty to the Iwasaki family.

If we think Mitsubishi Limited Partnership had an imperfect multidivision system, it was no wonder that the imperfect multidivision system appeared in Japan in 1908, much before the 1921 date which is said, by Professor A.D. Chandler, to mark the first establishment of a multidivision system in U.S.A.. Because Japan was a more underdeveloped country than the U.S.A., the accumulation of capital was realized by the sales of government enterprises, and diversification needed to be rapidly executed by Japanese entrepreneurs.

I–3

Management Organization of Vertically Integrated Nonzaibatsu Business

Moriaki Tsuchiya
University of Tokyo

1. What is Nonzaibatsu Business?

The definition of a zaibatsu is not clear. Sometimes it refers to any rich businessmen whose activities were conspicuous to the general public. The word *zaibatsu* was originally used to designate a group of businessmen who were from the same region, such as the Ko-shu zaibatsu and the Go-shu zaibatsu. A group of businessmen from Ko-shu (Yamanashi Prefecture) conspired to speculate in the stock market and invested their large profits in various electric companies. Merchants from Go-shu (Shiga Prefecture) were very famous for their trading ability.

By the term *zaibatsu* I mean those rich families who owned many industrial companies and financial houses. Such families as Mitsui, Iwasaki, Sumitomo, Yasuda, Furukawa, Asano, and Okura owned mining, industrial, trading, and financial companies, had close relations with government officials, and diversified their business into various fields under the patronage of the government. These zaibatsu were able to earn large profits from their main businesses, such as mining and banking, and reinvest these profits in new fields.

Even though each zaibatsu subsidiary was under the tight control of its headquarters, the capital necessary for its growth was usually supplied without difficulty. Even if it had the legal form of a joint-stock company, its stock was not listed on the stock market. It did not have difficulties with marketing because the trading company of the zaibatsu played the role of its sales department. All it had to do was to concentrate every effort on engineering and manufacturing. In this sense, each company under the zaibatsu can be considered as a single-function unit.

Needless to say, all Japanese industrial firms did not enjoy this advantage. One of the biggest problems of many industrial companies was the chronic shortage of capital. The securities of these companies were listed on the stock market, and sometimes they became victims of speculators. When they happened to have rational management, their business experienced steady growth. On the contrary, if they happened to have very aggressive managers, they had some possibility of becoming new zaibatsu. But when they were too aggressive in their new ventures, they suffered from a shortage of capital. Strange to say, they sometimes had to take a more aggressive diversification policy in order to raise money from the stock market. Two typical cases of this overaggressiveness in the 1920s were Naokichi Kaneko of Suzuki & Company and Konosuke Matsukata of Kawasaki Shipyard, who eventually failed through lack of operating capital.

The successful cases of aggressive diversification policy were the so-called new zaibatsu such as Ayukawa, Kuhara, and Noguchi. When the old zaibatsu were reluctant to cooperate with the army in the new territory in continental China in the 1930s, the new zaibatsu leaders took full advantage of the patronage of the military leaders. Although they grew rapidly enough to be called new zaibatsu, they had a different policy from the established big zaibatsu in that they continued to raise new capital from the stock market.

I would say that the typical zaibatsu businesses had the following attributes:

(1) They had their main business such as mining or banking from which they earned stable and large profits with little risk.

(2) They therefore had a large amount of capital to invest in new fields:

(3) Through their sound financial reputation, zaibatsu banks operating as divisions of the main zaibatsu business continued to absorb more and more deposits from the public in every bank crisis and financial panic.

(4) They enjoyed close relations and great leverage with high-ranking government officials.

(5) They were owned and sometimes controlled by their founding families.

(6) They could easily recruit talented managers whenever they wanted.

I would define a nonzaibatsu business as any business which was lacking some of these attributes. Moreover, I think the typical nonzaibatsu businesses differed greatly from these characteristics:

(1) Even if their business was very profitable, they had to pay a high-rate dividend to stockholders who were usually avaricious enough to ask for more dividends. (2) Managers of these businesses were expected to concentrate their efforts on one industry. They were sometimes very proud of being one-industry men. (3) Even if they had banking divisions, they did not enjoy strong financial reputations and were not always able to survive repeated banking crises. (4) Although some nonzaibatsu businesses could not stand without government help, others were proud of being independent from the government. (5) They were usually owned by public stockholders. (6) They suffered from a scarcity of talented managers.

Among modern industries, it is in cotton spinning that we find the typical nonzaibatsu business. It is for this reason that I limited my research to this industry. I will use the cases of Toyo-bo, Kurashiki-bo and Nisshin-bo, each of which had its own characteristics, as I will mention later.

2. Some Patterns of the Development of Growth Strategy

In any country during the early stages of industrialization, product markets were geographically limited and narrow; therefore manufacturing companies could not afford to specialize in one product but were forced to make any product which could be made in their plants. This could be called a jack-of-all-trades policy. In Japan, in their formative stage, shipbuilding yards had to make not only every part and accessory for their ships but also any product which their metal processing know-how could be applied to.

In the second stage of industrialization, due to the developing transportation system, markets for each product were enlarged, and manufacturing companies could specialize in one product which they could make most efficiently. As the market became competitive, the reduction of manufacturing costs also became critically important. This led to concentration on a single product, which was desirable for efficient production.

In the next stage, the success of existing companies invited new entry into the industry. The number of competitors grew too large and the fear of cutthroat competition became a serious concern. The movement for horizontal combination naturally started from these circumstances. Growth through company acquisition would most likely be the strategy utilized in this stage. But new problems of management arose. They had to revise their management organization to suit the evolving multiplant operations.

In the fourth stage, when oligopolistic market structure had been accomplished in the industry, each company desired to stabilize its supply of raw materials and the demand for its products. Vertical integration would be the new growth strategy. Again, however, there were new problems. Managers had to revise their management organization in order to coordinate various functions of the company.

In the fifth stage, when a company had some idle resources or the market for the existing product was saturated, it had to search for new product lines to diversify its business. Product diversification became the new growth strategy for the company. A new management structure suitable for diversified business was important in this stage.

In the next stage, the internationalization of the operation was adopted as the new growth strategy. If some of the oligopolistic competitors took advantage of the favorable conditions in foreign countries, other competitors were inclined to follow them. New management problems confronted the multinational company.

This development process of growth strategy which I have outlined is very simple and abstract. In real terms I think each industry had its own pattern. But I would like to apply this abstract pattern to the Japanese cotton-spinning industry.

3. Starting of the Business

Japan had had traditional hand cotton spinning, and the market for cotton yarn had already developed before a flood of the imported cotton yarn from India had stimulated the cotton-weaving business in Japan. It was natural that the Meiji government, suffering from a large and persistent deficit in the balance of payments, wanted to develop modern cotton-spinning mills using machinery. In 1877 the government imported two sets of 2,000-spindle spinning machines to establish two national mills. In 1880 the government imported ten sets of 2,000-spindle spinning machines to sell to private entrepreneurs. Ten private mills were established in each of the domestic cotton regions. Almost all of them were destined to fail because of inefficient scale and lack of capable management.

Eiichi Shibusawa, the most influential leader of modern industry in Japan, also thought that Japan must have successful cotton mills to produce a substitute for imported yarn. In view of the past failures, he thought it was necessary to establish a new large-scale mill with 10,000 spindles at least. In addition, he thought the would-be manager of the new plant should know everything about cotton spinning, and asked Takeo Yamanobe, who was staying in London to study economics, to undertake the study of cotton-spinning technology.

Thus, Osaka Cotton Spinning was established in 1882, under the leadership of Shibusawa, who raised the initial capital of ¥250,000 from aristocrats and Osaka merchants. When the new plant started operation in 1883, Yamanobe, chief engineer, decided to keep operation on a twenty-four hour schedule in order to take full advantage of the fixed capital.

A market would develop for the product from the new plant, if it could produce good products cheaply. Needless to say, the machinery of cotton spinning was highly specialized, and there was no need for early cotton millers to be jacks-of-all-trades.

Following the successful operation of Osaka Cotton Spinning, many local entrepreneurs and city merchants wanted to establish new cotton mills. In 1887 the Kurashiki Cotton-Spinning Mill was initially planned by three local youths who wanted to stimulate local industry. The Kanegafuchi Cotton-Spinning Mill was established by city merchants in the same year.

If we look at the management organization of these cotton-spinning mills in their starting periods, the presidents were not full-time managers, but occupied nominal positions. The first president, Denzaburo Fujita, and the second president, Jutaro Matsumoto, were both Osaka businessmen who had wide connections with many companies in Osaka. Shibusawa was merely a promoter of the company and an honorary board member. It may be that Yamanobe, chief engineer, was actually functioning in the role of full-time president, but it was not until 1898 that he was nominated to the presidency. Yamanobe was a captain of the industry and did not venture beyond the cotton industry.

Koshiro Ohara, the first president of Kurashiki Cotton Spinning, was the largest shareholder and nominally directed the management of the firm from his home without bothering to go to the office of the company. Seiichi Kihara was recommended to be the chief of the full-time directors by the prefectural governor. But it may be that two of the three initial planners were the most important managers. Keitaro Komatsubara was a manager in charge of production, but he was not experienced in engineering. Ritaro Kimura was in charge of commercial activities.

They thought it was important to separate commercial activities from production. Sales of the product and purchasing of raw material were very important for the success of the business but were considered traditional activities. Kimura visited many local wholesalers of cotton yarn and asked them to become sole agents in their territories. In fact, Kimura was the only person who conducted the purchasing, futures transactions, and negotiations with wholesalers. In 1893 the company opened a new, separate office for commercial activities in Osaka.

Engineering of spinning machinery was also very important in the industry's early stage of development. In Osaka Cotton Spinning, Yamanobe and other engineers who had studied machine operations in existing mills took charge of this function. In Kurashiki Cotton Spinning, Takeshi Yamaguchi was recommended as a chief engineer. Although he had no experience in cotton mills, he was a talented mechanical engineer and had graduated from the University of London. After he left the company in 1894, he worked for other cotton mills, including Kanegafuchi, as a chief engineer or director.

It was very common for an engineer to work for several companies.

Kyozo Kikuchi, for example, worked for Hirano Cotton, Amagasaki Cotton, and Settsu Cotton simultaneously. Yamanobe often recommended chief engineers for other companies.

In the case of the Nisshin Cotton Spinning Company, its establishment was much later. In 1906, the boom year just after the Russo-Japanese War, Momosuke Fukuzawa, a famous speculator on the stock market, needed new stocks to buy because stock market prices had already been boosted by speculators. He asked Heizaemon Hibiya, a leading merchant of cotton products, to cooperate in a project to establish a new cotton-spinning company.

The first chairman of the board of directors was Senzo Hiranuma, a reputable businessman in Yokohama. But this was merely a nominal position. Momosuke Fukuzawa was one of two executive directors, but he was concurrently busy with other business ventures. The other executive director, Fukutaro Sakuma, took full responsibility for building mills and starting the business. Among the directors of the new company, he was the only one who worked for the company on a full-time basis.

Figure 1 shows the organization chart when the company started operations in 1909.

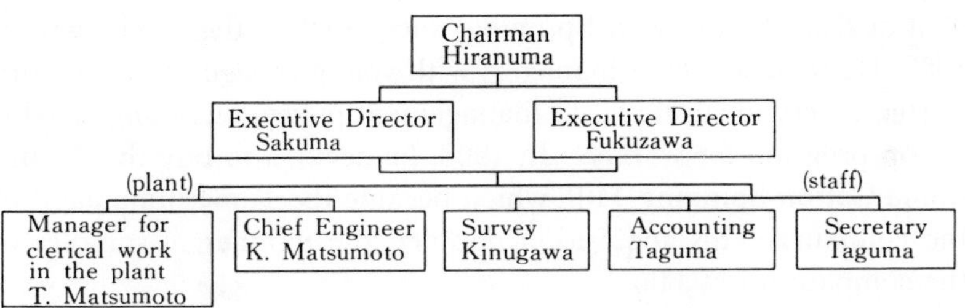

FIG. 1.

Clerical work for sales and purchasing was under the manager for clerical work in the plant. But Executive Director Sakuma made every decision about purchasing and sales transactions. He also took full responsibility for short-term financing. Sakuma, a former merchant and a subordinate of Hibiya, rather disregarded production control in the mill, and as a result, efficient production could not be attained. For example, he was so nervous about the market trend of products that he frequently changed counts of yarn for production.

Sakuma died in a traffic accident in 1911. Secretary Kumaichi Tanabe succeeded him as managing director. But he was also a congressman, and had no experience in commercial activities. He was more a politician than a company manager.

4. Consolidation of Multiplant Operations

The merger movement in the Japanese cotton-spinning industry began at the turn of century. In 1899 Seishu Iwashita, a reputable Osaka banker, pointing out the trust movement in the United States, argued that Japanese cotton-spinning mills should merge to increase their international competitive power. Kanegafuchi Cotton Spinning, having financial backing from Mitsui, started to promote an aggressive acquisition program in 1900, which resulted in the company having ten plants with 210,000 spindles by 1902. This program stimulated other companies to follow the same course and the number of cotton-spinning companies was reduced from seventy-eight in 1900 to forty-six in 1903.

Magosaburo Ohara, a young and aggressive son of the first president of Kurashiki Cotton Spinning, succeeded to the presidency in 1906. He replaced older managers with young college graduates and started a very idealistic labor management policy, including an education program for workers. In 1908, he decided to buy the Tamashima Cotton-Spinning Mill, which became the Tamashima plant of the company. This acquisition doubled the number of spindles of the company to 60,000.

During the two years following the acquisition, existing managers of the Tamashima plant continued in their management roles, and no attempt at consolidation was carried out. The quality of the product of the Tamashima plant was good enough, and the brand of the product continued to be used. But the production cost was higher than that of the Kurashiki mill.

In 1910, Ohara studied the multiplant organizations of other companies. Following the organization of Kanegafuchi, he started the consolidation program. Figure 2 shows the organization chart of Kurashiki.

Ohara forced the existing managers to retire and sent young managers there to reorganize the operation. The brand name of Tamashima was abolished, the commercial activities department in Osaka was enlarged, and a committee for cost reduction was appointed.

Ohara was very aggressive in his expansion plans. During the 1910s the company absorbed two additional companies, built two plants, and established two subsidiaries for weaving. In 1921 the company had nine plants with 174,000 spindles and 500 power looms.

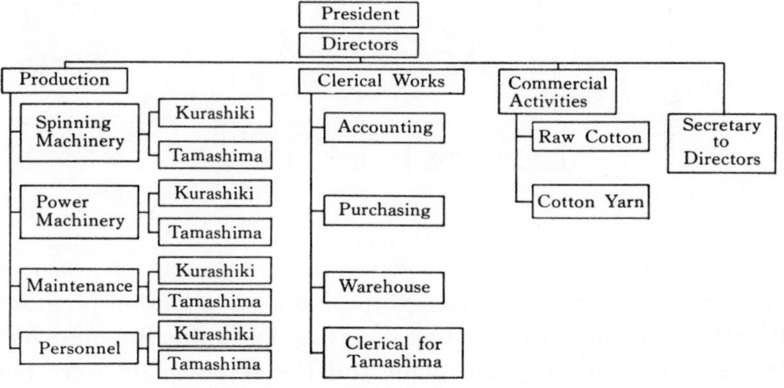

FIG. 2.

In the case of the Nisshin Cotton Spinning Company, it was in 1910, three years after its establishment, that it bought a second plant in Kyoto. This decision cannot be considered as a rational one because the offer came through a relative of Hibiya, Nisshin's largest shareholder and creditor. The company had to buy it at his request. The only merit of this acquisition was that it enabled Nisshin to stop operation of this plant, not its first plant with its efficient machinery, when the Japan Cotton Spinners' Association ordered curtailment of operations by member companies under depression conditions.

As already stated, Tanabe succeeded to the position of executive director after Sakuma's death in 1911. Being impatient with the consistently low rate of profit of the company, a group of stockholders proposed the replacement of Tanabe. The new executive director recommended was Seijiro Miyajima, who had had successful experiences in the management of another cotton-spinning mill.

In 1914 Miyajima started his rationalization program for the company. He curtailed every unneccessary expense and fired unnecessary employees.

He built a new management structure operating under new decision rules. Figure 3 shows a brief outline of the new organization chart. It seemed that the management of the Kyoto plant was left to Taichi Kinugawa, plant manager.

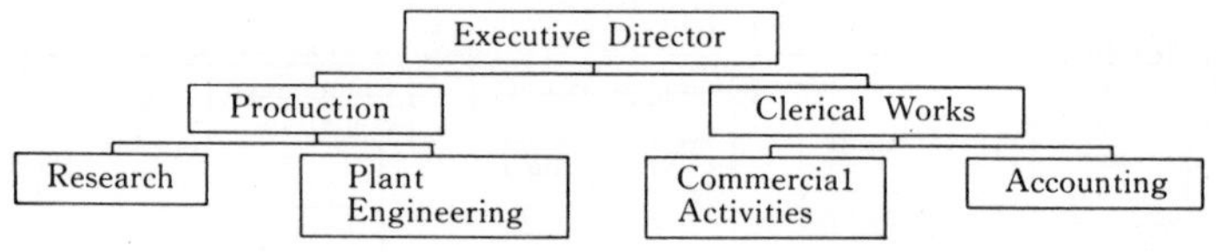

FIG. 3.

Having succeeded in a raw cotton futures transaction, the company earned profits large enough to plan new expansion programs. In 1915 the company purchased the Takaoka Cotton Spinning Mill. In the next year the main plant and the Kyoto plant were both enlarged. With large profits earned during World War I, an additional cotton-spinning mill was established as a subsidiary which would later be merged with the company in 1923. Vertical integration into weaving had been launched.

After Miyajima was appointed president in 1919, more aggressive expansion programs were initiated, including the construction of new plants in Nagoya and China. To each additional plant, managers were sent from the main plant. But there is no evidence that formal procedures were taken for administrative consolidation of the many plants. The number of employees at the head office was not increased even in this expansion. Even during the long depression period of the cotton industry from 1926 to 1933, the rapid growth of Nisshin Cotton Spinning was not slowed. In 1933 the company had eight plants with 464,000 spindles and 3,540 power looms, and was counted as one of the big five of the cotton industry.

5. Management for Integrated Operations

In the case of Osaka Cotton Spinning, forward integration into weaving came earlier than horizontal combination policy. In 1887, when spinning operations had started to run smoothly, Yamanobe planned to establish a weaving company as a subsidiary. He thought cotton cloth was also important for military demand, and in a follow-up move he went to England to buy power looms. In 1889 the Osaka Cotton Cloth Company started operation. But this company did not specialize in one type of product because each market was too small. In 1890 Osaka Cotton Spinning absorbed this subsidiary as a division.

In 1907 Osaka Cotton Spinning acquired another weaving company. Kanekin Cotton Weaving Company, established in 1888, was an exceptional case which had started as an integrated company. Because of the lack of domestic demand, it proceeded to exploit the Korean cloth market.

Mie Cotton Spinning Mill, which had been established in 1886 and would later be merged with Osaka Cotton Spinning in 1914, also started its weaving operations in 1901. The motive behind the policy of forward integration was to secure a market for cotton yarn and to export cotton cloth to the Chinese market.

In the domestic cloth market, these integrated companies could not be too aggressive because they had to avoid infringing upon their customers' markets. Just after the Russo-Japanese War, Osaka Cotton Spinning dispatched their salesmen to Korea to organize a network of special agents. A cutthroat price war in the Korean cotton cloth market broke out between the three companies. Mitsui Bussan, which had close connections with the three companies in handling their raw materials, machinery, yarn, and cloth, embarked upon a course of arbitration between the three companies in an effort to stop the price war and set up a common sales organization. Three months after the armistice, Kanekin was merged with Osaka Cotton Spinning with the promotion and support of Mitsui Bussan.

Osaka and Mie began to cooperate in order to expand the export markets in China and India. In 1914 the two companies arrived at an agreement to merge, on the advice of Eiichi Shibusawa, in order to establish a reorganized company known as the Toyo Cotton-Spinning Company (*Toyo-bo*). This new company had fifteen spinning mills with 441,700 spindles, and eight weaving mills with 10,130 power looms. In a true sense, this was a multiplant and multifunction company.

During the first few years after the merger, however, the new company was in reality a loose federation of many plants which lacked cohesion and central direction. Each plant had its own way of operating. Sometimes the quality of products of the same brand was not standardized. Also, a comparison of production costs among plants could not be attained.

The depression after World War I made it urgent to consolidate all operations of the company. Central staff departments were strengthened by recruiting new graduates from universities. Early in the 1920s the company adopted a cost accounting method based on a uniform price list. Production costs of all plants were compared monthly. When defects were found, the cause was thoroughly investigated and analyzed by the central staff. This method made it possible to attain a great degree of cost reduction in every plant, and was introduced to and adopted by the other companies.

A technical committee was organized under the leadership of the central staff in 1923 in order to increase the productivity for each spindle and to standardize operations in all plants. Procedures for machinery maintenance were standardized, which contributed to quality control and cost reduction. Improvement programs for each step of spinning and weaving were intensively promoted by central staff departments. Administrative consolidation was attained through these improvement programs.

6. Conclusion

When we look at the development of selected companies in the cotton-spinning industry, we can find some characteristics of management organization displayed by these companies.

Although initial circumstances leading to the establishment of these companies varied with each case, it was necessary for a new company to have a figurehead president, with a well-known reputation and extensive personal contacts, in order to raise sufficient funds. But he was not the man who contributed most to the development of the company. For the sound growth of the company, a full-time manager was needed who would never venture beyond the cotton industry. It was exceptionally lucky for Osaka Cotton Spinning to have found such a manager in Yamanobe, who was with the firm from its inception. In other companies it had taken several years before a full-time cotton man succeeded to the position of chief manager.

The function of marketing was usually carried out by a small number of employees. Cotton merchants were so powerful and reliable that it was not necessary for the company to deal with users directly. Although the brand of the company's product was important, cotton products could be called a standard product, and the price was more important for the cotton merchants.

Futures transactions for purchasing raw cotton were so vital to the success of the company that a chief manager was usually responsible for this function, and the company had a department which was engaged in researching business trends.

When the company had developed to the point of having more than two plants, it was very difficult to standardize the operations of these plants. For a few years after the acquisition, the acquired plant continued to be run by the old management or dispatched management who ran it independently. There is a famous story that the Tokyo plant under the management of Toyoji Wada, and the Kobe plant under the management of Sanji Muto, competed with each other in the Kanegafuchi company. It was not until the depression after World War I that administrative consolidation was attained in its true sense.

With regard to vertical integration, Osaka Cotton Spinning was an exceptional case because it was a pioneer in the industry. This company was very concerned about other functions besides manufacturing. It was this company which took the initiative in the importation of Chinese and Indian raw cotton, and in the exploitation of foreign markets. It was this company again which started the modern weaving business in the first place, and instituted a model organization for administrative consideration.

Generally speaking, however, it was at the time of World War I that vertical integration into weaving was adopted as a common growth strategy of cotton-spinning companies. The domestic market was growing because of the increase in population and the elevation of living standards, and Japanese cotton products were able to monopolize the Chinese market with the suspension of imports from Europe.

A growth strategy of diversification was taken in the 1930s when new artificial fibers were becoming popular and the domestic market for cotton products was saturated because of the deep depression. The new business taken up at this period was usually managed independently as a subsidiary.

As for internationalization of operations, some of the big companies had spinning and weaving mills in China, but it was not until the 1960s that Japanese fiber companies had the management problems of the multinational corporation.

COMMENTS

Tadakatsu Inoue
Kobe University

Before I go into details, I must tell you that I shall be unable to play the part of a commentator because I had almost no time to prepare a comment on Professor Tsuchiya's paper. So I would rather put some questions to the reporter in the capacity of an ordinary participant.

1. Professor Tsuchiya's paper induces me to compare the strategy of the Japanese cotton-spinning companies with that of the U.S. textile mills. As Professor Chandler points out, the textile industry belongs to that category of industries in which the adding, combining, and integrating of many units did not provide any special competitive advantage in terms of lower cost or customer satisfaction. Thus, the American textile industry remained highly competitive until well into the twentieth century. If I remember right, the top four companies represented together only 4 to 6% of the total industry in the number of spindles in operation in the 1920s and 1930s. On the contrary, as Professor Tsuchiya points out, the Japanese cotton-spinning industry adopted the strategy of horizontal combination on a large scale. If my memory serves me, the top fifteen companies represented together about 70% of the total industry in the number of spindles installed in the late 1930s. So I would like to know what factors brought about such a difference in the strategy of the U.S. and Japanese cotton-spinning industries.

2. According to Professor Chandler, horizontal combinations were rarely successful unless the constituent companies were well consolidated. One of the means of attaining consolidation is to shut down the old and poorly located mills and to build new ones. But mergers in Japanese cotton-spinning industry were seldom followed by this kind of consolidation. According to some data at hand, the

Toyo-bo Company closed only one of about forty mills for the period from its formation in 1914 to 1941. And the Kurashiki-bo Company had maintained all its mills combined for the period from its formation in 1887 to 1941. Judging from the facts, it may be said that the merger movement in the Japanese cotton-spinning industry facilitated keeping the old mills rather than closing them down. I would like to know Professor Tsuchiya's opinion on this point.

3. Professor Tsuchiya's paper makes its contribution by illuminating the problem-area of what type of management organization was adopted at the modern cotton-spinning mills in their initial period and how the organization was later revised to suit the evolving multiplant operations. If I may be allowed to hope for more, I wish I could gain a better sense of what structural changes followed after the vertical integration into weaving, which was a common growth strategy of the Japanese cotton mills at the time of World War I.

I-4

The Tradition of Family Business in the Strategic Decision Process and Management Structure of Zaibatsu Business: Mitsui, Sumitomo, and Mitsubishi

Shigeaki Yasuoka
Doshisha University

Four years ago I wrote a book titled *Zaibatsu keiseishi no kenkyu* [A historical study on the formation of zaibatsu], in which I analyzed the changes of the internal structure of two zaibatsu enterprises. Although I had in mind that a case study would provide us with both the peculiarities of each enterprise and the common features of all enterprises, in this study the abstraction of the common features in business behavior of zaibatsu was not always sufficient. Since then I have paid some attention to the behavior of some other zaibatsu enterprises, aiming at a generalized historical study of zaibatsu as my future goal.

In this paper I would, first, like to throw some light on the business behavior of zaibatsu by taking up three big zaibatsu, Mitsui, Mitsubishi, and Sumitomo, for the period up to the end of the nineteenth century; and secondly, I would like to look at the process of adopting corporate forms in their central offices with the public offering of stock. I feel, however, it will take some more time to complete this study, so this paper is a preliminary report of my present study.

To begin with, I would like to explain the term *zaibatsu*. This term is said to have come from a popular word and it is difficult to define strictly. So I will here tentatively define zaibatsu as follows: Zaibatsu are families or their firms which as a whole hold ownership, with huge capital, in many monopolistic (in reality, oligopolistic) incorporated enterprises, or enterprises of nearly the same size and various legal forms, in each of the industrial fields to which they become committed.

In the following, I would like to treat two problems. One is the problem of the entrepreneurship of big merchants who later became zaibatsu, and this will be explained through a review of the formative era of zaibatsu up to the 1890s. The second problem is related to the conditions under which occurred the disintegration of the closed character of the family, that is, the exclusive ownership of capital, which is considered to be one of the essential features of zaibatsu in Japan. In relation to this point, also to be treated is the problem of the adoption of a corporate form of organization in the central office of zaibatsu and the mutual holding of stock between the parent companies and their subsidiary companies in the period from 1937 to 1945. These two problems may seem to be unrelated, but in the sense that both are related to enterpreneurial activities and risk-evading as well as family-tie-keeping devices, there is a close relationship between the two.

1

As is already known, some of the zaibatsu families had their origin in the Tokugawa period, doing business as big merchants. These big merchants, however, found it difficult to adjust themselves to the rapidly changing environment of the Meiji period, and many of them were ruined. But some merchants who had skillful managers were able to tide over the crisis and eventually became zaibatsu. Admittedly, whether the merchants of the Tokugawa period could become modern industrial entrepreneurs depended on whether such merchants had skillful managers. In other words, the credit and capital they accumulated through the Tokugawa period were not enough to meet the needs of businesses responding to the development of Japanese capitalism.

It should, however, be noted here that modern industries were not yet rooted in the early part of the Meiji era, so even progressive and skillful entrepreneurs could not have been confident that they would succeed in their business. They had to have an understanding concerning the directions of the Japanese economy at the time as well as a perspective for future development. These situations can be seen in many industrialized nations, especially in their formative era, and therefore the same type of entrepreneurship should have taken place. In the early Meiji period, the development of banking, cotton spinning, and the railroad was conspicuous, but the young zaibatsu did not invest large capital in these ventures and they were rather cautious of direct investment to control them, although they did invest large sums of capital in their traditional businesses. It therefore becomes necessary to examine the ways in which the big merchants who became zaibatsu established their diversified businesses. I am inclined to regard the diversification of business as an important requisite for zaibatsu, though we must keep in mind the fact that such so-called finance zaibatsu, such as Yasuda and Konoike, had many enterprises in one industry.

Concerning the characteristics of zaibatsu, it has often been pointed out that zaibatsu would invest capital in any field to establish a business, regardless of its relation to their own business, as long as profit expectations existed, and they eventually came to own various kinds of business enterprises which had nothing to do with one another. I am not sure how strongly this remark is supported now, but as far as the above-mentioned three zaibatsu in the formative era are concerned, this remark appears not to be sustained. Let us examine this point.

First of all, I would like to point out the fact that the three zaibatsu, Mitsui, Sumitomo, and Mitsubishi, did not undertake diversification on a full scale before the 1890s. In the following we will analyze the business activities of these three zaibatsu up to this period and make the above point clear.[2]

MITSUI: This family ran a drapery business together with a money exchange in the Tokugawa period, but in 1872, accepting the suggestions of Kaoru Inoue and Eiichi Shibusawa, who were then influential officers in the Ministry of Finance, they transferred their drapery business to the Mitsukoshi family. The Mitsukoshi was a new family which was separated from the Mitsui in order to conduct the drapery business. Drapery now became the business of the Mitsukoshi so that even if this business were ruined, the Mitsui could evade damage. However, Mitsui continued to supervise Mitsukoshi and unofficially kept the potential ownership of the drapery business. In 1876 Mitsui established two firms, the Mitsui Bank and the Mitsui Bussan Company. As in the case of Mitsukoshi, Mitsui had two family members, Takenosuke and Yonosuke, removed from their family register at this time, and made them the owners of Mitsui Bussan, delegating their management function to an able manager, Takashi Masuda. In this way, the Mitsui family and their Mitsui Bank were again freed from damage in the case of failure of the new Bussan company. But also in this case, the Bussan company's assets and profits were under the control of the Mitsui family, and neither Takenosuke nor Yonosuke could have any rights to them. Using the family resister system in these ways, the Mitsui solved the problem of keeping the potential ownership of the two firms (Mitsukoshi and Mitsui Bussan) and at the same time evading the risks of their new business.

In 1888 the Japanese government disposed of the Miike Coal Mine, transferring it to Mitsui. It is, however, said that in this purchase, Masuda, the manager of Bussan took the intiative, and indeed this mine was sold to the Bussan company.[3] The Miike mine took the form of a joint property of the Mitsui family and Bussan for some years.[4] And it was not until 1892, a year before the Commercial Law was put into force, that Mitsui's mines, including the Miike Coal Mine, came to be the direct business of Mitsui, and in this year the Mitsui Mining Company was organized by the investment of eleven family members of Mitsui.[5]

In July of 1893, the Commercial Law was partly put into force, and just before this enforcement, Tokuemon Mitsukoshi of the Mitsukoshi Drapery Company returned to his original family register, so that Mitsukoshi Drapery came to be legally owned by Mitsui. At the same time, the same procedure was taken with Takenosuke and Yonosuke, and Mitsui became the owner of the Bussan company. In July of this year, the mining, banking, drapery, and trading businesses were respectively organized as partnerships and started operation. The liablity of these partnerships was unlimited, and Mitsui tried to find a way to avoid risks. Although the assets of these four partnerships were the joint property of eleven family members, Mitsui divided these eleven families into four groups consisting of five, two, two, and two families, and each group took responsibility for one of the four partnerships.[6] (See Table 1.)

TABLE 1 The List of Family Members of the Mitsui.

(July 1893)

	Mitsui Bank	Mitsui Bussan	Mitsui Mining	Mitsui Drapery
Hachiroemon (head family)	×			
Motonosuke (main family)	×			
Gen-emon (main family)			×	
Takayasu (main family)	×			
Hachirojiro (main family)	×			
Saburosuke (main family)			×	
Fukutaro (branch family)				×
Morinosuke (branch family)	×			
Takenosuke (branch family)		×		
Yonosuke (branch family)		×		
Tokuemon (branch family)				×

SUMITOMO[7]: This family was able to evade the confiscation of their Besshi copper mine in the Meiji Restoration, but their financial condition was so bad that they had to sell the Besshi mine to make business funds. On this occasion, Saihei Hirose, who was then the general manager of this family, became famous for his effort to check this sale.

Sumitomo reexamined their business strategy to tide over the crisis and decided to quit all of their side work lines, including the money-exchange business, and concentrate their efforts on the management of the Besshi Copper Mine. In 1876 Sumitomo began a commodity mortgage loan business, but they did not go into banking despite the national bank boom at the time. Recalling these days, Hirose remarked that the reason why they did not begin the banking business was as follows: "The Sumitomo could not afford to extend their business farther than mining."[8]

Hirose organized a reforesting project in the Besshi region and purchased woodlands. He also acquired such coal mines as Shoji and Tadakuma in 1894, shortly before his retirement, the motive of which was to secure the fuel for copper manufacturing as well as to increase Sumitomo's property. Among the new ventures that Sumitomo undertook were the Sumitomo Silk-Reeling Mill and the Sumitomo Camphor Works, but these businesses were only short-lived. However, the rationalization of management in the Besshi Copper Mine seemed to have resulted in the improvement of their financial condition, and around 1888 they appeared to have sufficient economic power to invest in businesses other than their traditional business. It was, however, not until the retirement of Hirose in 1895 that Sumitomo established their own private bank. Then, with the expansion of the mining-related businesses, Sumitomo's enterprise began to be diversified, and on this point Professor Morikawa has also pointed out that the full-scale diversification of Sumitomo's business began only after the retirement of Hirose.[9]

As shown in the foregoing examples of Mitsui and Sumitomo, we can see that the zaibatsu entrepreneurs were very cautious, at least up to the middle of the Meiji era, about side works and diversification, evading direct management of the large-scale enterprises. And these facts would suggest that even a capable manager could not manage effectively a number of operating units because he had to pay so much attention to managing the family business and property.

IWASAKI (MITSUBISHI): Mitsubishi was a newly-established business house with government affiliation in the Meiji era, and was often considered to be different from such traditional business firms as Mitsui and Sumitomo. Let us reexamine this firm with reference to their business strategy. The first business of Mitsubishi was shipping, and it earned big profits in military transportation in the Taiwan Expedition in 1874 and in the Satsuma Rebellion in 1877. In order to secure the supply of fuel to their ships, Mitsubishi began in 1871 to run the Manzo and Otokawa coal mines in Kishu, and in 1875 they started the Yokohama Iron Works to repair ships.[10] The following year they opened a money-exchange office to handle bills of lading for the purpose of competing effectively with their rivals, and this organization later became the Mitsubishi Bank.[11] In 1881 Mitsubishi acquired the mortgaged Takashima Coal Mine from the debtor, Shojiro Goto. In 1884 they got the right of using the government-owned Nagasaki Shipbuilding Yard, and the next year Mitsubishi's shipping business was merged with the Kyodo Unyu Company to form NYK (Nippon Yusen Kaisha). Since the shipping business was separated, the basis of their business was shifted to shipbuilding and ship repairing as well as coal mining, and in this respect the acquisition of the Nagasaki Shipbuilding Yard in 1887 would have been an invaluable addition to the Mitsubishi Company. At any rate, as long as they were in the shipping business, their business area was limited to shipping and its related ventures.[12] So we can safely say that the diversification of Mitsubishi took place as an extension of the shipbuilding business, and therefore the area of diversification was closely related to their original business. The purchase of the Yoshioka Copper Mine in 1873 was rather an exception. I at first had the impression that Mitsubishi was a newly risen entrepreneur compared with Mitsui and Sumitomo who had a history of two or three centuries, and therefore the former should have been more innovative and aggressive than the latter, but the results of my re-examination have shown almost the same business behavior in terms of the diversification of business activities.

If the behavior of these three big businesses is representative of the cautious attitude of the businessmen in the early part of the Meiji era, there would have been many businesses who were restricted to traditional pursuits. So, let's examine some other examples.

The house of Yasuda was established by Zenjiro Yasuda, who went up to Edo (Tokyo) when he was nineteen years old. Having opened a money-exchange shop, he earned lots of money through dealing in old coins and taking advantage of the fluctuations of paper money. After the revision of the National Banking Law in 1876, Yasuda established the Third National Bank with a joint investment, and in 1880 he transformed his Yasuda Company into the Yasuda Bank. Then Yasuda established as well as purchased a number of banks and integrated them together to form a huge Yasuda Bank. After the integration of the operating units along the same lines, Yasuda made his business come to be called a zaibatsu. But here again, it was not until the 1920s that the Yasuda Bank showed tendencies toward diversification.

Among other successful traditional merchants were drapers, whose success was brought about by their decision to transform their original Edo-period drapery businesses into modern department stores. Although they tried to keep the closed family system, as the result of diversification of the lines and eventual enlargement, they came to need more capital, and to meet this need they began to adopt a corporation system, so the family tie gradually disintegrated.

Still, there were other merchants who, while keeping their traditional business, gradually changed its character and finally built up a small-scale integrated concern. The case of the Kashiwabara Paper Company would illustrate this type of merchant. Kashiwabara was an old family with relations by marriage to Mitsui and Naba. He was called *Edo tanamochi Kyo akindo* (a merchant having an office in Edo and living in Kyoto). In the Tokugawa period Kashiwabara opened Edo stores to handle cotton goods, lacquer wares, and Japanese paper, and in the Meiji era they quit the business of cotton goods and Japanese paper, becoming a dealer in foreign paper. Having become the agent of the Walsh Company and the Mitsubishi Paper Manufacturing Company, the Kashiwabara later came to handle from 40 to 60% of the products of the Mitsubishi Paper Manufacturing Company. In 1910 the Kashiwabara acquired the Nishinari Paper Manufacturing Company, which then went into bankruptcy, and managed this enterprise. The Kashiwabara Paper Company was twice reorganized. In 1916 it became a limited partnership, and in 1924 it was incorporated. Three years before this, a holding company named the Kashiwabara Goshi Company was established to control the paper company, the Kuroe Lacquer ware Shop, the Nishinari Manufacturing Company, and some other businesses. After that Kashiwabara built and controlled several companies for insurance, real estate, transportation, and warehousing. Eventually Kashiwabara combined these enterprises into one integrated organization. As shown in this example, among the nonzaibatsu businessmen there were some merchants, originally specialized, who expanded their business related ways by building affiliated companies in the form of corporations, and finally established a holding company to integrate and control them from a central office. After the 1920s we can see similar examples among the newly risen zaibatsu in the chemical industry.

2

In the foregoing section I have discussed business behavior in the early part of the Meiji era, that is, to say, up to the 1890s, and have pointed out that many of the big merchants were rather cautious in the diversification of business. So in the following I would like to briefly examine the reasons why they were so cautious in their business activities, and the industries they willingly entered.

Industrialization was clearly the goal of the nation when Japan opened the door to foreign countries, but at that time no one knew whether Japan could become a highly industrialized capitalist nation such as the countries of Western Europe or the United States, and it was a serious problem, especially for the businessmen, whether the industries such as those developed in the advanced countries would bring any stable profit. For at that time there was no country in Asia that had succeeded in industrialization. Even if the success of certain enterprises in the future was predicted, stable profits immediately after the beginning of an enterprise were still questionable.[14] Therefore, even the big merchants who could hire capable managers hesitated to invest large capital in risky new ventures, and instead they tried to accumulate capital in rather familier businesses in which they had already had some previous experience. Banking, trading, shipping, and mining were the ventures they could enter with confidence.

Banking had long been practiced by money-changers since the Tokugawa period and was known as a profitable business, and the big merchants were very eager to establish their own private banks in the early Meiji period.

Commerce, and especially domestic commerce, was one of the important conditions for the establishment of the Tokugawa shogunate system, for one of the preconditions of the shogunate system was the commercialization of rice, an indispensable food for the Japanese people. As for foreign commerce, merchants had no experience except for Sumitomo, who had exported copper. For this reason Mitsui did not directly manage the Mitsui Bussan (trading) Company at first, and they restricted the latter to the commission business.

Shipping had also shown conspicuous development in the Tokugawa period, and in the Meiji era, as the feudalistic local government (*han*) was abandoned and communications were freed, the basis for further development was established. With the introduction of the steamship the nature of this industry was completely changed.

Mining was also a long experienced industry, and products such as gold, silver, and copper were used for export. In the Meiji era, coal and copper were largely exported and therefore the market for them was secure. Mitsui Bussan, which exported Miike coal, wanted to acquire this coal mine because of its profitability.

As indicated in the foregoing examples, the industrial areas in which the zaibatsu-oriented enterprises acted in the Meiji era were either already experienced fields or areas to which their traditional businesses were closely related. Here we can see the common behavior of the large family enterprises. They invested capital in such industries as railroads or cotton-spinning mills, but never managed them directly, although sometimes they elected an executive from among the stockholders and sent him into the industrial enterprises.[15]

The industrial division of Mitsui was somewhat exceptional. This division was organized in November 1894 with several factories and other properties, some of which the Mitsui Bank acquired in the recession of 1890–91 as mortgage forfeit. This division consisted of seven factories in three industries, namely, the Shibaura Manufacturing Works for electrical machinery; the Maehashi Spinning Mill, the Oshima Spinning Mill, and the Shinmachi Spinning Mill for silk spinning; and the Tomioka Reeling Mill, the Mie Reeling Mill, and the Nagoya Reeling Mill for silk reeling. Hikojiro Nakamigawa, the capable manager of Mitsui, worked hard to bring up these young industrial enterprises, ignoring profitability to some degree, but it seemed to be difficult for him to manage them effectively. This division was disintegrated in December 1898, and Shibaura Works was transferred to the Mitsui Mining Company and other mills to the Mitsui Drapery Company. In 1902 Mitsui sold out these silk industries. Shibaura Works was, however, in order to obtain a favorable licensing agreement with the General Electric Company as well as capital saving, separated from Mitsui Mining and became in 1904 an independent corporation.[16]

The example of the industrial division of Mitsui indicates how difficult it was to effectively manage unexperienced enterprises. Mitsui's and Sumitomo's decisions to reduce their diversified business at the time of the Meiji Restoration would indicate the same difficulty in management in this fluctuating period. It would, therefore, be quite natural for these businessmen to have started diversification from the business which, in the light of their experience, seemed to have the strongest possibility for success. In these respects, the problem of choosing between the alternative of direct management or the establishment of an affiliated company in the businesses in which they entered, remains for future investigations.

3

We have already seen common features in the behavior of zaibatsu businesses. It should, however, be noted that there were different characters as well among the zaibatsu families. One of the differences would be found in the location of the supervising power in the enterprise. Mitsui and Sumitomo developed from merchants in the Tokugawa period, and the supervising power or authority was materially in the hands of one or several managers (*banto*); but in the case of newly risen zaibatsu such as Mitsubishi, Yasuda, Furukawa, and Okura, the head of the zaibatsu family had the power to supervise the enterprise. That the originator of an enterprise was often a dictator was a well-known fact, and, indeed, the head of the Mitsubishi family practically had the right of command over the enterprise for two generations. In the following, I would like to analyze the first case by taking up Mitsui and Sumitomo, with an emphasis on the structures for decision making.

The Mitsui's business capital was owned jointly by eleven families of the Mitsui, and so were their branch offices, of which there were about thirteen. As early as 1710 they organized a kind of central office called *omotokata* to decide the business policy for these thirteen branch offices. Members of the family were sent to the branch offices to manage them with the help of hired executives. Their authority was, however, gradually delegated to the hired executives, and finally the family members came to "reign but not rule." This structure continued even after the Meiji Restoration, and therefore, as long as they could not hire a capable man as the top executive, they could not respond to the changing environment. But the Mitsui's eleven families were generally conservative, so they were often opposed to Minomura and Nakamigawa, who were hired as reformers. In 1914 Takuma Dan became the leader of the enterprise, but he was so slow to coordinate the different opinions of the eleven families that he was nicknamed *Kimezu no Dan* (Indecisive Dan).

Contrary to Mitsui, Sumitomo was a single family, but the head of this family seemed not to be dictatorial, and like many other big merchants, he appeared to have delegated the right of management to his managers. This system was not changed even in the Meiji era. When the general office of Sumitomo was transformed to a limited partnership and became a holding company in 1921, this managerial structure was formally established.

In the case of Konoike, who was one of the largest merchants in the Tokugawa era, business had been managed by hired managers since the eighteenth century, and the head of the family did not directly control the business. The family code of Konoike in 1889 was stated as follows: "Rōbun [the top manager] shall, on behalf of the head of the family, execute not only the management of the family property but also the internal and external businesses related to the family." Also, according to the family code of 1899, it is stated that the head of the family should not participate in either management of the property or business activities.

The organizational structure of the family enterprise, in which the head of the family did not participate in business but delegated the authority to the hired managers, was the generally adopted system in the Tokugawa period, the merit of which was that even though chance determined whether the head of the family was capable or not, the probability that the managers, who were selected from among many servants, would be capable was very high. And because of this delegation of the managing power to the employees, the right of ownership should presumably be restricted to the family members. This managerial structure was, however, institutionalized or traditionalized at the end of the Tokugawa period, and rather conservative men often became managers so that many of the merchants could not respond to the changes following the Meiji Restoration. For this reason, the big merchants had to hire capable and progressive talent from outside. The case of Saihei Hirose of Sumitomo, who had grown up in the traditional family enterprise, was one exception.

4

Now I am going to refer to the changes in the capital ownership. It was a well-known fact that the zaibatsu with strong family ties tried not to have their capital joined with others, although they did endeavor to keep their family property and business. Investment in the parent company of the zaibatsu was generally restricted to family members. After 1937, as business became gradually involved in the wartime economy, the zaibatsu companies including Mitsui, Mitsubishi, and Sumitomo began to incorporate their head offices, selling a part of their stock to the public. In this process, there can be found the elements which would show the characteristics of the zaibatsu enterprises and the postwar business group. I would, therefore, like to investigate at first the process of the public offering of stocks of the subsidiary companies of the zaibatsu firms, and then that of the parent companies.

Having received the patronage of the government, the zaibatsu realized a higher accumulation of capital, and, as monopolistic business units of capital, they came to control the Japanese economy. Through the years from 1909 to 1923, the zaibatsu were preparing to control their affiliated companies by having their head offices reorganized in the form of unlimited or limited partnerships, having most of their affiliates incorporated, and having the head office hold stocks of the subsidiaries. In this case, the prime motive of the incorporation was the rationalization of control as well as of ownership (tax reduction, limited liability, etc.) rather than the effective supply of capital.

In some cases, however, a few companies offered stock for public subscription when they made new issues, although it was only a small portion. In 1917 the Sumitomo Bank, in 1919 the Mitsui Bank, and in 1920 Mitsubishi Mining offered part of newly issued stocks for public subscription. On these occasions, all three companies gave the need for cooperation with the public as a reason for these public offers. It can, however, be presumed that World War I brought an opportunity for their business expansion, and as the demand for capital increased the zaibatsu tried to gather the additional capital from the public by offering a part of their stock, while at the same time they tried to give an impression of opening the zaibatsu to the public. It is not clear how great the need was to introduce outside capital by offering a part of their stock (less than 30%) to the public, but it is certain that they did this reluctantly.

In March 1920, when Mitsubishi Mining offered stock to the public, the company promised to keep the dividend rate, but the next year the company had to reduce the dividend. On this occasion, Koyata Iwasaki, then the head of the Mitsubishi zaibatsu, felt his responsibility so seriously that he refused to receive his several million yen dividend and requested that it be used to increase the dividend rate to general stockholders.[17] The subscribers to the offered stock of Mitsubishi Mining were not the general public but those who had personal connection with the company; nevertheless, Koyata treated their stocks as if they were bonds. Again in October 1945, when the head company of Mitsubishi was disintegrated, Koyata Iwasaki vainly made a request to the finance minister, Keizo Shibusawa, for the final payment of dividends to general stockholders.[18] These examples would suggest that with the public offering of stock, the heads of the zaibatsu had to be more considerate of society as well as of general stockholders. This might be seen as a kind of moral obligation. Since the public offering of stock was accompanied by such a a moral obligation as well as by bothersome obligations to outside stockholders, it was by no means desirable, but in order to soften the public criticism against zaibatsu and introduce outside funds, it was inevitable. It was, therefore, necessary for zaibatsu to have a device to assure that they would not be interfered with by outsiders in their efforts to keep the closed character of the business. This scheme was carried out in two ways.

First, they achieved this purpose by restricting the subscribers for the offered stocks to those concerned with the company, which meant in this case the officers and employees of the company or its affiliated companies. On this occasion, the company often put various limitations on the stock holding. The stockholders had to keep the stocks for a given period of time, and when they disposed of them they had to sell them to the company; examples can be found in the public offer of the stocks of the newly established Mitsubishi Trust Company in 1927, and that of the Mitsubishi Bank and Mitsubishi Mining in 1928.[19]

Secondly, they developed the first method of the mutual holding of stock among the concerned companies. The easiest way to be able to keep the controlling power as well as to supply large capital was to have the affiliated companies have the stock. When this procedure was applied among the affiliated companies of the zaibatsu, the mutual holding of stock among the affiliated companies took place. Although there is a view that the mutual holding of stock is a phenomenon which appeared after World War II,[20] the available evidence shows that even before the war the mutual holding of stock among the affiliated companies of zaibatsu was already being done on a scale similar to the postwar pattern.[21] Although the mutual holding of stock in the postwar period was devised to restore and strengthen the identity which was lost by the disintegration of the headquarters of the zaibatsu enterprise, that of the prewar period was devised to reduce the share of the investment by the zaibatsu family (headquarters), and at the same time to keep the controlling power over the affiliated companies. The final form of such a mutual holding device was the holding of the stock of the head company of the zaibatsu by its affiliated companies.

5

On the eve of World War II, as the whole nation became involved in the wartime system, the social criticism against the monopolization of national wealth by zaibatsu became severer, and the so-called *zaibatsu tenko* (conversion) was demanded. To this end, the rate of income tax and inheritance tax to the wealthy class was greatly raised. In addition to this obligation, the zaibatsu enterprises were required to expand into war-related industries, especially heavy industry.[22] Furthermore, the investment in new fields of industry was also necessary to compete with such newly risen zaibatsu as Nitchitsu, Mori, and Nisso, who had entered such new industries as electrochemicals and light metals. In accordance with these movements the zaibatsu enterprises reorganized their structures in various ways. In March and December of 1937 Sumitomo and Mitsubishi, the legal forms of which had been limited partnerships, were incorporated, and in August 1940 the head office of Mitsui, which was an unlimited partnership, was merged with the incorporated Mitsui Bussan Company, and again this central division was separated in March 1944 as the incorporated Mitsui Honsha (central office). In the following, we will see these processes in relation to their stock holding.

Referring to the reorganization of the head office of Sumitomo, a publication of the company stated as follows: "The reorganization of the headquarters in Sumitomo went ahead at a time when other zaibatsu were still contemplating the refomation of headquarters according to the social and political situation which appeared after the Manchurian incident."[23] This statement is the only evidence to indicate the organizational reformation of Sumitomo, but at that time the affiliated companies expanded their business to such an extent that the necessary funds for three years was estimated to be from ¥200 to ¥250 million. Nevertheless, Sumitomo's financial agencies had to subscribe to government bonds and to meet the demand for funds in general, so that it was difficult to supply the necessary capital for the Sumitomo zaibatsu as a whole. Consequently, they were gradually relying on public sources of funds through a new issue of stock and an issue of bonds, and they also came increasingly to rely on government funds.

Although Sumitomo had its central office incorporated earlier than Mitsubishi and Mitsui, its stocks were never offered to the public but were held by family members. In March 1945 they increased the capital to double the amount, and the total capital came to ¥300 million. The distribution of the capital among the family members at the end of the World War II was as follows:

Kichizaemon Sumitomo	470 (1,000 shares)	78.3%
Kanichi Sumitomo	1 (〃)	5.0
Yoshiteru Sumitomo	1 (〃)	
Motoo Sumitomo	1 (〃)	
Sumitomo Bank	7 (〃)	16.7
Sumitomo Trust Co.	2 (〃)	
Sumitomo Life Insurance Co.	1 (〃)	

Immediately before the end of the war, Sumitomo finally allowed its affiliated financial agencies to hold its headquarters's stock, though Sumitomo was one of the zaibatsu families who had continued to keep a strong closed character.[24]

In Mitsubishi, Koyata Iwasaki, the head of Iwasaki zaibatsu, had been offering the stocks of affiliated companies to the public one after another, but since the later part of the 1920s, as the criticism against zaibatsu became severer, he worked out a plan for reformation and decided to have the central office incorporated. In this respect, he said, "While our affiliated companies are opened to the public and have a public character, the fact that our central office alone has been maintained as the Iwasaki business is out of step with the progress of the times." The newly organized central office gave up its controlling position and temporarily ceased management of its affiliates as a holding company, but this did not bring good results, so the central office turned, in May 1940, back to the original position of controlling the affiliated companies.[25] In May 1940 the Mitsubishi Honsha (central office) increased its capital from ¥120 million to double the amount, and on this occasion stock was offered to the outside. But stock was "to be assigned to the stockholders who hold a given number of stocks of our affiliated companies, and to the officers, and the employees who have done good service." Then this did not mean a real offer of the stock to the public. According to the list of the leading stockholders at the end of this year, as shown in Table 2, except for five family members, most of the outside stockholders were either banks or insurance companies.[26]

TABLE 2 The Main Stockholders of the Mitsubishi Honsha (Dec. 1940).

Hisaya Iwasaki	75,000	shares	
Koyata Iwasaki	285,000	〃	
Hikoyata Iwasaki	480,000	〃	
Takaya Iwasaki	150,000	〃	
Tsuneya Iwasaki	150,000	〃	
Meiji Life Insurance Co.	80,000	〃	(affiliate)
Tokyo Marine Fire Insurance	55,000	〃	(〃)
First Mutual Life Insurance	50,000	〃	(〃)
Mitsubishi Trust	35,810	〃	(direct affiliate)
Nihon Life Insurance	35,000	〃	
Nihon Yusen (Japan Line)	35,000	〃	(affiliate)
Chiyoda Life Insurance	15,000	〃	
Teikoku Life Insurance	15,000	〃	
Mitsubishi Bank	10,840	〃	(direct affiliate)
Mitsubishi Marine Insurance	10,300	〃	(affiliate)
Meiji Fire Insurance	10,000	〃	(〃)

Like other zaibatsu businesses, in Mitsubishi the directly or indirectly affiliated subsidiaries came to hold a large part of the stock of the parent company, and the rest of the stock was assigned to insurance companies, which were expected to have no desire to control other companies.[27] The zaibatsu families' share of the stock was reduced to 1.14 million of the total 2.4 million, and dropped below 50%.

In the case of Mitsui, the following three situations influenced the incorporation of their central office[28]:

First, the unpaid inheritance tax of five of the eleven families had reached more than ¥45 million, but their unlimited partnership could not supply enough money to meet this urgent need. In addition to this, as long as their organization maintained this kind of legal form, they could not issue bonds which were convertible into currency.

Second, the need to get more funds increased because they had to subscribe to the newly issued stock of their affiliates and they also had to invest in new industries in order to respond to the business expansion which occurred with the outbreak of the Manchurian Incident.

Third, the government regulations on money supply were strengthened, so that they could not be furnished with sufficient funds by their affiliated financial institutions.

Under these circumstances, the incorporation of the central office of Mitsui came to be inevitable, but if they had done it alone, they would have had to liquidate their partnership, in which case they would have had to pay a heavy liquidation tax, which was estimated to have been from ¥300 to ¥380 million. In order to avoid such an unnecessary expenditure, the central office was said to have once been merged with the incorporated affiliate, the Mitsui Bussan Company.[29]

Two years after this merger, Mitsui decided to offer 25% of their ¥300 million capital stocks, the purpose of which was to acquire business funds. The subscribers were again restricted to "employees of the affiliates and customers of Mitsui Bussan." On this occasion, the share of the eleven Mitsui families became 75%, and in August 1945, with a new issue of stock, it dropped to 63.6%. In the meantime, the central office was again separated from the Bussan in March

1944 and became an independent corporation, the Mitsui Honsha, and among the stockholders were included insurance companies as well as the affiliates of Mitsui.[30]

As is shown in these examples, under wartime conditions, the public offering of stock proceeded to a certain extent, although the scope of the offering was limited to a small circle. In Sumitomo subscribers were the subsidiaries of the zaibatsu. In Mitsubishi and Mitsui all offered stock was held by their related firms, including financial institutions or insurance companies. Nevertheless, there was a certain degree of progress in terms of the public offering of stock when compared with the days when all stock was held only by the zaibatsu families. Here the subsidiaries came to be stockholders of their parent companies, which had formerly controlled the subsidiaries through the holding of their stock. Thus the mutual holding of stock entered the zaibatsu system, and this was an extreme form of the zaibatsu business, with which they could, under wartime conditions, secure the supply of necessary funds for business expansion without losing the closed character of their capital ownership. With the end of the World War II, the zaibatsu disappeared, but the mutual holding system created by the zaibatsu did survive and presumably provided the business world with the foundation for the postwar business groups.

References

1. As to this term, see Yoshio Togai, *Zaibatsu to shihonkatachi* [The zaibatsu and the capitalists] (1956) p. 151.
2. The following descriptions rely on Shigeaki Yasuoka's *Zaibatsu keiseishi no kenkyu* [A study on the formation of zaibatsu], 1970.
3. *Ibid.*, p. 363.
4. Mitsui had already acquired the Iwaonupuri mine in Hokkaido for sulpher in 1877, and Kamioka mine in Gifu Prefecture for gold, silver, lead, and tin in the next year.
5. *Mitsui bussan shoshi* [A Short History of the Mitsui Trading Company], p. 143.
6. As to the diversification of Mitsui in later periods, see Hidemasa

Morikawa, "Mitsui zaibatsu no takakuteki jukogyoka katei" [The process of the diversification in the heavy industry of Mitsui], *Keiei Shirin* 4, nos. 4–5 (1968).

7. On this company, see *Sumitomo ginkoshi* [A history of the Sumitomo Bank], 1955.
8. *Saihei iseki* [The achievement of Saihei], p. 200, cited in ibid., p. 16.
9. Hidemasa Morikawa, *Nihonteki keiei no genryu* [The origin of the Japanese-type business] (1973) p. 171.
10. Masaaki Kobayashi, "Kindaisangyo no keisei to kangyo haraisage," [The formation of the modern industry and government sale], in, *Nihon keizaishi taikei* [Economic History of Japan], ed. Mitsuhaya Kajinishi, 1956.
11. *Mitsubishi ginkoshi* [A history of the Mitsubishi Bank].
12. See Kobayashi, "Kindai sangyo," p. 341.
13. *Kashiwabara yoshiten hachijunenshi* [Eighty years of the Kashiwabara Paper Company], 1964.
14. On this point, cf. J. Hirschmeier, *The Origins of Entrepreneurship in Meiji Japan,* 1964, p. 197. Translation by T. Tsuchiya and T. Yui, *Nihon ni okeru kigyoshaseishin no seisei* (1965) p. 166.
15. For example, Hikojiro Nakamigawa became the president of Kanebo (Cotton Spinning Co.) and Nihon Tetsudo (Railroad).
16. See Yasuoka, *Zaibatsu keisei.*
17. *Iwasaki Koyata den* [A personal history of Koyata Iwasaki], p. 291.
18. *Ibid.*, p. 356.
19. Hisashi Masaki, *Nihon no kabushiki kaisha kinyu* [Corporate Finance in Japan] (1973) p. 129.
20. For example, see Hiroshi Okumura, "Hojin no kabushikimochiai ni Mesu o!" [Let's criticize mutual holding of stocks among the corporations!], *Kosei Torihiki,* no. 276 (October 1973).
21. Mochikabukaishaseiri Iinkai, ed., *Nihon zaibatsu to sono kaitai* [Japanese zaibatsu and its disintegration], 1951, pp.98–99: Kazuo Shibagaki, "Zaibatsu kara kigyoshudan e" [From zaibatsu to business group], *Keizai Hyoron,* March 1971.
22. The following are indebted to Mochikabukaishaseiri, *Nihon zaibatsu.*
23. *Sumitomo no rekishi to jigyo* [History and business of Sumitomo], 1956.
24. *Ibid.*, p. 20; Mochikabukaishaseiri, *Nihon zaibatsu,* p. 121.
25. *Iwasaki Koyata den,* pp. 206–12.
26. *Mitsubishi Shashi* [Mitsubishi Company Journal] (1940) p. 1,652.
27. See Mochikabukaishaseiri, *Nihon zaibatsu,* p. 114.

28. The following descriptions are indebted to the *Mitsui honshashi* [A history of the Mitsui Company], vol. 2.
29. Mochikabukaishaseiri, *Nihon zaibatsu,* p. 57.
30. When Mitsui was appointed the holding company, such incorporated insurance companies as the following held a large share of stock in the Mitsui: Mimotokai (263,720 shares), Daiichi Life Insurance (220,000 shares), Daihyaku Life Insurance (82,000 shares), Mitsui Life Insurance (81,500 shares), and Chiyoda Life Insurance (70,000 shares). Mochikabukaishaseiri, *Nihon zaibatsu* (document edition), p. 12.

COMMENTS

Yoshio Togai
Senshu University

Professor Shigeaki Yasuoka, after investigating the behavior patterns of the zaibatsu, points out two characteristics of the tradition of the zaibatsu (the family business).

First, they were very cautious and prudent about diversifying their businesses. In other words, they had a tendency to avoid risks in diversifying their businesses.

Secondly, he points out their mechanisms of family ties, in other words, the exclusive ownership of capital by their own family.

Professor Yasuoka explains the first point using data on the business activities of the three big zaibatsu (Mitsui, Mitsubishi, and Sumitomo) in the middle of the Meiji era (from about 1887 up to about 1896).

Concerning the second point, he tells us as follows: From the end of the Meiji era up to mid-Taisho, namely, from about 1909 up to about 1921, the headquarters of the zaibatsu were reorganized from private enterprises into *gomei kaisha* (partnerships) or *goshi kaisha* (limited partnerships), and their subsidiary companies were reorganized into *kabushiki kaisha* (joint-stock companies). At that time, the zaibatsu as family combines (*Konzern* in German) were built up, and, after that, the zaibatsu headquarters became holding companies with controlling power over their subsidiaries. At the same time, they sold a part of their subsidiaries' stocks for the first time to friendly third parties.

Then, when wartime came (1937–45), the zaibatsu headquarters were reorganized into joint-stock companies, in order to obtain more funds, and some part of their stocks were sold, mainly to their own subsidiary companies. But this measure did not break their family ties, because most of the headquarters' stocks remained in the hands of the zaibatsu families as before.

Although I agree with Professor Yasuoka, I want to bring up some other problems for topics of later discussion.

First, was this tendency to avoid risks peculiar characteristic only of the zaibatsu, or of Japanese family business?

I think this tendency is very common to every business unit that is a going concern. In the case of the zaibatsu this tendency was so, only because of the special relationship between masters of the zaibatsu houses and their employees (*banto* = manager). Particularly Mitsui and Sumitomo, which developed from large merchant houses in the Tokugawa era, had a special decision making system. In Mitsui and Sumitomo the controlling power and responsibility for business management was entrusted to their *banto* (single or plural), so that it was only natural for the *banto* to be cautious and prudent (and sometimes timid) in decision making.

Thus, in the case of the zaibatsu, the tendency to avoid risks originated in their unique master-employee relations, that is to say, in their own tradition of family business.

Secondly, in this sense, this tendency can be said to be a characteristic of the zaibatsu business, but I want to raise another question about this point. As Professor Yasuoka says, the zaibatsu were very cautious and prudent in diversifying their businesses, but was this the case even after they completed their diversification, namely, after they built up their combines? After that did this tendency change or not?

Thirdly, when family combines were built up, systems of controlling subsidiary companies by the zaibatsu families were also established. Did those systems have any unique characteristics of family businesses or not? If they had, what kind of characteristics were they?

Fourthly, as for the characteristics of the zaibatsu strategy, I think that the zaibatsu had close connections with the Japanese government. Because it is a matter too common to warrant explanation, I suppose Professor Yasuoka did not mention it. But we can not disregard it, especially in investigating the pattern of behavior of the zaibatsu in contrast with foreign business. I want to hear the opinion of Professor Yasuoka on this problem.

Lastly, two characteristics, which were pointed out by Professor Yasuoka, had completely disappeared at the time of the "zaibutsu dissolution." But after that, the zaibatsu were gradually transformed into "enterprise groups" based on their former zaibatsu lineage, and now these groups are organized along the former zaibatsu lines.

Here I want to raise another question concerning the problem of these groups. Have these groups inherited any of the traditions of the former zaibatsu? If they have, what part of the tradition is it? Each "enterprise group" is closely united, but group member companies nevertheless compete and struggle severely against one another. Is this behavior pattern inherited from a tradition peculiar to the zaibatsu? I think it is worthwhile to investigate this problem.

I–5

The Traditional System of Middlemen and Marketing Policies of Food Manufacturers

Tsunehiko Yui
Meiji University

In Japan, marketing methods for mass sales developed after World War II. This development is popularly called the distribution revolution. Today, very sophisticated marketing practices prevail among the big manufacturers. Prewar Japanese manufacturers, in contrast, were not interested in their own marketing activities toward the general public. This indifference could be explained by the low purchasing power of the general public and the continuing existence of the traditional trade system and distribution channels controlled by established wholesalers (*tonya*).

There were some exceptional fields of industry, however, where manufacturers poured every effort into creating new demands, and their marketing policy was the most important factor in the success of the firms. They belonged to industries such as food processing, cosmetics, and medicines. Even in these exceptional cases, their marketing policies and practices were very different from those of American firms in their initial stages, because the traditional trade system was more strongly established in Japan.

Firstly, this paper will outline some features of the prewar traditional trade system. Then, cases of the representative manufacturers of wheat flour, seasoning, and candy in the food processing industry will be presented. Their marketing policies for adapting, and sometimes effecting, changes in the traditional system will be examined.

1. Traditional Trade Systems and Distribution Routes

I will briefly explain the development of the merchant and his sales organization in preindustrial society. In traditional Japanese society of the Tokugawa period (1603–1867) a large number of sedentary merchants in towns and villages as well as in big cities were engaged in commerce. Consistent and stable trade organizations and distribution routes were the two constituent aspects of merchant life.

The feudal period of Tokugawa Japan was peaceful and lasted for 250 years. Three great cities, Edo (Tokyo), Osaka, and Kyoto, were prominent during this period and were connected to all castle cities by main highways. From merchant to merchant the selling organization developed like an unraveling cord, from big city wholesalers (big *tonya*) through middlemen (middle or small *tonya*), and finally to retailers.

In particular, it was in Osaka and Edo that many commodity exchanges had developed and where a large number of specialzed wholesalers possessing both capital and financing potential were located. Principal goods and merchandise were brought to the wholesalers in these big cities from each region of the entire country, and redistributed to numerous wholesalers in medium and small cities and finally to towns and village retailers.

Wholesalers and retailers in each region formed strong guilds which were given protection by feudal lords. The existing guilds and their protected distribution routes were not easily bypassed, and those who attempted to do so were punished.

The wholesalers in the big cities held great power over their trade systems. They extended credit up to sixty days to their buyers, medium and small wholesalers, and in some cases a credit period of six months to one year was given. By means of their great financial resources and credit, the wholesalers in the big cities (especially Osaka) came to control city and town wholesalers, who in a like manner controlled town and village retailers.

In the Tokugawa period, the static social order and the fixed trading system did not generally stimulate merchants to develop aggressive entrepreneurship. Advertising and marketing activities for dynamic demand creation did not exist. It was common for city merchants to inform customers of their business by means of *noren* (a dark blue cloth with the store's name) and *kanban* (a wooden plate with the store's name). Wholesalers tried to avoid mutual competition by their strong guild restrictinos, and were able to share big profits among themselves.

After the Meiji Restoration, the new government adopted a policy prohibiting guild restrictions. As a result, the static system of middlemen and their distribution routes was inevitably forced to change. Wholesalers had to compete more or less with each other. They had to diversify the commodities they dealt with. Not a few people opened new wholesaling businesses. However, even in the industrialization of the Meiji period, the merchant system of traditional society continued to exist.

In particular, the distribution of essential foods and commodities such as rice, grains, dried foods, sake, textiles, and paper could not produce major change because the daily life of the general public, which depended so fundamentally on these commodities, was itself changing only very slowly.

2. Milling: The Marketing Policy of Nihon Flour-Milling Company, Limited.

Many modern manufacturing companies which had been established during the Meiji period were generally not concerned with selling, especially in the field of daily commodities, because of the existence of a well-established marketing and distribution system. Manufacturing companies in their initial stage concentrated almost all of their efforts on mastering imported technology and manufacturing products whose quality would equal that of imported goods.

They thought that selling should be left to the existing wholesalers. When they had routinized mass production by the factory system, however, some companies began to reconsider their selling practices and adopted active selling policies to enlarge their markets.

First we will discuss the case of flour milling.

As high-grade machine-milled flour (so-called American flour), which was imported from the U.S., invaded the traditional flour market (the so-called noodle flour, which was milled by water wheel in the village), plans to establish modern companies for making machine-milled flour emerged. After a period of trial and error, the Nihon (Japan) Flour-Milling Company, Limited, was established in 1896 under the presidency of Nanjo Shinrokuro. Factory production in its true sense started with the setting up of roll machinery with a 200-barrel capacity imported from U.S.

The selling of flour at this time was handled by established grain wholesalers and flour wholesalers in the big cities, who mixed traditional noodle flour with imported American flour as they wished, and sold it as their own brands. It can be said that this was a transitional practice of traditional wholesalers encountering and responding to new conditions. In addition to this system, the local traditional grain wholesalers and flour sellers in each area continued to sell low-quality flour milled by the traditional water-wheel method.

In this market situation, the company adopted the following policy for selling flour milled in its new plant:

First, they registered a brand and a trademark of their own in order to show that their flour was machine milled and had a high quality, equal to that of imported flour. Then they graded the flour into three kinds according to its quality, and put the grade on the trademark.

Secondly, for their marketing channel, they adopted the general agency system in order to take full advantage of existing selling organizations of wholesalers. That is to say, they designated the biggest four among the traditional Tokyo flour wholesalers to be their general agents, who in turn forced their own subordinate dealers and retailers to handle only Nihon Flour Milling products. To make this policy effective, the company gave advertising signboards reading, "This store sells flour made by the Nihon Flour-Milling Company," to each of their general agents, dealers, and retailers, and forced them to display the signboard. In a subsequent move, the company also designated general agents in Osaka and Kobe.

Because the quality of Nihon Flour Milling products was as high as imported ones, and because their prices were set lower than those of imported ones, the general agents could easily stop the selling of mixed flour and concentrate on the selling of Nihon Flour Milling products. As a result, the existing selling system for mixed flour was changed suddenly to the marketing organization of Nihon Flour Milling.

It was natural for other milling companies to imitate this marketing strategy. Following Nihon Flour Milling's success, several modern flour-milling companies were established. They began operations using imported American machinery, and designated other grain wholesalers and flour wholesalers as their general agents for the selling of their products. Needless to say, however, Nihon Flour Milling was able to enjoy a competitive advantage because their general agents had at one time been the most powerful wholesalers.

After 1910 Nihon Flour Milling and Nisshin Flour Milling (the latter company, after prolonged effort, had succeeded in transforming the traditional local flour selling system into its own marketing organization) had grown to become the two dominant firms exercising oligopolic control over the flour market. Thus, almost all of the traditional selling system and distribution channels were divided between these two firms.

From this time on, however, the marketing strategies of these two firms became passive. Both of them introduced new products for bread, cakes, and soba. This introduction was based on cooperation with the general agents, and sometimes on the initiative of the latter. The marketing of these new products was left to the activities of the general agents and dealers. When they had firmly established their nationwide selling network, both Nihon Flour Milling and Nisshin Flour Milling redirected their management efforts toward reducing the costs of their manufacturing and raw materials.[1]

3. Seasoning: The Marketing Strategy of Ajinomoto

Although flour milling companies did not proceed beyond taking full advantage of the traditional wholesalers' system, Ajinomoto, a seasoning company, used the traditional system more broadly and effectively, and achieved great success after developing a modern advertising campaign.

Chemical seasoning (monosodium glutamate) is one of the few

industrial products which were invented by Japanese. Suzuki and Company (later the Ajinomoto & Company) began to produce it commercially in 1908.

As Saburosuke Suzuki and his son had engaged in the production and sale of medicines, they applied the sales organization for medicine to the marketing of seasoning, only to result in failure. Then they made aggressive plans to take advantage of the wholesalers' system for various foods (sake, beer, canned foods, dried foods, seafoods, etc.).

In order to carry out this plan, they asked more than ten wholesalers with large assets and good will among the many food wholesalers in big cities (Tokyo, Osaka, Kyoto, and Nagoya) to become general agents, and promised them that they would exclusively use their channel for the sales of Ajinomoto. But they could not expect the agents to make an exceptionally active sales effort, for their seasoning was an entirely new product, which the agents had never handled. Saburosuke Suzuki, therefore, visited each of the secondary wholesalers and retailers in the distribution channel of every general agent and explained the characteristics and qualities of Ajinomoto products, and entreated them to be more active in selling them.

In addition to these efforts, Suzuki looked for local wholesalers and retailers with goodwill in territories not covered by the general agents, and asked them to affiliate directly with the distributing organization of the general agent in each district.

The general agents appreciated this connection with the local agents because it promoted the interest of the general agents as well. In this way the general agents gradually became interested in the selling of Ajinomoto.

As a result, Suzuki obtained thousands of retail outlets covering cities, towns, and villages all over Japan. But this action was not sufficient to create new demand for his product. He thought it was necessary to initiate a large national advertising campaign. It was at this point, 1909, that one of the modern advertising sales had just begun. Although newspaper coverage had been established throughout the entire country, the bulk of advertising was limited to cosmetics, beer, wine, and books.

Suzuki thought a large newspaper advertising campaign was necessary in order to inform all housewives of his Ajinomoto and create large demand for it. In 1910, he presented full-spread advertising in major newspapers with such slogans as "the ideal seasoning," "a big revolution in food taste," and "a world shocking discovery." Thereafter he continued to place newspaper advertisements, adding pictures of seasonal foods and landscapes. Besides this, he utilized trams and electric poles for advertising, and urged all his retailers to display the Ajinomoto signboards with their various designs.

He also utilized the traditional advertising method on the streets (so-called *chindonya*). *Chindonya*, a group of musicians in fancy attire carrying advertising, were popular in Japan and China in this period as an advertising method appealing directly to the populace. Suzuki visited many cities and towns to acquire additional retail outlets and intensively used *chindonya* for advertising Ajinomoto.

This marketing strategy of using the traditional selling system on a large scale, and the modern as well as traditional advertising media, attained great success within a ten-year period. The general agents began to sell Ajinomoto in earnest, and their management and organization developed as result of the increasing sales.

Suzuki and Company launched a similar marketing campaign in Taiwan and China with great success in the 1910s. As Ajinomoto became popular as a seasoning, it provoked many producers of similar products in Japan and China.

In the 1930s a branch was established in New York with the brand name of Super Seasoning, and the company attempted a similar marketing practice based upon newspaper advertisement and personal visits to food stores. Although it did not succeed in creating consumer demand by using this marketing method, it sparked interest in Ajinomoto's usefulness on the part of large food processors such as Heinz and Campbell, and sold in volume. Thus, their selling effort in the U.S. could be considered a success in the prewar period.[2]

4. Candy: Marketing of Morinaga Confectionery Company, Limited

Morinaga Confectionery adopted American methods of marketing in addition to utilizing the Ajinomoto method, and grew to become the largest candy maker in prewar Japan.

The company's founder, Taichiro Morinaga, had worked during his youth from 1891 to 1898 in the United States as a laborer in a bakery and candy manufacturing plants, where he learned manufacturing technology for chocolate, marshmallow, caramel, and ice cream. After returning to Tokyo in 1900, he began the manufacture of Western confectioneries. At this time Western confectioneries were being imported in large volume and sold by imported liquor and candy stores in large cities.

There was no Western confectionery except for Morinaga, who built his own small plant and began selling directly to the imported liquor and candy stores. With its growing success in manufacturing and selling, Morinaga became well known as the largest and only Western confectionery marker.

In 1905, Morinaga invited Hanzaburo Matsuzaki, an import and export businessman in Yokohama, to join in his confectionery business, delegating to him full responsibility for marketing. Matsuzaki was an aggressive person, and with his enterprising spirit he set about planning an expansion of operations. A large-scale candy manufacturing plant was established and equipped with candy-making machinery imported from the United States. In 1910 the business was reorganized as Morinaga and Company, Limited.

Following Suzuki's example of merchandizing Ajinomoto, Matsuzaki aimed at establishing large-scale sales in each line of Western confectionery produced in the plant. Beginning with Tokyo, foreign liquor wholesalers and Japanese confectionery wholesalers throughout Japan were enlisted in large numbers as special agents. At that time, demand for Western confectionery was increasing in Japan, and in addition Matsuzaki began to advertise in newspapers, much to the delight of wholesalers who now sought to become special agents. Some sugar wholesalers changed business lines to become special agents for Morinaga's specialty line of Western candies. The number of special agents climbed to over 200 in a short time.

Matsuzaki was bolder in his advertising policies than Suzuki had been. He was the first to use full-page newspaper advertisements. The expense was considerable and equivalent to ten days' sales of the company. However, this one-page advertising was very effective. As a result, those desiring to become special agents increased in number, and nationwide demand quickly grew. The company concentrated its manufacturing, sales, and advertising efforts on four product lines, chocolate, caramel, marshmallow, and biscuits.

In 1918 Matsuzaki made a survey trip to the United States and Europe. He decided to adopt American marketing methods in use at that time. In 1923 he established sales companies for Morinaga's confectionery goods in Tokyo and Osaka. He also decided to try to promote the company's own retail outlets by furnishing a national chain-store system covering the main cities of the country.

These chain stores were called Morinaga Candy Stores. The store, with a marble front, was located in the business center or downtown area in each city. As Morinaga Candy Stores became known in the cities, some wholesalers and retailers wanted to go into the candy-store business instead of continuing their existing businesses.

In 1930 Matsuzaki organized a new chain-store system called Morinaga Belt Line, in which he included independent retailers. Morinaga Confectionery and the sales companies gave many services to the members of this organization. It was a great strategic success for the company to use the channels of both the special agents and the chain stores. Sales of the four products grew rapidly again.

Conclusion

I have outlined the marketing policies and strategies of three firms in the food industry. These three cases clearly differed from those of American food companies in their early stage. The difference could be explained by the existence of the traditional trade system and sales channel. We can also find some differences in the marketing policies among the three firms, each of which had a considerable impact on the traditional trade system.

In the first case, that of Nippon Flour Milling, the management did not go beyond utilizing the traditional flour wholesalers in their existing system. Once the retail outlets were controlled, advertisement was not relied on to create demand. Sales promotion was left mainly to the wholesalers.

In the case of Ajinomoto, almost every kind of food wholesaling system was utilized more broadly and more extensively. Along with big sales promotion efforts, both modern and oriental styles of advertising were jointly used to a remarkable extent in order to promote the selling activities of retailers. For example, Matsushita, the sole Osaka agent, was able to grow rapidly through the increase of Ajinomoto sales, and came to specialize only in this product.

In the third case, Morinaga Confectionery adopted their peculiar chain-store system in addition to utilizing the traditional wholesaling system, and had an impact in reorganizing the existing trade system. The advertising methods of Morinaga were mainly modern in style. In a sense, the marketing strategy of Morinaga could be called the most modern of the three cases.

In summary, the marketing policies and strategies of these three firms differed according to the nature of each firm's respective product line. In particular, Ajinomoto and Morinaga showed a pioneering spirit in their use of modern advertising, in their multiple utilization of selling organizations, and in the effort to reorganize the traditional trade system.

When the development and expansion of large-scale mass production required aggressive marketing activities in postwar Japan, it was these three firms which provided many manufacturers with prototypes of marketing methods.

References

1. This section is based mainly on *A Seventy-year History of the Nihon Flour-Milling Company,* by Tsunehiko Yui (1968), pp.76–94.
2. This section is based mainly on *A History of Ajinomoto & Company,* by Tsunehiko Yui (1971), pp.91–109.
3. This section is based mainly on *A Fifty-year History of Morinaga* (1955), pp. 52–175.

COMMENTS

Kin-ichiro Toba
Waseda University

Professor Yui's paper is different from the other papers presented to this conference. It discusses business firms which had no government patronage and did business mainly in the domestic market, while others deal with big zaibatsu firms which not only were under government patronage but also manufactured products mainly for the export market. This is a point which I would like to ask all of you to keep in mind.

In commenting on Professor Yui's paper, it is necessary to pay attention to the characteristics of market structure, particularly that of Meiji Japan (1868–1912). The character of a market changes in response to social changes. At the same time, however, the market is under the strong influence of the cultural pattern of the society. This means that, in considering the market structure of Meiji Japan, we have to emphasize the fact that the Japanese market had been secluded from the outside for long years because of the Tokugawa seclusion policy. There is no doubt that today's Japanese consumers are enjoying a western style of life in many respects, but it should not be forgotten that such changes in daily life have taken a long time. In short, producers for the domestic market faced more difficulties and modernized more slowly than producers for the export market, and the same situation can be seen in the relationship between the makers of consumer goods and the makers of producer goods.

Secondly, modern industries in Japan had started by introducing western technology. Therefore their products, particularly consumer goods, were difficult to adjust to the domestic market. Adjustment might have been easier if the technology had been transplanted from some more culturally homogeneous country such as China.

Most of the new products which the western technology produced were completely new to the Japanese of the Meiji period. Although Americans in the late nineteenth century were producing such new products as typewriters, sewing machines, and cigarettes for their domestic market, these products had some continuity with the life style of the day. In the Japanese traditional market, most of the products introduced from the West were not only new but had no connection with the life style of the day. Even such consumer goods as liquors and confectioneries, which Professor Yui discussed in his paper, were unknown.

Thirdly, the Japanese market had tended to be divided into two sectors by government policy from the beginning: the external (export) market and the internal (domestic) market. As the Meiji government tried to develop the economy without drastically disturbing the traditional life style, the development of the internal market had been rather neglected in spite of strong governmental stimulation of the external market. This resulted in a sharp contrast between the big zaibatsu firms which developed rapidly with the help of government subsidies and small firms which developed slowly through their own efforts. As the result of such governmental and entrepreneurial emphasis on the external market, *sogoshosha*, for example, quickly grew into modern big businesses, as Professor Nakagawa pointed out in his paper. In the internal market, on the other had, traditional distribution carried on by traditional entrepreneurs was continued without any drastic changes, as Professor Yui has mentioned. The effectiveness of this distribution system in the internal market should be emphasized here. It was a well-organized system which had developed through the long Edo period, and it was not only maintained but even encouraged under the strong protectionary policy of the government.

These basic characteristics of market structure in early modern Japan brought about some different patterns of development for the producers of consumer goods. It is true that modern industries in Japan had made remarkable progress; in many industries, rapid development not only in technology but also in marketing methods had been achieved. However, in considering the development of marketing methods in the consumer goods industries, it will be useful to divide the producers into three types: (A) those producers engaged in the production of such standard and traditional products as soy sauce, *sake* wine, flour, cloth, and so on, which were familiar to contemporary consumers; (B) producers of such new products as beer, whiskey, western drugs, western-type confectioneries, and so on, which were unknown to consumers; and (C) producers of such products as *tabi* (Japanese socks), seasonings, etc., which were half-way between new and old products.

These three types of producers responded differently to the marketing problems created by modernization in the Meiji era. Type (A) producers did not feel any necessity to modernize their distribution methods and paid no attention to modern types of advertising. They usually depended on traditional distribution channels and concentrated their modernization efforts mainly on technological development. Type (B) producers had difficulty using traditional distribution channels and tried to find new outlets for their products by establishing new channels of distribution. In so doing, they engaged in active advertising campaigns, using not only traditional media but also newly introduced media like newspapers and magazines. The Morinaga Confectionery Company is a good example of this type. Type (C) producers depended on the old distribution channels because of the similarities of their products to traditional ones. At the same time, however, they used advertising actively in order to popularize their brand names. Ajinomoto Company is an example of this type.

The differences in marketing and distribution methods among the three companies which Professor Yui discussed are mainly due to the differences in the technologies they used and the products they produced under the given marketing conditions. Therefore, in considering the development of modern marketing methods and distribution channels in an underdeveloped country like Meiji Japan, we have to take into account such factors as: (1) what type of product the company was producing, (2) what kind of technology it was using, (3) whether the existing channel of distribution was effective for its products or not, and (4) whether the new mass media for advertisement already existed or not. I believe that considera-tion of these four factors is very important in any discussion of the development pattern of business firms producing consumer goods. It was only after World War II that a big market opened up not only for the producers of export products but also for the producers of domestic products.

PART II

INTERNATIONAL COMPARISON OF BUSINESS STRATEGY

II–1

Institutional Integration: An Approach to Comparative Studies of the History of Large-Scale Business Enterprise

Alfred D. Chandler, Jr.
Harvard University

1

I am honored and greatly pleased by the invitation to participate in this conference. It has given me an opportunity to see Japan and to learn about the writing of business history here. As important, the invitation caused me to focus attention on a topic of major significance to business historians throughout the world, "an international comparison of the strategy and structure of big business." Such international comparisons are, I am convinced, one of the most promising areas for long-term continuing research in business history. Only by comparing developments of business activities, practices, and institutions in different nations operating under different sets of economic and political constraints and within cultures having different attitudes and values can we understand what in modern business organization results from the imperatives of the economic and technological processes and what reflects particular national economic, political, and ideological realities.

Any such comparison requires agreement on a common set of terms, concepts, and approaches. The purpose of this paper is to suggest some neutral (that is, nonideological) terms and concepts as well as an approach which can help to order the fund of information already available to business historians. As my research has been concentrated on American business history, these suggestions are based on the American experience. I would hope that in the discussion following the paper we can evaluate the usefulness of this approach for the analysis of large-scale business enterprise in other countries. A comparison with Japan should be particularly fruitful, for in this country the economic situation and the underlying attitudes and values are so different from those of the United States.

Big business, that is, large-scale business enterprise, is historically a new phenomenon. The modern enterprise differs from that of earlier centuries in its size, in the variety of its activities, in the number and types of its managers, and in the processes of its management. *The basic characteristic of large modern enterprise is that it is multiunit.* A *unit* is a regionally or functionally separate business component that could theoretically operate as an independent enterprise. It is managed by a full-time partner or salaried supervisor responsible to headquarters. Its books and accounts, locally kept, can be audited separately from the accounts of the organization as a whole. Thus, the units within a larger enterprise may be engaged in the same or different functions, handling the same or different products, and located in the same or different regions.

Before 1850 even the largest business firms in the United States rarely operated as many as two or three factories, or mines, or buying or selling offices, or transportation lines. By 1900, however, many American enterprises had become multiunit. By then, many multiunit firms had taken on several different functional activities. Thus, a single industrial enterprise came to manage not only many manufacturing units, but also many mining, selling, purchasing, and transportation units as well. Also in the twentieth century, many such multifunctional enterprises began to operate in several different industries and in a number of different countries. Modern enterprise had become multiindustrial and multinational.

The operation of many different units by a single enterprise required the recruitment and training of a new species of economic man, the professional salaried manager. These activities also demanded the formation of an organizational structure and other administrative arrangements to coordinate, control, evaluate, and direct the work of the many units and their many managers. At each stage of expansion, the enterprise added a new type of administrative office and a new level of managers. A multiplant manufacturing firm or a marketing enterprise with many branch offices required a set of managers at headquarters to coordinate, evaluate, and plan for the activities of the managers of the several factories or branch sales offices. As the firm became multifunctional, a central office had to be formed to coordinate, evaluate, and plan for the work of the headquarters of different functional departments. Finally, as an enterprise became multiindustrial and multinational it needed a general office to coordinate, evaluate, and plan for the activities of several central offices in different industries and in different nations.

Before the 1840s very few men worked as managers at even the lowest or field-office level and almost none at the higher levels of management. In 1840 all the managers in the United States who supervised a working force of over fifty men probably numbered less than 3,000 in a working force of 5.42 million. Not only was the managerial class tiny in 1840, but few enterprises used more than one manager. Except for a minuscule number of plantation stewards, no managers managed other managers. Professional middle and top managers made their first appearance in the United States only after 1840.

Theoretically, the large managerially manned multiunit enterprise can be created in two ways. One is by subdivision. As the volume of activity expands, the firm's operation becomes divided into specialized subunits. The other is by addition. The enterprise becomes large by adding, combining, and integrating already specialized operating units.

Economists since Adam Smith and management analysts since Frederick W. Taylor have tended to view the growth of modern enterprise, and with it the coming of modern management, as resulting from the first route to size, that of increased internal specialization. Economists such as George Stigler have done more than continue to accept Adam Smith's theorem that the division of labor is determined by the extent of the market. They have extended it into a theory of institutional specialization. The expansion of the market, they argue, not only permitted increasing specialization within the firm but also encouraged the firm itself to specialize in the single product or process for which it had the greatest comparative advantage. Thus in young and growing industries enterprises became increasingly specialized. As they did, these enterprises "disintegrated." In Stigler's words: "When the industry has attained a certain size and prospects, many of these tasks are sufficiently important to be turned over to specialists. It becomes profitable for other firms to buy equipment and raw materials, to undertake marketing of the product and the utilization of by-products and even to train skilled labor." Only in old and declining industries, when capacity outran demand, did integration and combination occur.

For Stigler and other economists, institutional specialization meant that market mechanisms continued to coordinate the flow of goods from one specialized unit to another. As important, investment decisions concerning facilities for future production and distribution became increasingly decentralized. The managers of these specialized firms, at least in growing and dynamic industries, thus concentrated on supervising and coordinating the work of specialized subdepartments within single-unit, single-function enterprises.

I believe that the second theoretical way of growth is much closer to historical reality than the first. Institutional specialization was indeed an important phenomenon in the development of the modern American economy. On the other hand, institutional integration played a much larger role than institutional specialization in the development of the modern American business enterprise. The great mass of data suggests that the modern firm came into being and continued to grow through the addition, combination, and integration of specialized units of a type that could, and often did, operate as independent businesses.

The large, modern firm can be viewed as an aggregation of units, each with its own supervisory office. It forms a network, usually spread over a large geographical area, through which flow decisions, orders, and information about present and also future operations. The functions of its managers are to coordinate, evaluate, and plan for a number of offices often carrying out quite different economic activities. The resulting industrial structure was precisely the opposite from the one posited by Stigler. Decisions concerning the flow of goods through the American economy became increasingly coordinated by administrative rather than market mechanisms; while the decisions as to investment for future production and distribution became increasingly centralized in the top offices of large multiunit enterprises.

I am convinced that the concept of institutional integration—institutional aggregation might be a better term—provides a far more useful approach to the study of the history of large-scale modern business enterprise than does that of institutional specialization. It permits a more precise probing into the beginnings and growth of the modern firm, a better understanding of the evolution of the processes and procedures of modern management, a more thorough explanation of interfirm competition and the resulting changing structure of American industries, and finally a deeper appreciation of the role and function of large-scale enterprise in the overall economy. This approach also allows, I believe, a more exact use of terms for similar offices, functions, structures, levels of management, and the like. If large-scale enterprise grew in other nations through the integration of specialized units, then this approach can help to provide the common set of terms and concepts so necessary for comparative analyses of the history of large-scale business enterprise in several different national economies.

2

A very brief look at the rise of modern large-scale business enterprise in the United States can document the basic proposition that it resulted far more from the addition of new units than from the subdivision of existing ones. At the same time, this review can indicate why and how big business first appeared, grew, and became managed. In the United States the first enterprises to grow large enough through a process of institutional integration or aggregation to require sets of managers and an explicit internal organizational structure were those in transportation and communication. The resulting improved transportation and communication, in turn, permitted the appearance and growth of large multiunit enterprises in marketing, mining, and manufacture.

It should be stressed, however, that the process of institutional integration was preceded by a half century of institutional specialization. From the making of the Constitution in 1789 until the 1840s, the activity of a general, unspecialized merchant, the dominant businessman of the day, became increasingly specialized. In the eighteenth century the merchant handled the buying, selling, transporting, financing, and insuring of goods. He bought from and sold to farmers, planters, artisans, manufacturers, and other merchants at home and abroad. With the rapid growth and geographical expansion of population and of the American economy and economic activity after 1790, specialized common carriers, banks, and insurance companies appeared in sizable numbers. At the same time, the merchants found their volume of business large enough to concentrate on a single product or commodity like cotton, grain, dry goods, hardware, drugs, and groceries. Nevertheless, before 1840, the growth of the market was not yet advanced enough to allow extensive specialization within the firm. Nor apparently were there any strong pressures or incentives for an enterprise to add new specialized units or to combine with others.

In transportation, the enterprises operating the new common carriers remained small. A transportation line rarely owned as many as five ships, boats, stage coaches, or wagons. The captains and drivers were often partners in the enterprise and,even if they were only paid a salary, they kept in close contact with the owners. The relationship between ownership and operation was close and personal. There was no need for organizational structure or for middle and top management.

Nor did the building and operation of rights of way—the turnpikes and canals—on which these carriers operated require much in the way of a managerial force. In the 1840s, the controller of the state of New York (one of the state's most powerful politicians), assisted by four clerks and a handful of engineers, supervised the operation and maintenance of the Erie Canal, the largest and most profitable of the nation's great artificial waterways. Each time an election overturned the political party in power, the entire working force, as well as the managerial staff, was replaced by adherents of the victorious party. The canals and indeed most of the turnpikes became public rather than private enterprises largely because of the high construction costs. While Americans were willing to let their government finance and operate costly rights of way, they never suggested that the government should take over the operation of common carriers.

With the coming of the railroad in the 1830s, a private business enterprise for the first time both built and maintained the right of way and operated all the common carriers that used it. Partly because of the belief that common carriers should be private enterprises, partly because of the costly failures of the canals, and partly because railroad operations required a permanent technically competent working staff that would not be rotated at each election, the railroads in the United States were built and managed by private enterprise. Government participation came only in the provision of financial aid in construction. From their beginnings, the railroads were the nation's largest business enterprises in terms of capital invested and workers employed.

They were also the most complex to manage. Railroad operations involved the integration of more functions than did the management of other transportation and industrial ventures of that day. Railroad equipment was technically more complex and required greater attention to maintenance than other contemporary machinery. Rails and roadbed needed more constant and detailed attention than did turnpikes or canals. As more employees handled money on a railroad than in any other contemporary business, new methods of financial accounting had to be devised. Finally, the movements of trains and traffic had to be coordinated with great care in order to avoid serious accidents and to insure that existing equipment was fully used and efficient service provided.

Nevertheless, railroad management remained relatively simple as long as their lines were short. Thus, on the forty-four-mile-long Boston and Worcester, trains left three times a day from both termini. After safely meeting at the midpoint, Framingham, each moved on to its destination without fear of collision. A single superintendent could personally supervise and coordinate the work of the managers in charge of each of five different functional activities, that is, the movement of trains and of traffic, maintenance of way, maintenance of locomotives and rolling stock,and accounting.

But on the longer roads built to connect more distant commercial centers, such as Philadelphia and Pittsburgh, or Baltimore and Wheeling, management became more difficult. These larger roads were built in sections of 75 to 100 miles, and when a new division went into operation it was given the same functional structure as the original unit. By the mid-1850s several roads had created from three to five divisions and were integrating their operations. Here, for the first time, American business managers had the problem of coordinating, controlling, and evaluating the work of several similar operating units. To do this, the companies set up central offices with a general superintendent and with managers of the five functional activities for the line as a whole. At this point, the new top managers had to define the relationship of the functional officers at headquarters —the very first middle managers—with those in each of the operating divisions.

In the United States this fundamental management problem of coordinating regionally defined, functionally organized units was answered by the invention of the line and staff concept. The president delegated his authority to the general superintendent and through him to each of the division superintendents in charge of transportation and their assistants. The managers on the line of authority were given power to order the movements of trains and traffic, as well as any emergency maintenance of equipment and road bed. The other functional executives became designated as staff officers (see Table 1). They set standards and evaluated, promoted, and hired and fired managers in their departments. In the terminology of the day, the line managers handled men; the other functional or staff managers handled things.

By spelling out line and staff relationships, the early roads devised an organizational structure that carefully defined the lines of authority, responsibility, and communications. The relationships were outlined in organizational charts—the very first of such devices to appear in American business. The top executives quickly developed elaborate daily, weekly, and monthly reports to flow up, and standardized orders and circular letters to move down these communication channels. Almost at once, they began to use for managerial purposes the detailed flow of operating information so essential for the coordination and control of the daily movement of hundreds of locomotives and thousands of cars over hundreds of miles of track. They employed these data to determine operational costs and so pioneered in the development of modern cost accounting. As important, they began as early as the 1850s to use costs and other statistical information to

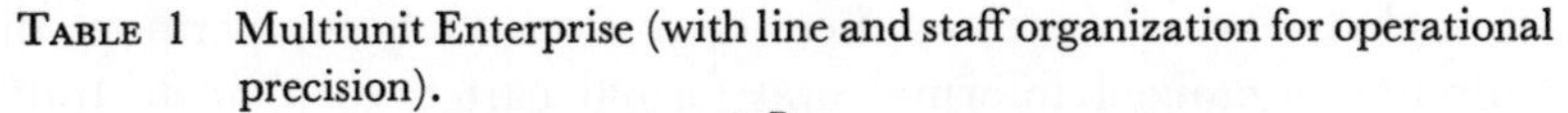

TABLE 1 Multiunit Enterprise (with line and staff organization for operational precision).

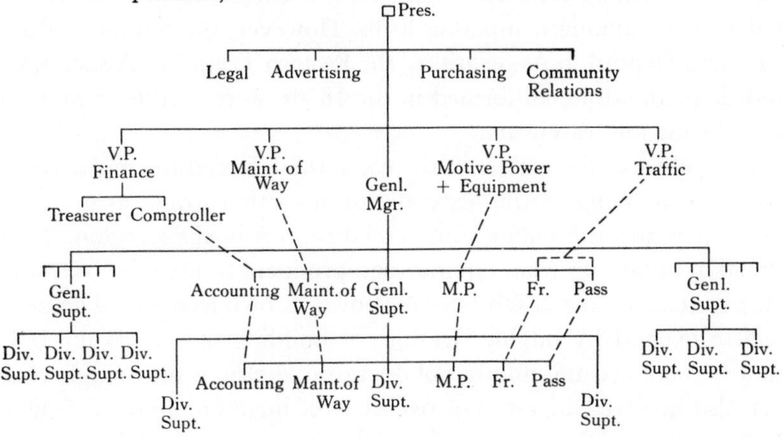

Used by: Railroads after 1840s and in modified form by air lines and large bus and truck lines.

Similar structure without precise line and staff distinction used by firms carrying on a single-function business over wide geographical area including insurance companies in late nineteenth century and banks with extensive branches in twentieth century.

evaluate the performance of the line and staff managers within each of the regionally defined operating divisions.

The railroads in the United States grew to greater size and their managers handled more divisions than did those of other countries. For example, by the mid-1870s only two nations in the world, Great Britain and France, had built more mileage than that operated by the Pennsylvania Railroad alone. One reason the American railroads had more operating divisions than those of European countries was, of course, the longer distances between commercial centers in the United States. After 1870, however, the primary reason for adding new units resulted from the need to assure a continuing flow of traffic over the road's existing costly roadbed and equipment. After the nation's main lines were completed, the pressure to keep their heavy fixed capital employed created an irresistible temptation to attract business from competing roads by cutting rates on through traffic. For most roads, financial solvency depended on a continuing flow of through traffic. To protect themselves from such competition, the railroads organized informal and formal cartels to allocate traffic and revenue among competing firms. However, the Southern Railways and Steamship Associations, the Eastern Trunkline Association, and their imitators, all formed in the 1870s, were unable to prevent rate cutting and rate wars.

The failure of the cartels in the early 1880s forced the major roads into a strategy of creating extended systems that would assure their own entry into the major commercial centers in their region. They aimed at obtaining what one railroad president termed "self-sustaining" systems where "each line must own its own feeders." The decision to expand by buying, leasing, or building new units not only greatly increased the number of operating divisions on a single road but also involved investment decisions of huge amounts of capital. This meant that financiers, particularly investment bankers, came to sit on railroad boards and have a say in the overall strategy of expansion.

To manage their greatly enlarged transportation empires, the new systems fashioned still larger management units. This resulted in the creation of two new levels of middle and top management. A number of territories managed by general superintendents were combined into an organization headed by a general manager with his staff. The larger systems had two to five such regional organizations supervised by a vice president in charge of operations and by his staff. On the Pennsylvania, the Burlington, and the Santa Fe, the general managers of these great administrative organizations had the same autonomy and profit responsibility that the division managers of large industrials such as General Motors and Du Pont came to have in the mid-twentieth century.

At the same time that the roads were increasing the size of their operating domains, they were cooperating with each other to develop techniques to move trains and traffic efficiently from one system to another. By the 1880s they had made mutual arrangements that permitted a car to go from one major commercial center of the country to almost any other without a single transshipment. Both internal organization and external cooperation thus permitted the railroads to provide the transportation of freight, passengers, and mail on a continental basis with a speed and regularity that was unprecedented in world history.

In these same years came a comparable increase in the speed and, with it, volume of communication. The experience of the great private enterprises that came to operate the new forms of communication, the telegraph and the telephone, had many parallels to that of the railroads. As nearly all the business of the many telegraph companies was long distance, and not local messages, cooperation between these enterprises in the handling of such messages was essential. As a result, consolidation came quickly. By the late 1850s, less than a decade after the telegraph became commercially viable, six regional systems were operating nearly all the mileage constructed. By 1866 these had been consolidated into Western Union. At its start Western Union was already managing a network of over 2,500 offices, and it continued to add from 500 to 1,000 a year. The new consolidated enterprise administered this network through a number of regionally defined territorial offices whose managers were responsible for supervising groups of operating units, for the functional activities of maintenance and repair, and for the development of procedures to assure a smooth and steady flow of messages between towns and cities in all parts of the United States.

In its early years, the telephone differed from the telegraph in that it was used primarily for local rather than long-distance messages. Local companies using Bell's patents and equipment operated the first telephone enterprises. As local companies became interconnected and patents expired, the Bell interests maintained control over these many units by means of the American Telephone and Telegraph Company, which operated the nation's "long lines," or through long distance traffic. The operations of AT&T were quickly organized through a regionally defined administrative structure similar to that used at Western Union.

From the start the new forms of transportation and communication were operated through multiunit enterprises. These enterprises were, therefore, forced to pioneer in the ways of modern big business. By making possible an unprecedented level of speed, regularity, and volume of transportation and communications, they in turn permitted the rise of modern large-scale business firms in both the production and the distribution of goods.

Between the 1850s and the 1880s a revolution occurred in American marketing based entirely on the new forms of transportation and communication. Within a single generation all the modern types of mass marketing enterprises had replaced the merchant who for centuries had handled the distribution of goods. Although by the 1840s merchants had become specialized in handling a single line of commodities or products, their modes of operation differed little from those of the merchants of Venice and Florence a half a millenium earlier. They sold primarily on consignment and commission, operated through the same types of partnerships, and used the same double-entry bookkeeping.

As the American farmers in the early nineteenth century moved west, the merchants moved with them. By 1840 distribution of agricultural commodities and finished goods was carried on through a chain of middlemen. Cotton and wheat moved from farms to processors, and dry goods and hardware from manufacturers to farmers, through the hands of at least three or four commission merchants, each residing at one major point of transshipment.

As soon as the railroads and telegraph provided fast, reliable, all-weather transportation and communication, the chain of middlemen disappeared. Commission merchants were replaced almost overnight by marketing enterprises that purchased on their own account directly from the farmer or the manufacturer and sold directly to the processor or local retailer, or in some cases to the ultimate consumer. In the marketing of agricultural crops, the commission merchants lost out to commodity dealers who purchased corn, wheat, and cotton at the rail head, stored and shipped the commodities, and sold them directly to processors. To finance these transactions, the dealers relied extensively on the grain, cotton, and other exchanges formed in the 1850s and the 1860s on the basis of telegraphic communication. In the distribution of manufactured or processed goods, the full-line, full-service wholesalers (who were specialized in the same product lines as their predecessors including dry goods, hardware, drugs, and groceries) began to buy directly from the manufacturer and sell directly to the local retailer. These new wholesalers pioneered in the developing of modern marketing techniques such as branding, advertising, and the use of an extensive sales force. Before the railroads, the country storekeepers in the South and West had come twice a year to the eastern cities to purchase their goods. After 1850 the new wholesalers sent salesmen and delivered their goods directly to those retailers. The modern mass retailers—the department store, the mail-order house, and the chains—which would in time replace the wholesaler, also had their beginnings in this same period. First came the department store that catered to the growing urban markets; then the mail-order houses—Montgomery Ward and Sears, Roebuck—which concentrated on the rural markets. Although the A & P and Woolworths had become large by the 1880s, the chains did not begin to grow rapidly until after 1900.

All the new mass marketers had extensive purchasing and selling organizations. Mass distributors of finished goods had buying offices in the major commercial and manufacturing centers in the north-eastern United States and in Europe. For each major line these enterprises had a buying staff which set the prices, volume, and specifications of their purchases and arranged for the shipment of the goods to the offices or departments responsible for marketing that line. The latter units handled the advertising, the actual selling, and the delivery of goods to the customer. For all managers the criterion of successful performance was volume, or in their terms "stock turn." The greater the turnover of inventory, the greater was the volume of business and the resulting profits. These enterprises were, then, integrated networks of buying and selling units whose function became to coordinate the flow of goods across the new transportation systems directly from the processors to the retailers or final consumers. And these enterprises expanded their activities not only by increasing the volume of their current lines but also by adding new lines of goods that could effectively use the firm's buying and selling facilities.

The first large multiunit enterprises to appear in any numbers in American manufacturing were those which found the new mass marketers inadequate for the sale of their products. These firms grew first by building large distributing networks of their own. In most cases they used new types of continuous or mass production processing techniques. The high volume of production and of sales, in turn, caused them to create extensive purchasing organizations to assure a continuing and steady flow of materials into their manufacturing plants. These firms were the first to integrate mass production with mass distribution and so become responsible for coordinating the flow of the goods from the sources of foodstuffs and raw materials through the processes of production to the retailer or ultimate consumer.

The first manufacturers to become large by building a network of national and often international branch sales offices were the makers of brand-new types of mass-produced machines which required specialized marketing services such as sales demonstrations, installation, continuing service and repair, and consumer credit. Such enterprises included the makers of sewing machines, complex agricultural machinery such as harvesters and threshers (but not the simpler plows, harrows, etc.), and business machinery such as cash registers, typewriters, and finally, somewhat later, electrical equipment. The pioneers among these types of manufacturers began to build their marketing organizations in the 1850s and perfected them by the 1880s.

A second type of manufacturer not only added an extensive network of marketing offices but also built a large purchasing one. These were the producers of semiperishable, low-priced packaged products who had in the late 1870s and early 1880s innovated in devising high-volume mechanical, continuous process machinery and plants. These included the makers of cigarettes (but not cigars), matches, breakfast cereals, soaps, and soups and other canned foods. The new continuous process machinery permitted an enormous increase in volume. For example, when the Bonsack cigarette machine was perfected in the mid-1880s, five machines could meet the current world demand. To market this volume the manufacturers added a worldwide sales network. Then to assure a steady flow of materials into their plants, they added a large purchasing organization network. Unlike the mass producers of machinery, they concentrated more on selling by advertising than on the use of salesmen. While they often continued to use the wholesaler to handle the actual distribution, they became responsible for scheduling the flow of goods from the factories to distributors and large retailers.

In the same decade of the 1880s, a third type of manufacturing firm began to build comparable integrated enterprises. However, these firms were forced to do so because of their reliance on new techniques of mass distribution rather than on those of mass production. When the processors of fresh meat and beer began to use refrigerator cars on railroads to market their products, they could no longer rely on the existing wholesalers. They had to put together a national network of branch offices with refrigerated warehouses and sales facilities and then to create large buying organizations. Because of the perishable nature of their products, they devised even more sophisticated and intricate techniques than did the makers of cigarettes and matches, to assure a continuing flow from the purchase of the raw materials through the processes of production to the retailer or ultimate consumer.

All the industries in which manufacturers created large enterprises by adding a network of sales and purchasing offices were from the start dominated by a very small number of such integrated enterprises. They were from the beginning oligopolistic, and in some cases monopolistic. They were never competitive in the traditional sense.

The first oligopolists also became the nation's first multinationals. After extending their marketing organizations abroad, they often built manufacturing facilities in foreign countries, largely because of local tariff and other restrictions. Then they began to supply these plants from local sources. So in a short time, overseas activities were operated through autonomous, integrated subsidiary enterprises.

Nearly all the manufacturers that pioneered in creating large, integrated enterprises had been forced to do so because the existing mass marketers were unable to handle their products. For those manufacturers who could distribute their goods through existing channels, the normal route to size was that of horizontal combination in the form of a cartel, followed by legal merger and then the administrative consolidation of hitherto independent manufacturing firms. Only then did such multiunit enterprises begin to add extensive marketing and purchasing networks.

The initial cause for horizontal combination was the rapid decline in prices after the early 1870s. In a wide variety of industries the response to the price drop was the formation of cartels operating through trade associations. In the 1880s a few industries using continuous process techniques of production went one step further and merged the members of the cartel into a single multiunit enterprise, first in the form of a trust and then, after the passage of the New Jersey law of 1889, of a holding company. These new corporations then consolidated the manufacturing facilities into a few large plants in order to obtain the economies of scale permitted by their technological processes. One or two, such as Standard Oil, began to integrate vertically by buying or building marketing organizations and then obtaining and producing raw materials. Others, like those in sugar, cotton, linseed oil, and lead, were content to exploit the competitive advantage of low-cost, high-volume production. A number of comparable consolidations in a wider variety of industries occurred in the early 1890s.

Then, after the depressed middle years of the decade, came the first great merger movement in American history. Mergers occurred in all types of industries. One reason was that the depression again gave convincing proof of the difficulty of maintaining cartels. Another was that, after the passage of the Sherman Antitrust Act, court rulings appeared to declare the cartel illegal and the holding company legal. Still another cause was the realization by promoters and financiers of the sizable profits promised through promotion of such mergers. But certainly one of the most important reasons for the merger movement at the turn of the century was the desire of manufacturers to imitate the success of those enterprises that had in the 1880s consolidated production and then built sales and marketing organizations.

In any case, manufacturers soon learned that mergers were rarely successful unless the constituent companies did consolidate their production into a single manufacturing department and did build national marketing and purchasing networks. The mergers that were generally financial failures were those that essentially used the holding company form to maintain earlier cartels, with constituent companies operating independently. Even those that did consolidate and vertically integrate continued to dominate their industries only if they were able to combine the advantages of mass production with those of mass distribution. And this occurred when their production processes involved capital-intensive, high energy-consuming, high-volume techniques (that is, those of mass production, continuous, or large-batch processes). It also occurred when the standardized goods they produced for the mass market could be differentiated by branding and advertising. Finally it occurred when special marketing services such as demonstration, installation, service and repair, and consumer credit were required.

These conditions existed for the mergers in industries producing semiperishable packaged goods such as sugar, whiskey and other distilled products, biscuits, and candy. They also existed for the mergers in standardized but relatively complex machinery, such as radiators, shoe machinery, printing machinery, brake shoes, and locomotives. And they occurred in the chemical, oil, rubber, and explosives industries which used continuous or large-batch techniques of production. These new consolidated and integrated enterprises quickly dominated their industries, and the new oligopolists as quickly joined the ranks of the nation's early multinationals.

Large-scale enterprises resulting from merger and integration also proved successful in the capital-intensive steel, iron, and nonferrous metals industries and in those making specialized heavy machinery. Here high-volume production required careful scheduling and coordination of the flow of raw materials into the plants and of the deliveries to the consumer. The resulting organization differed somewhat from that of enterprises making more standardized mass-produced products in that their marketing organizations remained much smaller, while their purchasing, especially their raw materials producing, departments were much larger. While these industries became oligopolistic, the dominant firms in them did not become multinational as did the oligopolies created by mergers in the metal mass production and continuous process industries.

On the other hand, in those industries where the advantages of mass production and mass distribution could not be combined, mergers were less successful. The new integrated mergers failed to play a dominant role where the process of manufacturing was labor-intensive, where the application of additional energy did not necessarily speed up the process, where the product was difficult to differentiate by performance, branding, or advertising, where it required little in the way of special marketing services, and where capital and scheduling of production and distribution were less critical.

One or more of these characteristics occurred in the following industries: textiles, leather, lumber, clothing, hat, shoe, saddlery, furniture, carriage-making and other wood-processing industries, cigar and many food-processing industries, simple fabricated metal products and machinery which did not require special installation, service or credit, and specialized machine tools and instruments. In these industries the adding, combining, and integrating of many units failed to provide any special competitive advantage in terms of lower cost or customer satisfaction. In these businesses, single-unit enterprises, selling through mass marketers or manufacturers' agents, continued to operate successfully. Such industries remained highly competitive until well into the twentieth centry.

Where there were technological or marketing advantages to the incorporation of additional units, the successful strategy of expansion for industrial enterprises in the late nineteenth and twentieth centuries thus was one of vertical integration. Some of these enterprises had been forced into this strategy by their marketing requirements. Others had come to it after trying and finding inadequate a strategy of horizontal combination. In both cases the resulting structure had been one of functional departments (manufacturing, sales, purchasing, raw materials, and finance) controlled by a central office consisting of the heads of functional departments, one or two general executives, and a staff (see Table 2).

If large-scale enterprise—big business—first appeared in the United States in the second half of the nineteenth century through the process of adding new units to existing ones, it also continued to grow in much the same manner throughout the twentieth century. In mass marketing, for example, the department stores expanded first by adding new lines and then new outlets. The mail order houses grew first by building new mail order plants in different parts of the country and then by moving into direct retailing through the building of a chain of retail stores. Existing chains expanded rapidly by adding new stores, and new chains appeared in an increasing number of trades. All these marketers continued to maintain their central purchasing organizations and to coordinate the flow of goods from

TABLE 2 Multiunit, Multifunctional Enterprise.

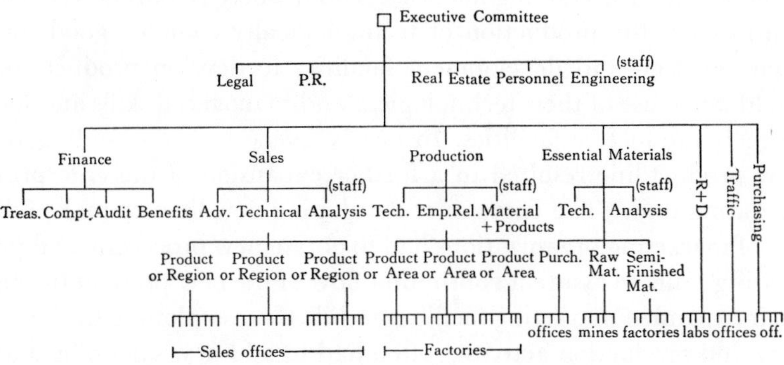

Used by: Integrated manufacturing companies from 1890s on.

supplier to consumer. The great increase in the number of outlets created by expansion intensified the problems of scheduling the flows. Many met these challenges successfully and high "stock turn" was maintained. The success of the branch unit operations in marketing led to the adoption of comparable enterprises in the finance and service industries. Banks, brokerage houses, hotels, restaurants, rent-a-car services, and others grew by adding new operating units and by centralizing basic functions that could service these operating units.

In manufacturing, growth at first followed existing patterns. As the economy expanded in the first three decades of this century, the integrated enterprises added new sales and buying offices and new factories. As technological innovation made it possible for capital-intensive, high-volume methods of production to replace labor-intensive processes, many manufacturers who had sold through the wholesalers and other mass marketers began to build their own branch sales offices and purchasing organizations.

The more significant continuing road to growth in manufacturing was not that of adding new units to existing departments but that of diversifying into new markets and new types of production. This strategy of diversification, in turn, resulted from a desire of the manufacturers to use more fully their costly facilities and highly developed managerial skills. The mass producers of perishable and semiperishable products began to take on new product lines that could use their marketing facilities. Those whose resources were concentrated in the production of technologically complex goods used their research and development facilities to develop products that could make use of their technological and managerial skills and some of their productive facilities. In nearly every case the adding of a new product line resulted in a further expansion of the enterprise's operating units. The companies developing new lines to make fuller use of marketing organizations had to obtain new processing and purchasing units to assure a continuing flow of the new product through their expanded marketing facilities; while those exploiting the laboratory and production activities often had to add new sales offices and new purchasing units to assure a continuing flow of the new product through their expanded production facilities.

In both cases this strategy of diversification led to the creation of a new operating structure—the multidivisional type (see Table 3). Here the autonomous divisions handled all the functional activities involved in producing and distributing a major line of goods while the general office concentrated on evaluating overall performance, planning strategy for the corporation as a whole, and allocating resources to implement these policies and plans. The divisions became responsible for the coordination of all activities involved in the production and distribution of goods with a constantly changing

TABLE 3 Multiunit, Multifunctional, Multiindustrial Enterprises.

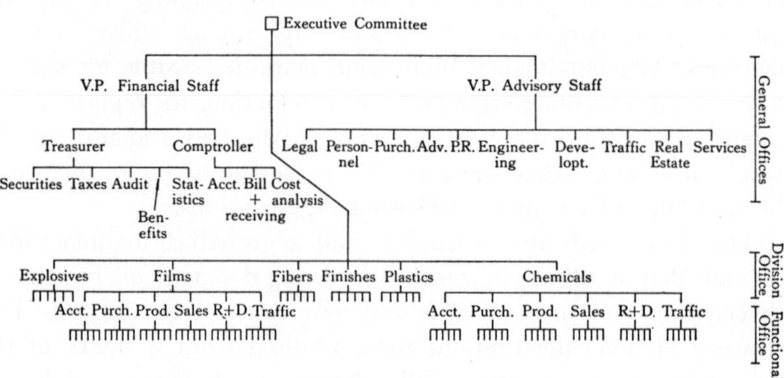

Used by: Diversified industrial enterprises from 1920s on.

market; the general office, for the long-term allocation of capital funds and managerial talent.

This review of the growth and the continuing strategy and structure of big business in the United States does document the proposition that large-scale enterprise first appeared and then continued to grow through the addition, combination, and integration of operating units that could and often did operate as independent specialized business enterprises, and it emphasizes that the process of growth had been one of *institutional integration* rather than one of institutional specialization or disintegration as defined by George Stigler and others. Economists from Adam Smith to Stigler have been quite right in emphasizing that the expansion of the market led to increasing specialization both within the enterprise and by the enterprise itself. Certainly a large market was one precondition of the rise of modern large-scale enterprise.

But another was just as significant. That was the development of the new technologies in the nineteenth century that permitted an unprecedented increase in the speed and volume of the processes of production and distribution. And nearly all these processes depended on the energy stored in fossil fuels. The increased speed and volume permitted, and indeed often required, the creation of an organization to coordinate and schedule the flow of goods from one unit to another. If this was not done, the new processes could not be fully exploited. Thus, while the increase in specialization resulting from the expansion of the American market did intensify the need for overall coordination, that coordination was handled by the existing marketing mechanism until the coming of the new technologies after 1840. Then when the new technology forced much greater speed and volume in production and distribution, the coordination came to be handled on a national scale by the large multiunit enterprises.

The managers in these new multiunit organizations operated at three levels. At the lowest level the heads of factories and other specialized units supervised the actual processes of production, distribution, transportation, communication, and finance. At the middle level, managers supervised, coordinated, and evaluated the work of a number of plants, offices, or other units carrying out one basic functional activity in one region. They also became responsible for the development of techniques to assure the steady flow of goods from one functionally or regionally defined multiunit department to another. At the top level, the managers evaluated the performance of the functional or regional managers, checked their coordinating procedures, and, most important of all, planned for the enterprises as a whole and allocated managerial talent and capital funds to carry out these plans.

Because the American market during the twentieth century continued to expand rapidly, and because at the same time the technology of production and distribution became increasingly capital-intensive and energy-consuming and so increased enormously the speed and volume of the output and flow of goods in the American economy, the multiunit enterprise that efficiently coordinated and integrated such flows became an increasingly important institution in the American economy. In fact, it has become the dominant economic institution in the United States, and its managers—a brand new class in history—have become its most powerful decision makers. These managers have more to say about the processes of current production and distribution and about the investment of goods and manpower for future production and distribution than does any other group in the economy.

3

The approach I have used to describe, to analyze, and to begin to explain the rise of large-scale business enterprise in the United States should have value for the study of comparable organizations in other nations. In other economies, enterprises which are large in terms of capital invested, number of workers, volume of output, and values are multiunit ones. They, too, are networks of offices normally carrying out more than a single economic function. If they became so through a process of combination and integration of specialized units rather than from one of subdivision and specialization within existing units, then they have had much the same problems of coordination, control, and evaluation and direction as had the large American firms. They all appear to have an organizational structure, either formal or informal, that makes possible the coordination, evaluation, and planning for their many units and the offices managing them.

They have salaried managers at the different levels of management. Therefore, the terms multifunctional, multiindustry, and multinational, as well as multiunit, appear to be descriptions that would be valid for business enterprises in most advanced economies. So should the terms of lower, middle, and top management. While the types of organizational structures probably differ, they have the same functions of integrating regional and functional activities involved in the production, transportation, and distribution of different products. Even the most cursory look at the history of large-scale business enterprise in other nations suggests that the concept of institutional integration provides a useful common approach to its study.

In the first place, the large, multiunit, managerially-manned enterprise does appear to be historically a new phenomenon. Multiunit enterprises, of course, did exist before the 1850s. The great Italian banks of the Renaissance had their branch offices. The eighteenth-century London brewers had integrated both forward and backward. The shipping companies of the early nineteenth century had a sizable number of officers and ships under their control. But these were exceptions in economies where single-officed enterprises flourished. And, more important, even the largest enterprises had a very small number of managers, rarely employing as many as ten or fifteen. The relations between the managers and the owners were direct, close, and personal. There was no middle management and almost always top managers were also owners. There was, therefore, no need for an internal organizational structure nor explicit internal administrative procedures.

I suspect that the first large modern enterprises in nearly all economies were those that operated the railroads and the telegraph. Such enterprises, either public or private, had similar problems of coordination, control, and evaluation. Yet they often came to rather different operating solutions. The British tended to use a functional departmental structure, rather than the line and staff divisional one developed by American railroad managers. One reason was the shorter mileage one company operated, but there were probably others. The strategy of railroad expansion also differed in Great Britain primarily because railroad pools were permitted. In France, Germany, and Japan, where the government constructed and operated many railroads and the telegraph, competition, of course, had still less impact on the growth of the enterprise. At the same time, bureaucratic concepts and techniques used by the political departments responsible for the operation of the new networks must have had an effect on the organizational structure and operating procedures. A comparative analysis of the growth, organization, and operation of the railroad and telegraph systems in various economies would surely indicate how different attitudes, values, and legal practices, as well as local needs and demands for transportation and communication, affected the coming of the first large business bureaucracies.

A comparative analysis of the growth and management of modern mass marketing enterprises would be more difficult to make than a comparative review of transportation and communication systems. Much less information is available on the former than the latter. That small amount of data does indicate that the timing and process of the growth of mass marketing differed in different countries. While the railroad and the telegraph appear to have precipitated a marketing revolution in other economies, the process varied. The wholesaler seems to have had a larger role in Germany than in Britain, the modern retailer appear to have grown more rapidly in Britain than even in the United States; while in Japan the traditional distribution system continued to operate in the domestic market well into the twentieth century. A comparative analysis of the rise in mass marketing should, therefore, reveal much about the rate and direction of flows of goods through the different economies, the nature of the markets for different products, and also the impact of tastes and traditions on industrial and economic changes.

In Europe and Japan, as in the United States, the first large manufacturing enterprises appear to be those which built extensive marketing and purchasing organizations. In the different economies, however, these organizations have come into being in somewhat different ways—ways that clearly reflect basic differences in the nature of their markets. Manufacturers in Europe and Japan with smaller domestic market to exploit relied much more on international customers than did American producers. In Britain the first to use the new steam-driven machines and capital-intensive, energy-using processes—including the makers of textiles, steel, nonferrous metals and shapes (rails, beams, etc.), and heavy machinery—concentrated as much on foreign as domestic markets. They usually sold abroad through exporters who, in turn, sold to importers in a colony or foreign country. The chain of middlemen, therefore, continued in foreign trade and possibly in these same industries at home. The first enterprises in Britain and on the Continent to build their own marketing organizations and so to link the processes of production and distribution were those that produced low-priced packaged goods by continuous process, capital-intensive machines and plants. These were the makers of soap, margarine, and other vegetable oil products, kerosene, cigarettes, and canned and processed foods. Such manufacturers, soon competing oligopolistically at home, began to compete with comparable American multinationals in all parts of the world. The Europeans may have produced similar ogranizations for the production and sale of mass-produced sewing, agricultural, and business machines, but if so, they never reached the size of their American counterparts. It would be interesting to know why this was so and if this resulted from the small size of their domestic markets. In any case, the first large European multinationals were those manufacturing enterprises that were the first to eliminate the middleman.

In Japan, as Professor Nakagawa has shown, manufacturers and processors produced for two quite different markets. After the Meiji Restoration, the domestic market continued to be supplied by small producers and even traditional craftsmen who distributed their products through traditional middlemen. Here neither a rapidly expanding market nor new technologies created pressures for institutional integration. At home, then, the small single-unit processors continued to sell through small middlemen.

In the brand new overseas trade, however, a wholly different type of enterprise appeared. To reach markets already dominated by British and Continental shippers and exporters, the Japanese had to develop new marketing techniques and organizational methods. The zaibatsu which formed great trading companies with the support of the government to carry on this new business continued during the following century to dominate the external trade and to make inroads into the domestic market. Unlike the British and Continental companies which sold through middlemen, these Japanese enterprises had direct contacts with the foreign markets and, like the European and American multinationals, they coordinated the flow of goods from the supplier through the processes of production to the consumer. So where in the United States, and to a lesser extent in Europe, the growing domestic market laid the basis for the large, modern multinational enterprise, in Japan they were created by the needs of international trade.

In the twentieth century, manufacturing processes in all parts of the world had become increasingly capital-intensive and energy-consuming. With the lowering of trade barriers since World War II, markets for European and Japanese manufacturing enterprises have expanded greatly, especially in the affluent advanced economies. The larger European enterprises have become multinational and have grown like the American firms by adding new units. Many have integrated and become multifunctional. Others have then become multiindustrial by following a strategy of diversification. Nearly all came to operate in more than one country. As in the United States, they have come to adopt variations of the multidivisional organizational structure. In Japan the nonzaibatsu firms also appear to have integrated and diversified. In recent years they and the zaibatsu also have paid closer attention to a careful articulation of their internal structure.

In the past two decades, the large-scale enterprises in all technologically advanced market economies have developed much the same types of organizational structure. Many have similar strategies—essentially based on the exploitation of the product cycle—a strategy for which the multidivisional organizational structure is particularly well suited. The structure and the functions of the large firm in any one nation have indeed become much closer to those of modern enterprises in other nations than they are to their own predecessors in their own economy of a century or even half a century earlier.

Yet important differences remain. Surely one of the best ways to understand the differences as well as the similarities is through historical comparative analysis. I would hope that the approach offered here and the terms and concepts that it can generate may have some value in making such comparative analyses more fruitful.

Note: This paper is based on a study of the history of large-scale enterprise in the United States on which I have been working for several years and which is now nearing completion. The views of Professor Stigler and other economists on institutional specialization can be found in George J. Stigler, "The Division of Labor Is Limited by the Extent of the Market," *The Journal of Political Economy*, 59 (June 1951): 185–193; also Allen C. Kelley, "Scale Economies, Inventive Activity, and the Economics of American Population Growth," *Explorations in Economic History* 10 (Fall 1972): 35–52.

COMMENTS

Koichi Shimokawa
Hosei University

I am honored to have the chance to comment on the report to this conference by Professor Chandler, from whose writings I have obtained a number of lessons and suggestions for my study of American business history. The following points in his report today have been particularly interesting to me. The first point is that in the behavior and growth of big business, the historical formation of administrative structure in association with functional divisionalization, diversification, and business concentration is very important. The second point is that in the growth of big businesses an active approach to the mass market through the formation and development of mass marketing or mass distribution is decidedly important.

On the first problem, it is emphasized in the report that the advent of multiunit enterprises has necessitated a change in their administrative structure. Perception of the importance of strategic decision making and of the general coordination function in administrative management of big businesses, the report points out, led to the formation of top management administrative structure made up of professional managers. The development of line and staff organization in the nineteenth-century American railroad industry was the earliest symptom, and then centralized functional organization and decentralized divisional organization began to appear. In this connection, I think it is very suggestive that Professor Chandler emphasizes the historical significance of the formation of the general administrative structure. It is also instructive that he thinks that the organizational principle at the top levels of big businesses (institutional integration) is not a simple extension of Adam Smith's principle of division of labor or of F. W. Taylor's shop management organization (institutional specialization). Because, without any need to go back to Smith, we understand that the business management organization was formed on the basis of shop and field organizations, which led to the separation of planning and operating functions, to the segregation of planning room, to Taylor's functional foreman system. And we think the formation of managerial hierarchy, and distinction of responsibility and authority at managerial levels of functional departments, were all based on settlement of management tasks in field work. However, such an understanding is appropriate only when improvement of operating efficiency can reduce costs and can expand the market with little effort. Therefore, Professor Chandler's clear indication merits our attention. It is that the administrative structure was formed to cope with the need for coordination of the operations of various units of multifunctional or divisional enterprises, such coordination being indispensable for grappling with market problems and for setting business strategy. Professor Chandler shows that with the formation of administrative structure, the flow of information and communication within the American business organizations has become much smoother. This he has established by studying the history of American big businesses since the days of the railroad industry.

On the second problem, namely, mass marketing, Professor Chandler points out that the development of transportation and communication in the nineteenth century has done away with the middlemen merchants, has stimulated the appearance of mass retailers, and has caused the advent of industrial marketing facilities which were spreading networks of national branch sales offices and which did not depend on middlemen but tried to reach the customers directly. Towards the end of the nineteenth century, the productive capacity of main industrial enterprises improved rapidly, business integration and combination proceeded apace, and successful enterprises in this concentration movement combined mass production with mass marketing or distribution. Then these big businesses had to diversify themselves in order to efficiently serve the new markets, and they adapted their administrative structure to such developments. I think that Professor Chandler's report enables us to see why and how mass marketing developed in America, which enjoyed rich market opportunities and which possessed a wide and deep internal mass market.

While appreciative of these positive contributions by Professor Chandler, I should like to raise some questions and points of dissent. First, Professor Chandler says that those enterprises which came out of the merger movement as victors were those which combined mass production with mass distribution. But were there not among these successful enterprises those exploiting their monopolistic positions, and were there not those which took to stock watering or those which merely tried to raise the prices? We can probably cite the cases of U.S. Steel or Standard Oil before its breakup. More generally, is it not necessary to make a clear distinction between innovative big businesses and noninnovative ones?

I turn to my second point: Professor Chandler repeatedly emphasizes the importance of mass marketing in the formation of big businesses. Marketing here is understood in its broader sense, namely, the direction of the flow of goods. If so, marketing simply means distribution in general. Is there not a danger of overlooking the more specialized aspect of marketing? That is, is there not a danger of losing sight of marketing's significance for systematic managerial techniques in businesses? Does not marketing mean not only organized sales activity but also a body of systematic techniques which consist of market forecasting, product planning, sales promotion, advertising, brand, packaging, and integration of production schedule?

My third point is associated with my second point. In making international comparisons of marketing development, I think it is necessary to take account of the nature of the mass market in each country; that is, there are those markets which are consumer-oriented and have the possibility of product differentiation by mass production and there are markets which do not have such possibilities. For instance, *shosha* in Japan were not mass marketers or marketing promoters, for Japan was heavily dependent on foreign trade. *Shosha* were largely concerned with distribution to domestic small producers. Were not *shosha* only organized general merchants sensitive to foreign market opportunities?

My fourth point is that, although there are many similarities in administrative structure between American big businesses and Japanese businesses, particularly zaibatsu businesses, there are a number of differences, if we look at the actual operation of their administrative organizations. For example, in American businesses the formation of administrative organization was traditionally associated with the clarification of individual responsibility and authority. Institutional integration went hand in hand with such establishment of individual responsibility. On the other hand, in Japanese businesses authority and responsibility were left unclear, and administrative organization was operated by informal groups which connected superiors and subordinates in the management hierarchy. This may explain why the adoption of line and staff organization, which had early been established in America, was delayed in Japan, and the *ringi* system, based on corporate responsibility, served its function. Thus, Japanese businesses could carry out informal institutional integration without the establishment of institutional specialization based on individual responsibility.

II–2

A Comparison of Choice of Technology among Three Nations: Great Britain, United States, and Japan

Akio Okochi

University of Tokyo

Industry started to develop in three different nations, Great Britain, United States of America, and Japan, at different times. This simple historical fact seems to have significance in two ways. First, at the starting time of America's industrial development, she was technically behind Great Britain, and there was a gap of technology between the two nations. It was the same in the case of Japan, compared with either Great Britain or America, and the gap was larger than that of the case of America versus Great Britian. Secondly, the difference of starting times between these three nations meant that the technology available to each country at its starting time would differ from that of the others.

A technology gap between two nations means a technical leader on the one side and a technical follower on the other. For the purpose of simplification of comparison, I would like to classify the technologies chosen by business enterprises into only two categories: fundamental innovation and unchanging traditional technology. Every method of improvement and application mediating between innovation and tradition will be eliminated in this simplification. Upon this premise as to classification, the technology choice for the business in the leading country is the choice between an innovative method and an unchanging traditional one. For the business in the following country, the choice is between a new method for the purpose of imitation, from several ready-made methods developed by the leading nation, and a traditional method. The technical gap between leader and follower is, however, a phenomenon which will not be uniformly found in every sector of industry of both nations at the same time. The conditions in one sector are different from those in other sectors. In some sectors, for example, we could find a large gap between America and Japan, while in other sectors we could perceive no technical gap. Such a state of technical gaps and the difference of available technology would naturally lead to different choices of technology between different nations and different sectors, and such differences in technological prerequisites would cause the differences in the business behavior of each nation.

In the following, four important sectors among modern industries before World War II are selected for the purpose of comparing the choice of technology among three nations, mainly of comparing Japan with the forerunning nations. Two sectors are ones in which American, and especially Japanese, enterprises started very late, with big gaps in technology—the cotton industry and the iron and steel industry. The other two sectors chosen here are electrical manufacture and ammoniac inorganic chemical industries, in which gaps of technology were not so large among the three nations when they started these sectors. Tables 1–4 are international chronological comparative tables, separately prepared for each of the four sectors, showing the main inventions and improvements, their diffusion into the following nations, and specific events which seem to be indicating the level of technology in the sector of each nation.

Cotton Industry

During the industrial revolution, as is well known, various spinning frames and weaving looms were invented in Great Britain, and, based upon these inventions, the technology of the cotton factory system was created. Their main equipment was the mule for spinning and the power loom for weaving, powered by a water wheel or a steam engine. With the creation of this new technology which realized high productivity and quality as well as low cost, British cotton enterprises enjoyed a dominant position in world cotton trade during the nineteenth century.

When Americans thought to have a cotton industry of their own, in rivalry with the influx of British cotton, they had to imitate the supreme British technology. For the Americans, three kinds of spinning frame existed at the time—jenny, water frame, and mule, and they chose the water frame and mule. Samuel Slater's spinning mill in Rhode Island was equipped with the water frame, and was the first successful mill in America. Within a few decades after the start of Slater's mill, however, Thorp and Mason invented and improved the ring spinning frame. This new frame, which appeared in the years between 1828 and 1833, is considered to be the most important technical improvement in the cotton industry after the industrial revolution.

The ring frame is, compared with the mule, technically more suitable for spinning medium and coarse yarns sub forty counts, while the mule is more suitable for higher counts of yarns. The ring frame has, however, advantages over the mule in two ways. Firstly, the output per ring-spindle for a given count of yarn exceeds that of the mule. Secondly, the ring frame needs only unskilled or semiskilled female labor as an operator, while the mule requires skilled male labor.[1]

The state of technology being thus, American cotton manufacturers rapidly installed the ring frame, with improvements. The number of ring spindles in 1870 was 3.7 million, which was well over the number of mule spindles installed in America, 3.4 million.

Northrop's automatic loom was another important invention which was completed in 1890. Although the Northrop loom proved highly productive without skilled labor, it required a strong yarn. Ring yarn was more suitable for this loom than mule yarn. In consequence of this technical requirement, the invention of the Northrop loom gave an impetus to diffuse the ring frame in the United States on the one hand, while it accelerated the extinction of the mule. The mule disappeared from America before World War II.

After the appearance of the ring frame, the British cotton enterprise might have had opportunities to install the new ring frame in place of the old mule. The British attitude toward the ring frame was, however, not receptive, when compared with that of America or Japan. As late as 1913 the British cotton industry kept 45.2 million spindles of the mule, approximately four times as many as that of the

TABLE 1 Development of Technology in Cotton Industry.

	U.K.	U.S.A.	Japan
1774	*Mule*		
1784	*Power loom*		
1790		Slater's mill est.	
1814		Lowell's mill est.	
1825	*Self-acting mule*		
1828–33		*Ring spinning frame*	
1867			Mule introduced (1800 spindles)
1872			Ring introduced (547 spindles)
1870s		Number of ring spindles exceeds that of mule	
1873			Osaka Spinning Co. est., installed with 10,500 spindles of mule
1885			Power loom introduced
1886			Osaka Spinning Co. installs ring
1889			Number of ring spindles exceeds that of mule
1890		*Northrop automatic loom* (patented in 1894)	Osaka Spinning Co. integrates weaving with spinning
1891			First exportation of cotton yarn
1895		Draper Co. sells first Northrop loom	
1897			*Toyota loom*
1900			Introduction of Northrop loom is failure
1902	Northrop loom introduced		
1907			First *electrification* of cotton mill power (Fuji Spinning Co.)
1914			Toyo Spinning Co. est. (merger). Spinning of fine yarn started
1916			*Toyota automatic loom*
1919			Northrop Loom introduced at Toyo Spinning Co.
1930			Toyo Spinning Co. becomes the largest cotton enterprise in the world (1.24 million spindles and 16,000 looms)
1933			Exportation of cotton cloth exceeds that of U.K.

Table 1 (cont'd)
Number of Mule and Ring Spinning Frames Installed (million spindles)

		U.K.	U.S.A.	Japan
1913	Mule	45.2	4.1	0.1
	Ring	10.4	27.4	2.2
1937	Mule	28.0	0.4	—
	Ring	10.8	26.5	11.9

Table 2 Development of Technology in Iron and Steel Industry.

	U.K.	U.S.A.	Japan
1708	*Coke blast furnace*	—	
1740	*Crucible process*		
1783	*Puddling-rolling process*		
1828	*Hot-air blast*		
1856	*Bessemer converter* (acid)		
1856–63	*Siemens-Martin open hearth furnace*		
1857			Charcoal blast furnace introduced
1859	H. Bessemer & Co. installs Converter		
1867		Cambria Iron Works makes steel rails utilizing converter	
1869			Puddling process introduced (navy yard)
1870		Cooper-Hewitt Co. installs open hearth furnace	
1873		E. Thomson Steel Works installs converter	
1879	*Thomas converter* (basic)		
1882			Crucible process introduced (navy yard)
1890			Open hearth furnace introduced (navy yard)
1894			Coke blast furnace is blown at Kamaishi Mines Tanaka Iron Works (25 t/d)
1896			Yawata Steel Works est. (state-run)
1901		United States Steel Corp. est. (73 BF, @313 t/d)	Yawata blows in a 160 t/d coke blast furnace

Table 2 (cont'd)

	U.K.	U.S.A.	Japan
1908		Production of steel by open hearth furnace exceeds that of converter	
1912			Nippon Steel Tube Co. est., utilizing Indian pig iron and U.S. scrap iron First importation of Indian pig iron
1916			Abolition of import customs upon scrap
1925		*Continuous hot strip mill*	
1926		Columbia Steel Co. installs strip mill	
1930			First large-scale blast furnace (500 t/d) designed and constructed in Japan
1934			Japan Iron and Steel Co. est. (merger)
1936			Cold strip mill introduced at Yawata (begins operation in 1940)
1937			1,000 t/d blast furnace built
1941			Hot strip mill installed at Yawata

TABLE 3 Development of Technology in Electrical Manufactures.

	U.K.	U.S.A.	Japan
1866–73	Gramme and Siemens improves *Generator*		
1879		Edison's *incandescent lamp*	
1881	Edison & Swan Electric Lighting Co. est.		
1882		Edison's electric lighting in New York (*direct current*)	
	Electric lighting of Holborn viaduct station		

Table 3 (cont'd)

	U.K.	U.S.A.	Japan
1882		*Hydroelectric power station*	
1880s	Various types of *electric motor* developed in Europe and U.S.A.		
1883			Tokyo Electric Co. est.
1886		Westinghouse Electric Co. est.	
			Electric lighting of Osaka Spinning Co.
		Alternating Current System by Westinghouse	
1887	London Electricity Supply Corp. est.		Electric lighting service starts in Tokyo (direct current)
1888		*Induction Motor* of Tesla	
1889	Deptford power station (alternating current)		Electric lighting in Osaka (alternating current)
1890		Electrification of factory power	Hydroelectric power station (Shimotsuke Flax Spinning Co.)
1891			Tokyo Electric Co. introduces alternating current
1892		General Electric Co. est. (merger)	
1890s			Small dynamos manufactured
1895		Induction motor becomes a commercial machine	Tokyo Electric Co. installs Japanese dynamos in its station
		Niagara Falls power station (11,190 kw.)	
1900			Electrification of factory power
1909			Shibaura Mfg. Co. affiliates with General Electric Co.
1914			Inawashiro power station operates with highest voltage for transmission in the world (115 kv, 37,500 kw.)
1917			More than half of the factory power is electrified
1920			Hitachi Mfg. Co. est.

Table 3 (cont'd)

	U.K.	U.S.A.	Japan
1921			Mitsubishi Electric Co. est., affiliated with Westinghouse Co.
1935			Choshinko Hydroelectric power station (400,000 kw.)
1941			Suiho Hydroelectric power station (800,000 kw.)

TABLE 4 Development of Technology in Ammoniac Inorganic Chemical Industry.

	Europe and U.S.A.	Japan
1895	*Fixation of air nitrogen* by electric arc (Lord Rayleigh)	
1905	*Frank-Caro process of calcium cyanamide*	
1907	*Rothe process of calcium cyanamide*	
1908	*Haber-Bosch process of synthetic ammonium*	
		Frank-Caro process introduced at Nippon Nitrogenous Fertilizer Co.
1909		Frank-Caro process operates successfully
1910		Conversion of calcium cyanamide into ammonium sulfate
1913	Haber-Bosch process operates successfully at Badische Anilin und Soda Fabrik	
1917	Union Carbide Corp. est.	
1920	*Casale process of synthetic ammonium*	
		Tokyo Industrial Technology Laboratory process of synthetic ammonium
1921	*Fauser process of synthetic ammonium*	
1922		Casale process introduced at Nippon Nitrogenous Fertilizer Co.
1293		Casale process operates successfully
1926	Imperial Chemical Industries Ltd. est.	
1930		Showa Fertilizer Co. succeeds in industrial use of Tokyo Industrial Technology Laboratory process
1931		Nippon Nitrogenous Fertilizer Co. succeeds in synthesizing ammonium by electrolytic process

ring frame. The same tendency was observed in the introduction of the Northrop loom into Great Britain. The British cotton enterprise had, indeed, good reason for such a conservative choice of technology, as was analyzed by L. G. Sandberg.[2]

In the case of the last comer among the three nations, Japan, the cotton industry, equipped with modern technology, started in 1867, when 1,800 spindles of the mule were imported from Great Britain. As is easily seen in Table 1, the Japanese cotton industry could equip their mills either with the mule or the ring frame according to their choice. At the beginning, however, no serious technical assessment seems to have been done. Both the mule and the ring frame were huddled together in Japan. For example, the Kashima Spinning Company installed the ring frame in 1872 (first installation in Japan), and a few years later they made an imitation mule; the Osaka Spinning Company, the first successful cotton spinning enterprise based upon foreign technology, started in 1883 with 10,500 spindles of the mule, and in 1886 they installed 4,000 spindles of the ring frame. Such a confusion in technology was resolved within a very short term of years, and Japanese cotton enterprises finally chose the ring frame to install in their mills.

As early as 1889 the number of ring spindles exceeded that of the mule. After that time the Japanese cotton-spinning industry developed with the ring frame. It should be noted that Japanese cotton-spinning mills were, in fact, from the very start of their business, installed with ring frames.

Besides the high productivity, another factor made the ring frame more preferable for the Japanese cotton industry. That is, Japanese cotton staple was short and suitable for spinning coarse yarn.[3] Spinning such a coarse yarn was, as already mentioned, where the ring frame was at its strongest.

Thus, until World War I, it was a common technology choice among Japanese cotton enterprises to install ring frames in their mills and to specialize in the spinning of coarse or medium yarns, expecting to bring the high productivity of the ring frame into full play. Such a strategy proved successful within a short time. Before World War I Japanese coarse cotton yarn rushed into the Far Eastern and Indian markets.

Another common strategy among Japanese cotton mills was to

integrate both spinning and weaving processes within a firm, as was common in the American cotton industry, F. C. Lowell's Waltham plant taking the lead. The Osaka Spinning Copmany was again the forerunner and installed 333 sets of power looms in 1890.[4] After World War I, improved technologies were introduced successively—high-draught mechanism, Northrop loom, Toyota loom, electrification of the power engine. Installed with this much improved equipment and technology, Japanese cotton enterprises began to spin finer yarn and to export cotton cloth, both of which had been British specialties before the war. In 1933 the exportation of cotton cloth amounted to 2,090 million yards, which was 60 million yards more than the British, and Japan stood first in the list of world cotton exportation in this year.

The Osaka Spinning Company was the most aggressive, through these years concentrating many rivals and small companies. After changing its name to the Toyo Spinning Company in 1914, it grew to be the biggest cotton enterprise in the world by 1930, with 1.24 million spindles and 16,000 sets of looms installed in its mills.

The Iron and Steel Industry

During the years between the industrial revolution in Great Britain and World War II, the iron and steel industry experienced three epochs of innovation in technology. The first epoch took place in Great Britian with the inventions of the coke blast furnace (1708, by A. Darby) and the puddling-rolling process (1783, by H. Cort), together with the adaptation of the Watt engine for blowing the blast furnace and forging. The second epoch was opened with the invention of H. Bessemer's steel converter in 1856. Although the Bessemer converter was invented in Great Britain, and was the first technology of mass production of steel, British iron makers did not welcome the new process at its inception. Technical reasons could explain their attitudes to some extent.

From the viewpoint of metallurgy, Bessemer's acid converter was not applicable to most British iron ore, which includes a lot of phosphorus. Moreover, most British iron makers at that time specialized in the process of either the blast furnace, the forge, or the crucible. Installation of the Bessemer converter, which requires melted pig iron, would mean either the integration of the two processes of pig iron making and steel making, or the invasion of the pig iron maker into the steel converter, or vice versa. Although H. Bessemer & Company, John Brown & Company, and some others installed the Bessemer converter, their achievement was poor until the improvement of the basic converter by S. G. Thomas in 1879.

In America, on the other hand, stimulated by the enormous demand for strong and durable rail, Cambria Iron Company of Jones Town (1867) and Edgar Thompson Steel Works Company (1873), and their rivals, installed the Bessemer converter with great success, and opened the era of mass production of steel. From the metallurgical viewpoint, it was lucky for American iron manufacturers that the available iron ore contained only a little phosphorus.

After 1908, however, as the demand for steel diversified along with the rise of several new steel-consuming industries, steel makers were required to supply not only large amounts but also various qualities and large amounts of uniform quality steel. To meet such market demands, the open hearth furnace was preferable to the converter, for its large capacity, uniform quality, and greater flexibility of quality. Since that time the United States Steel Corporation and other steel makers replaced the converter with the open hearth furnace, and the process was elaborated with many subsidiary technical improvements.

The third epoch was characterized by the automatic-continuous high speed process of rolling and finishing the steel plate, accomplished by the hot and cold strip mills, which were American innovations. Since the first strip mill was installed in the Columbia Steel Company in 1926, many strip mills were installed in American steel works, and very soon American tin plate, manufactured by their strip mills, overwhelmed the traditional tin plate made in South Wales.

Compared with those forerunners, the modern iron and steel industry started very late in Japan, although she had a long history of steel making (*tatara*). The first integrated iron and steel works in Japan was the Yawata Iron Works, established by the government in 1896. The Yawata Iron Works started to blow in its blast furnace in 1901, inheriting nothing from the traditional *tatara* technology. At the beginning, the Yawata Iron Works chose German technology, and built two blast furnaces and Bessemer converters.[5] By the beginning of World War I, however, Yawata decided to introduce the American mass production system, planning to make 650,000 tons of manufactured steel. Although this original plan of expansion was just a moderate scale, if we consider the 10 million tons of steel produced by U.S. Steel in 1901, Yawata tried to install the newest equipment and technology, increased the number of open hearth furnaces, blew in a 1,000 t/d blast furnace in 1923, and installed a cold strip mill (1940) and hot strip mill (1941), which were the first strip mills outside of America.

A characteristic technical feature of Japan's iron and steel industry before World War II should be noted. Between the Russo-Japanese War (1904–1905) and World War I, many private steel making enterprises were established, such as the Nippon Steel Works[6] and the Nippon Steel Tube Company, with the expectation of a rapid increase in military demand for steel. Most of these newcomers specialized in the steel converting and forging process installed with open hearth furnaces. As they had no blast furnace at all, they had to buy pig ingot and scrap steel for their open hearth furnaces from outside sources. In the case of the Nippon Steel Tube Company, they were initially expecting to import cheap pig ingot from India, although the company built a blast furnace later, in 1922.

Compared with the American integrated iron works, such process specialization chosen by latecoming firms seems to be unwise and irrelevant from the viewpoint of technology as well as from the viewpoint of economy. There was good reason, however, for the newcomers to select only a part of the whole process of steel making. Abolition of the import customs upon scrap iron in 1916 stimulated the importation of American scrap iron. Importation of cheap Indian pig iron showed a remarkable increase in the 1920s. Such a state of pig iron supply, together with the technical trend in America above mentioned, made it preferable for Japanese steel makers to choose specialization in the steel converting and forging process with open hearth furnaces, rather than building expensive blast furnaces and fixing a large amount of capital in them.

Electrical Manufactures

The electrical manufacturing and generating industry was in its infancy in the 1880s, when this sector started in Japan. In this sector America took a lead among the three nations, and Japan followed America in building power stations and in the industrial application of electricity. Both American and German technologies in electrical manufactures were imported into Japan hastily, resulting in nation-wide confusion of electrical technology such as 50 Hz versus 60 Hz, direct-current generation versus alternating-current generation, direct-current power transmission versus alternating-current power transmission. Apart from these confusions, it deserves to be noticed that with this imported technology and equipment Japan skipped over the era of the steam engine as the main power source for the factory, and she advanced directly into the electric motor stage from the water mill.

Total housepower of electric motors installed in factories increased from 4,107 hp in 1903 to 200,834 hp in 1914, and in 1917 more than half of the factory power was electrified in Japan. Inawashiro Power Station, built in 1914, was a milestone for Japanese electrical manufactures based upon imported equipment. Although all of the equipment for this power station was foreign made, and although the generating capacity itself was never very large, it used 115,000 volts for transmission, which was the highest voltage in the world for commercial transmission of electricity. Its distance of transmission was also the third longest in the world. The successful operation of the most advanced power station in the world on the one hand, and the rapidly increasing demand of electricity on the other, stimulated the manufacturing of electrical equipment, such as the dynamo and electric motor. As early as in the 1890s several pioneers ventured to manufacture small capacity dynamos. Among others, the Shibaura Manufacturing Company took the technical lead in Japan through technical affiliation with General Electric in 1907, in both dynamos and electric motors, especially those of large capacity.

During the boom years of 1920–22, following Shibaura,[7] three heavy electrical manufacturing enterprises, Hitachi, Mitsubishi, and Fuji were established in succession. Among the last three, Hitachi was technically independent, Mitsubishi had intimate connections with Westinghouse of America, while Fuji received technical support from Siemens-Schuckertwerke of Germany.

Within a few decades after their establishment, these electrical manufacturers not only mastered the imported technologies, but they also improved and developed their own technology in some divisions which exceeded that of the foreign. Thus all the equipment of the Choshinko hydroelectric power station (400,000kw.) was made in Japan. Suiho hydroelectric power station (800,000kw.) completed in 1941, was also installed with Japanese dynamos and transformers. The Suiho power station was one of the largest hydroelectric power stations in the world at that time, and the transformer made by the Tokyo-Shibaura Electric Company had, indeed, the largest capacity in the world. These two power stations represented the achievement and the level of Japanese technology in this field. Quantities of electricity generated in Japan, with this advanced technology, exceeded those in Great Britain in 1937.[8]

The Ammoniac Inorganic Chemical Industry

Synthetic ammonium was one of the key products of chemical industries before World War II.[9] In this sector all of the main processes were invented in continental Europe. It should be noted that many of the infant processes, which were not yet technically established, were introduced into Japan as soon as they appeared, by venturesome enterprisers who had foreseen the possibilities of the process. These venturesome enterprisers were confronted with the difficulties of developing the blueprints into actual plants, and labored with great toil and trouble to acheive their goals. And indeed, some chemical enterprisers conquered the difficulties earlier than the European inventors and made great strides with new processes. Such a circumstance was not experienced by either the cotton or iron and steel industries, because technology in these sectors was well established when they were introduced into Japan. The experience of the chemical industry was also different from that of the electrical industry, because in the latter case the imported technologies were already ready for commercial use, even if they were in the immature stage.

The Nippon Nitrogenous Fertilizer Company,[10] for example, purchased the Frank-Caro's patent for making lime nitrogen (calcium cyanamide) from carbide (patented in 1905) in 1908 when it was not yet a great success even in Europe, and in the next year a plant built in the Minamata factory began to operate successfully. The company also introduced the Casale process of synthetic ammonium (patented in 1920) in 1922, and a plant using the Casale process was completed in the next year, which successfully produced the first synthetic ammonium in Japan. The company later built the second largest synthetic ammonium factory in the world in 1931.

Side by side with foreign processes, such as Casale's, Fauser's, and Claude's, new processes were invented and improved in Japan, as early as in the 1920s. With one of these Japanese processes (Tokyo Industrial Technology Laboratory process), the Showa Fertilizer Company succeeded in 1930 in producing synthetic ammonium.

In dealing with the rapid technical progress of the ammoniac inorganic chemical industry in Japan, we must not pass over the favorable environment for this sector—the ample supply of electricity on the one hand, and the demand for ammonium sulfate by Japanese agriculture, which began to use chemical fertilizers at this time,[11] on the other hand.

Conclusion

From the comparisons of the four sectors, the following might be said: In the case of the cotton and iron industries, Great Britain was the technical forerunner, while both America and Japan were followers. Between America and Japan, however, there was an important difference. Although America was a follower at first, imitating the British technology, she soon improved and invented her own technology, such as the ring frame and the strip mill, which made it possible for American enterprise to establish the new technology of mass production. Innovation in technology was, therefore, a trigger for the growth of big business in America.

When Japan started in these sectors, the technology employed in each sector was already at a matured stage, and the gap in technology between Japan and the leading nations was so big that it was all that Japanese enterprise could do to catch up with the forerunners. There was no opportunity for Japanese enterprise to create a breakthrough innovation which would become a trigger for the growth of big business. Only a skillful and sometimes very lucky choice of advanced foreign technology could effectively trigger the growth of Japanese enterprise in these sectors. Thus the attitude towards the choice of technology was, in J. A. Schumpeter's words,[12] an "adaptive response," biased to attach importance to foreign technology.

It should be noticed here, however, that in these sectors the latecomer grew more rapidly in any time of its growth, when compared with the forerunner. To explain this phenomenon, many reasons might be considered, such as cheap labor, potential market, encouragement by government, and so on. Among others, however, technological reasons deserve our notice. The difference of available technology at the starting time yields the difference of business growth; the latecomer could use the advanced and established technology from the beginning, free from any risks of developing new technology, while the forerunners could develop their technology only after many years of trial and error, which was always accompanied by risks, fruitless investments, and inefficient equipment.

In the latter two cases, electrical manufactures and the ammoniac inorganic chemical industry, there was neither such a big gap in technology nor a lag in starting time among the three nations. Japanese enterprise could introduce an infant technology which was still in its laboratory stage and improve it for industrial use, and very soon catch up with the leading nations, and even outrun them sometimes in applying the original technology in practical use and sometimes in further innovations. In these sectors, the prime trigger for the growth of big business in Japan was innovation and technical improvement, standing on a fairly equal footing with the forerunners. Thus the attitude of "creative response" was required of the Japanese entrepreneurs at the moment of the choice of technology, and the business enterprises led by technically aggressive entrepreneurs became the successful big businesses in the fields, as was typically observed in the case of the Nippon Nitrogenous Fertilizer Company.

NOTES

1. Lars G. Sandberg, "American Rings and English Mules: The Role of Economic Rationality," *Quarterly Journal of Economics* (February 1969).
2. *Ibid.*
3. Domestic cotton wool was not sufficient in quantity to meet the demand from newly established cotton mills. From the very early period, Chinese, and later Indian, cotton wool had been imported. Both of these cotton wools were similar in nature to Japanese cotton wool.
4. To be exact, the Osaka Drapery Company was established in 1889, installed with 333 sets of power looms. In the next year, the Osaka Spinning Company affiliated the Osaka Drapery Company for the purpose of integrating the weaving process with the spinning.
5. At the same time, Yawata installed open hearth furnaces, to which Yawata expected to supply the pig ingot made at the Kamaishi Iron Works, the forerunner of the coke blast furnace in Japan.
6. The joint concern of the Hokkaido Mining and Steamship Company and Vickers Armstrong Company of Great Britain, established in 1907.
7. Shibaura Manufacturing Company changed its name to the Tokyo-Shibaura Electric Company when it merged with the Tokyo Electric Company in 1939. The latter being specialized into light electrical manufacturing, the new company could develop a full-line products policy, from incandescent lamp to gigantic dynamo.
8. In this year, 9,910 million kw. of electricity was generated per month in U.S.A., 2,249 million kw. in Japan, and 1,909 million kw. in Great Britain.
9. Modern explosives before World War II were nitro-compounds or nitrates, which required nitric acid for the making. As nitric acid is easily converted from ammonia, developing the technology for synthesizing ammonia by fixation of nitrogen in the air became a matter of policy for every country in the early twentieth century, from the military point of view as well as from the viewpoint of supplying chemical fertilizers.

10. Established by Jun Noguchi, an electrical engineer, in 1906. Name of the company was, at first, the Sogi Electric Company. It changed its name to the Nippon Nitrogenous Fertilizer Company in 1908.
11. Ammonium sulfate was first imported into Japan after the Sino-Japanese War (1894–95).
12. J. A. Schumpeter, "The Creative Response in Economic History," *Journal of Economic History* (November 1947).

COMMENTS

Toshiaki Chokki
Hosei University

I am much honored to be here as a commentator on Professor Okochi's paper. I would like to add a few words to his statement.

As we all know, Great Britain was a leading industrial country and remains so even today. But around the mid-nineteenth century it was the only country that could produce modern industrial goods, and in that sense Great Britain was often called the workshop of the world. As Professor Okochi discussed, the U.S., Japan, and other countries owed much to her in the process of their industrialization. Especially in the case of the cotton industry, British technology was introduced in these countries. Great Britain was the starting point of technological diffusion in this sector of industry. However, in my opinion, there seemed to be two major differences between Japan and the U.S. in the technological introduction. One is the frequency of human contact. Great Britain and the U.S. are near to each other. They are not only geographically near, but also they have similarities in culture. Some British engineers and workers went to the U.S. and established new cotton mills. Those were the foundation of the modern American cotton industry. But in the case of Japan, being remote from England and having an utterly different culture, neither engineers nor workers came to Japan of their own will. New technology was introduced only through machine. So there arose some confusion or irrational choice of technology. For example, as Professor Okochi pointed out, the mule frame and the ring frame were found in the same factory. This was caused by being ill-informed of modern technology, and we could have avoided such a choice if we had had more frequent human contact with England.

The other difference is eagerness for new technology and the meaning of the foreign market. The American cotton industry was developed on the local demand. Its domestic market was very large. But for the Japanese cotton industry the foreign market was very important from the beginning. To compete with the foreign manufacturers the managers of the Japanese cotton mills were always looking for new technology. The top managers of the leading spinning companies often visited Great Britain and the U.S., and introduced new machines and tried to absorb new technology. For example, as Professor Okochi said, the Northrop loom was introduced into our country in 1900, several years after its invention in America. Naturally any manager in any country is eager for new technology. But Japanese managers at that time, having great concern about new things, were much more eager than any other managers in the world.

Even in the choice of technology in the iron and steel industry, the U.S. and Japan were in different situations. Between Great Britain and the U.S. there was some interchange of goods and people since the seventeenth century, when the U.S. was under British political control. An early American iron and steel works was built by British equipment and run by British workers. As far as economic activity was concerned, the U.S. was also under the British influence at that time.

In Japan, after the Meiji Restoration, when the new iron and steel technology was introduced, some foreign engineers came and assisted us in producing iron and steel. But ordinarily they did not stay so long, and moreover the result was not always satisfactory. Japanese materials—ores, coke, and fuel—were not adaptive to modern technology. In both the state and private enterprises, the Japanese were forced to proceed by severe trial and error. In the case of the Yawata Iron Works, based upon a German system of technology, it took several years before it could continuously produce iron and steel, even after its equipment was completed. As the level of technology became higher and higher, there arose lots of problems to be solved: more capital funds, more skilled workers, more related technology. It was not until World War I that Japan could produce iron and steel economically.

But after World War I, the Japanese government tried to strengthen the iron and steel industry, and established the Nihon Iron and Steel Corporation, a great iron and steel trust, by legal device in

1934. As Professor Okochi pointed out, it was the Nihon Iron and Steel Corporation that installed the cold-strip mill and the hot-strip mill, the first strip mills besides those in the U.S. at that time.

As for the electrical manufacturing and generating industry, I would like to comment on the Japanese dynamo and electric motor industry.

After World War I, the level of Japanese technology in this field became considerably upgraded. As Professor Okochi pointed out, following the Shibaura Manufacturing Company, Hitachi, Mitsubishi, and Fuji emerged as new producers, and began to produce large dynamos and transformers. We can say that they showed a "creative response" to the technological development in this field. But with regard to this, I think it is necessary to discriminate between two types of engineers.

One is the old type of engineer, having no formal technological education. Hisashige Tanaka, Shoichi Miyoshi, Kibataro Oki were this type of engineer. They established small factories and manufactured electric devices. Telegraphs were their favorite field. But they could not produce dynamos and electric bulbs by themselves. The Miyoshi Factory is known as the first one that produced dynamos and transformers. But Miyoshi was helped by Ichisuke Fujioka, an academic specialist in this field. Fujioka is well known as a pioneering electrical engineer and was one of the founders of the Tokyo Electric Company, which later on merged with the Shibaura Manufacturing Company and made Toshiba. In order to produce dynamos, electric motors, and electric bulbs, modern scientific knowledge was necessary. The old type of engineer lacked this knowledge. So there came the new type of engineer, having a formal technological education and scientific knowledge. I want to stress the emergence of this kind of engineer for the successful development of the Japanese dynamo and electric motor industry. Namihei Odaira, the actual founder of the Hitachi Limited, was another example of this kind of engineer.

The situation is almost the same in the ammoniac inorganic chemical industry. This is also one of the so-called science-based industries, and the technology was always advancing. So it was necessary to have excellent technological manpower. To introduce and develop the modern chemical industry, the top manager with scientific knowledge played an important role. Jun Noguchi, the excellent executive of the Nippon Nitrogenous Fertilizer Company in the early twentieth century,was one of those managers. Professor Okochi stressed that the ample supply of electricity and the demand for ammonium sulfate by Japanese agriculture were accelerating factors for the development of Japanese ammoniac inorganic chemical industry. I do not deny this fact. An industry does not run smoothly without its resources and market. But I should like to define the modern chemical industry as a science-based or research-intensive industry. From this viewpoint I choose technological manpower as a main factor for its development. Japan could have this kind of manpower around the 1920s to 1930s. In 1928 a governmental laboratory succeeded in improving the Harber process of synthetic ammonium. This was the process that the Showa Fertilizer Company adopted.

Furthermore, I should like to mention that even in the cotton industry excellent technological manpower became important in the twentieth century. The Toyota loom is very famous as a Japanese original invention. It was invented by Sakichi Toyoda. He was an old type engineer, having no formal engineering education. But it is a well-known fact that the Toyota loom was completed by Kiichiro Toyoda, son of Sakichi, an engineer having graduated from Tokyo Imperial University.

The situation is also the same with Japanese high-draught technology in the cotton-spinning industry. Kusuo Imamura of the Dainihon Spinning Company, and Kikutaro Honda of the Daiwa Spinning Company are famous for their high-draught devices, and they were both university-graduate engineers. The age of the old-type engineers passed away in the 1920s to 1930s. Any activities of the technological choice—in my opinion it includes R & D, technical assessment, and technological introduction—are now carried on by the assistance of professional engineers. The quality of the choice of technology has become determined by the level of science and technology. And compared with Great Britain and the U.S., Japan's level of science and technology was not much less advanced around the 1930s, especially in its application level. This helped greatly the development of new industries in Japan.

Closing my comments, I would like to present one point for discussion. As Professor Okochi pointed out, Japan's response to the technological choices in the cotton and iron and steel industries was "adaptive," while in the electrical manufacturing and the ammoniac inorganic chemical industries Japan made a "creative response." But when we look at the two groups of industries from the viewpoint of their sizes and industrial integration, it was rather the former group that made a considerable performance. The Toyo Spinning Company and the Nihon Iron and Steel Corporation were fairly diversified and vertically integrated in the 1930s. On the other hand, the Nippon Nitrogenous Fertilizer Company and the Showa Fertilizer Company, though some new zaibatsu came out from them, were considerably smaller and much less diversified than the world's largest—I.C.I. and Du Pont—in the 1920s and 1930s. Also Toshiba, Hitachi, and the Mitsubishi Electric Company were very small in size compared with General Electric and Westinghouse Electric before World War II. What caused this result? I hope this point will be discussed and cleared up in this conference.

II–3

Marketing Strategy and Market Structure in Three Nations: The United States, The United Kingdom, and Japan

Ryushi Iwata
Musashi University

1

Over a decade has passed since the appearance of Professor Chandler's provocative work *Strategy and Structure* in 1962. Recently, we have witnessed some signs that increasing numbers of students have begun to focus their attention on this promising perspective. Professor Louis Galambos, for example, wrote as follows in 1967:

> His manner of analyzing the changing structure of business organization and the related changes in strategy gave business historians the guidelines for a new synthesis.[1]

Professor D. F. Channon lately published a book entitled *The Strategy and Structure of British Enterprise.*[2] It is also not of little significance that this International Conference of Business History (in Japan) has chosen as the central subject of its first meeting the title "The International Comparison of Strategy and Structure of Big Business." Although Professor Chandler focused his attention, in his book, on the internal structure of business organization, the structure outside of unit businesses and the corresponding strategies also provide an interesting field of topics for analysis. His perspective can be effectively applied to this field as well.

Now, the discussion topic that I was given is as follows: A Comparison of Market Structure and Marketing Strategy among Three Nations: Great Britain, the United States, and Japan. However, I am not a student of "marketing" myself. It must be beyond my ability to carry out a precise analysis of the market structures and marketing strategies in these three countries. Therefore, I would rather try, in this paper, to raise several questions which have been developing in my mind since I had tried an overall analysis, several years ago, on the structural development of business in the three countries during the period between the 1880s, when big businesses began to appear, and the 1910s when they were firmly established in all these countries.[3] I would be very happy if I could give any stimulus to a further and deeper discussion on this topic.

Now, it is a widely accepted idea that the type of marketing strategy which is dominant in a business field largely depends on the market conditions, especially of the market structure of the field. Many analyses have been made on this relationship. Some of them insist that competitive productions were superceded by competitive marketing when an oligopolistic business structure had firmly established itself and the market condition reached its saturation point. Others explain the same phenomenon by saying that price competitions were largely replaced by nonprice competitions in an oligopolistic business structure. One of the classical examples of these views is that of Thorstein Veblen. His view on this relationship can be roughly summarized as follows: In the era of free competition when captains of industry were playing an active part in industrial development, increasing population and growing export provided a sufficient market for increasing production. Therefore, the industrialists of this period were mainly interested in attaining lower costs and extending their production. However, as the end of this era approached, they began to exert all their efforts in active marketing rather than in the improvement of the production processes. Sales competition (competitive selling in Veblen's term) began to take the place of competitive production. Shrewd marketing skill and sabotage in production became the main tactics in competition in this period.[4]

More modern students of economics or marketing propose that nonprice competition became dominant when an oligopolistic structure firmly established itself. Under an oligopolistic business structure, even big firms would have to suffer heavy losses before they would be able to kick out of the business field a marginal firm which also has a certain size and strength. Because powerful big opponents would be able to counteract price cutting, price competition was inutile. Thus price agreements became common among firms. In this state of affairs, price competition was largely replaced by nonprice competition.[5]

However, a historical overview tells us that this is a kind of oversimplification of the situation and further analyses are required, because nonprice competition, especially aggressive competition in marketing, was quite common in many of the U.S. industries far back in history before the oligopolistic structure had established itself in these industries at the turn of the century. Evidently, captains of industry fought their way to success up to the level of industrial kings by means of (and this was not the least of their methods) their ingenious marketing strategies and tactics. In many American industries, it was this kind of nonprice competition that resulted in the rapid growth of oligopolistic structure. Therefore, I propose to reconsider the accepted model on the relationship between market structure and marketing strategy.

2

An overall view of the U.S. industrial development during this period reveals two major growth patterns.[6]

First, let us look at one of the two types. A keen understanding of new market opportunities and great skill were required for an entrepreneur to make a respectable start in some industries. In some cases, for instance, ingenious marketing techniques were needed to sell new products to the public. Or a distribution network had to be established. Sometimes, the difficulty lay in collecting raw materials for the production process. Control of patents or transportation facilities affected the structural development of some industries. Whatever the obstacles, the outcome in these industries was that only a few were able to capture substantial market shares. These few often enjoyed enormous profits. Growing markets and competition encouraged heavy investment of these profits back into the same industry. Thus the few successful companies in industries of this type tended to grow rapidly. A highly centralized structure resulted in the very early stages of the development of these industries. On the other hand, combinations tended not to appear until relatively late in these industries. Mergers sometimes occurred ultimately due to the pressures of oligopolistic competition, once the possibilities for gaining control over strategic factors had been largely exhausted. The harvester, sewing machine, cash register, typewriter, photographic equipment, electrical manufacturing, cigarette, beef, and banana industries are examples of industries which exhibited this type of growth.

Now for the second major growth pattern. In other industries, no serious barriers to entry appeared. Thus, in these industries many firms survived. The market conditions these firms faced approached perfect competition. Although their markets were also growing, the productive capacity in these industries quickly surpassed what their markets could absorb. This was due largely to the growing numbers of firms which entered these industries.[7] Price cutting resulted. Also, market fluctuations produced serious repercussions in these industries. Firms responded to these conditions by attempting to control their markets through trade association. These attempts were generally ineffective. For example, Standard Oil sought to remedy its market problems by forming a horizontal combination. In 1872, when the association failed, it turned in 1879 to acquiring legal control by placing the control of stock of subsidiary companies in the hands of individual trustees. Then in 1882, it invented the trust form to secure tighter legal control over the properties it had purchased. Many other companies followed Standard's example and established trusts in the 1880s, and then again at the turn of the century after a brief pause from 1893 to 1897.[8] The legal form of the holding company proved to be an even more effective way of combining firms in this second wave of the trust movement. The cottonseed and linseed oil, whiskey, lead, sugar, and secondary steel production industries, etc., provide examples of this type of growth.[9]

Now, these two patterns of development in the United States reveal several interesting points which we must not overlook. From the structural viewpoint, the market conditions were alike in both types of industries. Large-scale, uniform, and unsaturated markets were growing quickly. However, the marketing strategies adopted by firms which followed the first type of growth are quite different from those which were common in the second type of industry.

In the second type of industry, the competitive efforts were directed mainly to cutting prices. When they finally found that price competition was inutile, they turned to forming gigantic combinations. The state of affairs in the industries such as cottonseed oil, whiskey, sugar, etc., clearly show this process. Although cottonseed oil had been manufactured in the South before the Civil War, it was not until the 1870s that this industry began to grow. There were only seven mills in 1866 in the whole United States.[10] However, various new uses for this product were discovered, and cottonseed oil mills began to increase in number in the 1870s. Although there were only 26 mills in 1870, by 1880 there were more than 40, and in 1885 there were about 130 mills in the South. It is said that "the market was 'drowned in oil,' and despite heavy exports it had driven tallow down to half its former price. . . ."[11] About seventy firms engaged in the manufacturing and refining of cottonseed oil were combined in 1884 to form the American Cotton Oil Trust. The members of this trust manufactured 88% of the total national output.

In the sugar refining industry, a limited number of refineries were in business and imperfect competition existed prior to the 1850s. However, the centrifugal machine, which was introduced in 1851, revolutionized the industry. This innovation made mass production and cost reduction possible. A large national market emerged due largely to the sharp price reduction. New entry became easy. This situation made the industry highly competitive. During the immediate post–Civil War years, the market condition came close to perfect competition.[12] "Agreements to limit output or fix the margin brought, at most, only temporary relief."[13] Many firms were forced out of business by the severe competition from the late 1870s to the late 1880s. Due to the increasingly unstable market condition, seventeen of the twenty-one sugar refineries still in business east of the Rocky Mountains were persuaded to join a combination, the Sugar Refineries Company, in 1887.[14]

In the first type of industry, however, because of the severe limiting factors for success, the competitive efforts in controlling the limiting factors had decisive effects on deciding which firms should continue to grow and which firms should lose and fail.[15] In those industries, therefore, the decisive strategies for carrying out a successful business were such efforts as (1) sales promotion by massive advertisement, the establishment of an effective nationwide market organization, etc.; (2) controlling patents, sometimes using a primitive form of patent pool; (3) setting up quota systems of markets; (4) securing swift and regular transportation; (5) securing materials, and so on.[16] Marketing strategies and activities, among others, played very important roles in many of the U.S. industries in this period because of their historical settings. In those industries, therefore, sales promotion by providing credits, product warranties and afterservices, gimmicks to attract the consumer's attention, in addition to extensive advertisement and nationwide market organization, had appeared far back in history before the oligopolistic business structure had firmly established itself.[17] The marketing strategies and tactics adopted by great industrialists and businessmen such as Cyrus H. McCormick, Andrew W. Preston, etc., provide interesting examples of these facts.

A large potential market for reapers had been developed by 1850. A severe farm labor shortage created a need for more efficient farm equipment. In 1848, just when the demand for the reaper began to grow, the original patents of both Hussey and McCormick expired. Numerous rivals entered the industry. There were several limiting factors to be surmounted, however. The ignorance and obstinate conservatism of farmers, when confronted with an unfamiliar new instrument, had to be overcome. No established distribution system was available. Thus, rigorous and ingenious marketing activities were an integral part of doing business in this industry. McCormick's mass distribution resulted from extensive advertising, public demonstrations, product warranties, and a credit system; an efficient organization which was built first around a dealer system, and later around a branch system, assured him the lion's share of the market for reapers. Cyrus H. McCormick, Jr., attributes the supremacy of the McCormick Harvesting Machine Company largely to its selling system.[18] The competitive efforts were mainly directed to active marketing and to supplying newer and better products. Judging from the amazingly high profit rates which McCormick attained in the early stage of his business, it is difficult to assume that severe price competition prevailed in this period. This industry affords an example of the type of industry in which marketing played by far the most important part. Industries such as meat packing, cigarette, sewing machine, cash register, and typewriter production followed the same path.

The banana industry provides us with another interesting case. In the banana industry, the uniquely unstable character of production and the perishable nature of the product made it difficult for banana traders to achieve permanent success and steady growth. Many firms entered the business only to fail. First of all, this fruit came from the tropical areas in the Caribbean islands and Central America. In these areas, floods, droughts, and especially hurricanes often destroyed the banana plantations, resulting in a disastrous failure for banana importers.[19] Furthermore, tropical epidemics and frequent "*revoluciones*" gave banana planters and importers much trouble. Secondly, the sources of production were far removed from the section of consumption. Because the banana is the most perishable of all tropical products, sure and swift transportation to banana ports in the United States was of vital importance. The delay of a ship sometimes caused the failure of a banana importer. Repeated shipwrecks also plagued importers. It is said that "during the five years between 1885 and 1890, about one out of every seven ships hired to the banana trade had been lost by storm or fire at sea."[20] Finally, distribution of this perishable fruit was difficult. C. M. Wilson remarks:

> In the struggle against crowded markets practically all importers were at the mercy of the broker or jobber . . . . Ports deluged with the fruit for a few days would have none at all the following week, and one port often would be flooded with fruit, while ports near by would have less than a dozen bunches.[21]

Because of these conditions, the commercial casualties in this industry were very high. Nearly a hundred banana firms are said to have failed by 1900.[22]

These difficulties could be overcome by (1) spreading of risks by planting bananas in widely separated places and also by introducing several other lines of products into the business, (2) building up an efficient and stable transportation system, and (3) building up an efficient distribution and marketing system. Andrew W. Preston, the manager of the Boston Fruit Company, was one of the few banana traders who realized the necessity of controlling these factors.[23] He initiated a policy aiming at "low but steady prices and year-around work." He introduced an honest classification system and official inspection of bananas by disinterested and respected business clubs. He also extended his marketing organization into Philadelphia, New York, and neglected inland areas, always choosing his fruit dealers with care.[24] He incorporated the Fruit Dispatch Company in order to make distribution more efficient. In addition to these efforts, he worked to build up an efficient fleet to carry bananas. Owing to Preston's policies, Boston Fruit had gained and held a position of leadership in shipping and selling bananas.

In those industries, it was not the oligopolistic structure nor market saturation that resulted in competitive marketing. On the contrary, it was the marketing strategies that played decisive roles in the successful development of the firm and, therefore, in the development of oligopolistic business structure.

These U. S. cases reveal that:

1) The types of business strategies depended largely on the form of the limiting factors for success which were dominant in the particular industries.

2) In some industries, it was nonprice competition that resulted in the rapid rise of oligopolistic structure, contrary to the popular views which insist that nonprice competition superceded price competition when an oligopolistic market structure had been developed.

3

Contrary to the rapid rise of big business and the early concentration of business in the United States, a decentralized business structure had remained in the United Kingdom, at least up until the First World War. I shall briefly review the state of affairs, focusing on two key British industries: the textile industry and the iron and steel industry.

In the textile industry, a decentralized structure persisted. In the cotton industry, for example, importing, spinning, weaving, dyeing, printing, bleaching, and merchanting, all constituted separate trades carried on by separate groups of manufacturers.[25] The situation was not far from this in the worsted and linen industries. Furthermore, each of these separate trades was carried on by numerous small businesses.

In this decentralized structure, big horizontal combinations were formed at the turn of the century. These included J. & P. Coats, Limited, Bradford Dyers' Association, Limited, Calico Printers' Association, Limited, Bleachers' Association, etc., as are well known. These combinations had several characteristics, which are as follows:

1) Many of them were combinations of a large number of evenly developed firms, without any decisively powerful core company which could buy out or force its competitors to join the combination.

2) They were horizontal combinations "embracing a majority of the firms and companies engaged in one branch of trade." Many of them were so-called process combinations and their "members were concerned with only one stage in production."[26]

3) Although their emergence was conspicuous, combinations resulted only between firms producing high-class goods such as sewing cotton and fine thread, or between firms dealing with special processes such as dyeing, printing, and bleaching. Their success resulted largely from exploitation of their technical superiority over foreign and domestic competitors, and their control of various strategic factors such as material resources, availability of water, and geographical conveniences. Firms producing standardized goods were quite immune to this movement, and remained decentralized. The situations in the chemical industries, such as the salt industry and the alkali industry, were not far from those in the textile industries.

These British cases reveal some interesting points. First, in the United Kingdom of this period, open markets seem to have played much more significant roles than in the United States or Japan, because of the extremely decentralized business structure. The fact that merchants small in scale and large in number played a substantial role shows this state of affairs. As a result, price competition seems to have prevailed in many of the British industries. However, the growth of big business introduced in this scene different elements, and price competition declined in those fields where oligopolistic structure was established. This British type of development might be close to the accepted model which was mentioned earlier in this paper.

Now for the iron and steel industry. The number of iron and steel concerns increased rapidly in the 1870s. Steel making was amazingly scattered as in the textile and chemical industries, in small-scale plants. Henry W. Macrosty reports in 1907 as follows:

> In the whole of the United Kingdom there are, after allowing for associated companies, some 101 blast furnace companies . . ., and thirty of these in Scotland and on the North-East Coast are responsible for half the total output. There are about ninety-five steel-making concerns, of which some twenty-eight also possess blast furnaces.[27]

This situation was quite different from that in the United States. In the U.S., three giant companies were dominant at the turn of the century, in primary steel production. These, then, almost immediately merged into the U.S. Steel Corporation in 1901. It is very interesting to compare the market structures of the two countries.

In the United States, the demand for iron rails rose in the 1850s and continued to increase until the early seventies. In 1869 iron rails shared more than 40% of the total rolled iron,and this figure reached about 50% in the early seventies. Thus, a large-scale and homogeneous potential market for Bessemer steel developed before its commercial introduction. The fact that steel rail accounted for over 90% of the total demand for rolled steel in the early eighties clearly shows the importance of the rail market to steel producers. The unique market structure in this industry had a substantial effect on the structural development of the U.S. steel industry. The members of the Bessemer Association adopted a quota system in the steel-rail market in concert with the major railroads. This, together with the patent pool of the Bessemer, Kelly, and Mushet patents, which were held by the Bessemer Association, contributed to the rapid concentration of the primary steel production in this country.

In the United Kingdom, however, wrought iron had "many centuries of successful use behind it" when steel came into prominence.[28] In addition, this country had a long tradition of high-grade steel. The markets for wrought iron were of a diversified character. In addition to this divergence in finished iron production, the markets for these products were further subdivided by the predominance of traders: factors in domestic trades and "merchants" in export trades.[29] This diversified character of the iron and high-grade steel market was carried over into the steel age. In the seventies, steel began to supercede iron. However, the old crucible steel and wrought iron were not entirely outmoded. Wrought iron was still preferred for ships, cables, anchors etc., where corrosion was feared, and the old crucible method continued to be used by manufacturers of high-grade cast steel.

The important point is this: Given this segmented and heterogeneous market structure, price competition was naturally limited. It is said that even small-scale firms had competitive strength in this state of affairs. D. L. Burn described the situation during the decade before World War I as follows:

> Not only was the number of firms virtually stable, but their relative strength also; probably most firms expanded their output and the increase in total output in the period was certainly not the result of the exceptional growth of a few plants.[30]

Obstacles to the elimination of competitors are, at the same time, obstacles to effective combination. In trades in which small and large producers flourish side by side, it is virtually impossible to form large combinations. Under these circumstances, one way in which the competing firms could improve their competitive position was by securing markets for their products by means of vertical integration of firms in the steel-consuming industries. This was the strategy which was actually adopted by some of the large British steel firms under the pressure of increasing competition from abroad. Among others, shipbuilding and armor provided relatively large stable markets. It is not without reason that many of the big integrated steel companies began with the integration of shipbuilding or armor companies. This comparison of the British steel industry with its counterpart in the United States shows significant impact of market structure on the corresponding marketing strategy. However, the unique strategy—a marketing strategy, in a sense—which was adopted by large British steel firms, provides an exceptional case to the accepted model. This strategy prevailed even before an oligopolistic structure was established in this field. Close to 100 steel firms were jostling each other when some of them were trying to integrate steel-consuming firms.

Now, one thing should be borne in mind. It is the fact that market structures and the form of limiting factors do not provide the whole picture of the factors which defined the marketing strategies in this period. Creative ideas of brilliant entrepreneurs, and their marketing strategies formed on these ideas, sometimes completely changed the "meaning" of market structure, and thus created an entirely new market structure for their products. The history of Unilever provides us with one of the most interesting examples. Professor Wilson's attractive analysis of the spectacular growth of this company clearly shows us the role of a creative idea.

In this industry, according to Professor Wilson's analysis, less than twenty well-known makers and a number of small makers were in business before Lever began soap manufacturing in 1885. Many of these firms were formed in the eighteenth century and the early nineteenth century, and had developed little by little over a long period. The market was of a limited and local nature. In Professor Wilson's words:

> A series of conventions, almost medieval in their parochialism, maintained a system of zones . . . . This was the confortable world, gentlemanly and harmonious.[31]

This quiet scene was rudely shattered by a newcomer, William H. Lever. Shrewdly perceiving his opportunity, he seized a national market and pushed his business armed with his shrewd mass marketing. He first improved the formula for his soap. Secondly, he launched a massive advertising campaign, adopting such gimmicks as a "prize system" and selling tablet soap in cartons carrying his brandname. He also tried to gain control of sources of certain natural resources. Among those innovations, the idea of selling soap in cartons revolutionized the soap marketing. The national market for soap was suddenly opened to the innovator, thus completely changing the "market structure." Lever achieved growth through intensive reinvestment of profits. By 1906 when "the Soap Trust" was formed, Lever Brothers had secured the leading position in this industry.

McCormick, Swift, Weston, and other American innovators provide other examples of this great impact of brilliant marketing strategies on the market structure. When Cyrus H. McCormick came to anticipate a larger demand than the early orders sent in, and built accordingly, while Hussey conservatively limited production each season to the number of orders he received in advance; when

Swift got the idea of sending to the Eastern market a large quantity of beef which was dressed in the Midwest; and when Andrew Preston turned his attention to hitherto neglected inland areas, and began to extend his market organization into those areas choosing his fruit dealers with care, the market structures of those industries were radically changed.

The success of these companies shows us that the entrepreneurial idea, rather than the old market structure, often had decisive impact on their marketing strategies and it was often their strategies that created new market structures and not vice versa. Those are very interesting examples which we cannot neglect when we consider the relation between the market structure and the marketing strategy.

4

For the analysis of marketing strategies and market structure in this period in Japan, it is of vital importance to consider the roles played by large trading companies, such as Mitsui Bussan, which opened new overseas markets and provided industrial companies with relatively large-scale markets which they could not find inside of the border. Secondly, large trading companies played significant roles in facilitating industrial growth by importing machines, by supplying industrial companies with credits, by providing those companies with information, etc.

As is well known, Meiji Japan suffered much from the unequal treaties signed with the then advanced Western countries such as the United Kingdom, France, Austria, and the United States. Among others, the extraterritoriality and the forfeiture of tariff autonomy, together with the immaturity of Japanese merchants, made it possible for foreign merchants to put Japanese foreign trade under their control. It was pointed out as follows:

> Our foreign trade is under the mercy of foreign merchants. It is not easy for our merchants to escape from their maneuver. We used to find Japanese merchants who had risen from small traders to successful merchants in Yokohama. However, few of them could successfully compete with foreign merchants, and most of them have failed.[32]

The natural reactions to this situation were great efforts to extend direct marketing channels to overseas markets by Japanese merchants. However, this was not an easy task for them, owing to their weak financial strength and inexperience in foreign trade. In other words, there were severe limiting factors ahead of them in order to attain brilliant success in this field. The Meiji government was eager to support those efforts.[33] However, as a result of the severe limiting factors to be overcome, only a few firms, which had government support, which were equipped with talent and efficient organizations at the same time, and which could exploit a certain economy of scale, were able to grow successfully. Mitsui Bussan was one of a very few successful trading companies of this kind. In spite of its humble start, this company attained a startling success mainly due to the talented people it could command, people who were endowed with business foresight, knowledge, and experience in foreign trade, and who were cautious and energetic at the same time. The fame of the Mitsui family and the support of the government were of course, of much

TABLE 1 The Percentage that the Mitsui Bussan Shared in the Japanese Foreign Trade: 1897–1932.

Year	Export	Import	Total	Year	Export	Import	Total
1897	5.9	14.5	10.7	1915	20.7	19.4	20.9
1898	7.5	13.2	11.0	1916	20.6	21.1	20.8
1899	11.3	17.1	14.2	1917	20.1	18.4	19.5
1900	10.3	15.0	13.0	1918	19.7	18.5	19.1
1901	8.0	13.9	11.0	1919	18.7	21.0	19.9
1902	9.1	15.6	12.4	1920	18.1	17.2	18.0
1903	11.0	14.6	15.3	1921	16.1	10.3	12.8
1904	13.2	14.4	13.8	1922	15.5	11.0	13.0
1905	15.5	17.0	16.7	1923	15.6	9.5	12.4
1906	16.5	17.2	16.9	1924	14.5	9.7	11.5
1907	18.6	20.7	19.7	1925	12.0	9.7	10.7
1908	18.4	22.6	20.5	1926	13.2	10.9	12.0
1909	20.1	18.8	19.4	1927	13.3	11.4	12.3
1910	21.7	17.5	19.6	1928	14.4	11.9	13.0
1911	24.0	20.5	22.5	1929	11.9	11.3	11.8
1912	22.7	17.9	20.1	1930	14.7	13.2	13.9
1913	23.5	17.3	20.1	1931	14.7	10.5	12.5
1914	27.6	24.1	25.8	1932	15.9	10.2	13.0

Source: Mitsui Bussan Kabushikikaisha, *Mitsui Bussan Shoshi*, p. 145.

help. Thus, it quickly attained an important position in foreign trade in Japan. (See Table 1).

Now, this Mitsui Bussan played a significant role in the rapid rise of industrial Japan. First, it created new markets for rising industrial companies, and gave much stimulus to their industrial activities.(See Tables 2 and 3.) Secondly, the large marketing organization, which covered many industrial fields and a wide geographical extent, provided industrial companies with a relatively large-scale market which they could not find inside of the border and which made it

TABLE 2 The Percentage that the Mitsui Bussan Shared in the Total Japanese Import of Machines and Cotton Material: 1897–1912.

Year	Machine	Cotton	Year	Machine	Cotton
1897	26.0	31.5	1905	18.1	23.1
1898	11.6	29.0	1906	14.0	31.7
1899	17.8	33.2	1907	20.1	32.7
1900	12.2	30.7	1908	41.7	31.4
1901	18.5	24.2	1909	42.6	28.1
1902	11.8	27.2	1910	50.5	25.2
1903	11.1	25.1	1911	31.1	30.7
1904	8.8	24.0	1912	29.2	20.9

Source: Yoshio Togai, "Sogoshosha toshite no Mitsui Bussan no teichaku" [The establishment of the Mitsui Bussan Company as a *Sogoshosha*], in *Japan Business History Review* 3, no. 1.

TABLE 3 The Percentage that the Mitsui Bussan Shared in the Total Japanese Export of Cotton Yarn and Cotton Cloth: 1897–1912.

Year	Cotton Yarn	Cotton Cloth	Year	Cotton Yarn	Cotton Cloth
1897	29.4	5.8	1905	32.2	9.0
1898	22.0	4.6	1906	52.4	20.0
1899	29.8	6.5	1907	29.2	40.0
1900	32.0	4.7	1908	36.2	47.0
1901	21.2	6.0	1909	33.3	42.0
1902	32.2	7.4	1910	33.0	51.0
1903	28.3	9.5	1911	37.5	34.0
1904	35.4	24.0	1912	33.3	26.0

Source: Yoshio Togai, "Sogoshosha toshite no Mitsui Bussan no teichaku" [The establishment of the Mitsui Bussan Company as a *Sogoshosha*], in *Japan Business History Review* 3 , no. 1.

possible for them to put their production on a mass basis. Mitsui Bussan played an active part, for example, in 1906, in forming *Sanei Menpu Yushutsu Kumiai* (The Sanei Cotton Cloth Exporting Association) and *Nihon Menshi Yushutsu Kumiai* (The Nihon Cotton Yarn Exporting Association). It pushed forward the exporting business of Japanese textiles into hitherto occupied overseas markets. As a result, vast markets in Korea and Manchuria were opened up to the Japanese textile firms. These cases afford interesting examples of the role played by large trading firms in early industrial Japan. Therefore, large industrial companies could find ready makrets for their products without much marketing efforts provided that the quality and price of their products were reasonable; and this was oftentimes assured by special long-term contracts. Cotton spinning, one of the most important leading sectors in early industrial Japan, provides a typical example of this kind of the relation between trading companies and industrial companies.

Japanese cases reveal that the marketing strategy of large trading companies and their well-organized marketing activities created new markets and determined largely the market structure for industrial companies. This situation saved industrial companies much marketing efforts, contrary to the U.S. cases. They could concentrate in the extention of production, because they could rely on trading companies both for importing machines and material and for exporting their products. Large trading companies could cut down the marketing costs overseas by their worldwide organization and by their experiences. On the other hand, large trading companies provided industrial companies, contrary to the U.K. cases, with relatively large-scale overseas markets, thus making it possible for industrial companies to follow a mass production process.[34] In other words, the rise of large-scale trading companies determined the market structure for industrial companies, and saved them much marketing effort and also marketing costs. The main strategy for those trading companies was the establishment of extremely efficient and worldwide marketing organizations on the one hand, and the securing of a constant supply of better products at reasonable prices by organizing industrial companies which were competing against each other, and the forming of special ties with better industrial company groups.

Conclusion

A historical overview on the relations between the market structure and marketing strategy in three nations reveals several significant facts. First, the popular view that competitive production turned to competitive marketing or that price competition was superceded by nonprice competition when oligopolistic business structure appeared cannot be fully supported by historical facts. Secondly, the market structure is not the sole factor which defined marketing strategy. Both the market structure and limiting factors, which resulted in corresponding business structure, were largely responsible for the specific form of marketing and popular marketing strategy. Thirdly, the marketing strategy of an entrepreneur sometimes drastically changed the meaning of "market" and thus changed the market structure itself.

References

1. Louis Galambos, *American Business History*, Service Center for Teachers of History, Publication Number 70 (Washington, D.C., 1967), p. 27.
2. D. F. Channon, *The Strategy and Structure of British Enterprise* (Mass., 1973).
3. Ryushi Iwata, "Entrepreneurial Opportunity and Business Structure: A Comparative Study of Business Conditions in the United States, the United Kingdom, and Japan," *Musashi University Journal* 20, nos. 2–3 (December 1972).
4. Thorstein Veblen, *Absentee Ownership and Business Enterprise in Recent Times: The Case of America*, Chapter IV, The Era of Free Competition. He says as follows:

   In great part this decay of the old-fashioned competitive system has consisted in a substitution of competitive selling in the place of that competitive production of goods that is always presumed to be the chief and most serviceable feature of the competitive system." (Ibid., p. 78)
5. See Mitsuharu Ito, *The Structure of the Modern Price Theory*, and Kojiro Niino, *The Theory of Modern Market Structure*, etc.
6. See Ryushi Iwata, "Entrepreneurial Opportunity."
7. The large numbers of firms which were incorporated into large trusts in this second type of industry clearly show this.

8. E. B. Andrews described the situation in 1889 as follows:

> The career of this Titan agency has stimulated on all hands the most earnest efforts to imitate or rival it. There is scarcely a single industry in the country which has not, either bodily or in some of its phases or departments, passed under this or that form of associate management. Reports of fresh schemes for business amalgamation literally crowd the press.

E. B. Andrews, "Trusts According to Official Investigations," *The Quarterly Journal of Economics* (January, 1889), p. 121.

9. The petroleum industry—the industry which established the prototype of the trust device—followed a somewhat different path of development because Rockefeller shrewedly exploited the opportunity to form a gigantic and monopolistic organization by controlling a strategic factor, that is, the transportation of oil, and so became an important variant of this type of industry.
10. Thomas R. Chaney, "The Cottonseed Oil Industry," in *One Hundred Years of American Commerce*, ed. Chauncy M. Depew (New York, 1895), vol. 2, p. 452.
11. Victor S. Clark, *History of Manufacturers in the United States: 1860–1914* (Washington, 1928), p. 45.
12. A. S. Eichner, *The Emergence of Oligopoly: Sugar Refining as a Case Study* (Baltimore and London, 1969), pp. 21–22.
13. *Ibid.*, p. 50.
14. *Ibid.*, pp. 83–85.
15. This concept, "the limiting factors for success," should be understood as a broader concept than the term "barrier to entry."
16. Most of the first type of industry show several of these features.
17. The Marxian economists use the word *oligopoly* as an interchangeable word with their term *monopoly*, which is a historical concept. This remark especially holds true with this Marxian terminology.
18. Cyrus H. McCormick, Jr., *The Century of the Reaper* (Boston and New York, 1931), pp. 112–13, 33, 50.
19. "Even large banana companies can be ruined by a single hurricane. . . ." Charles M. Wilson, *Empire in Green and Gold: The Story of the American Banana Trade* (1947), p. 91.
20. *Ibid.*, pp. 84–85.
21. *Ibid.*, p. 73.
22. *Ibid.*, p. 112. According to F. U. Adams, not less than 114 firms had been organized prior to 1899, the year the United Fruit Company was formed. However, only 22 were still in business in 1899. See F. U.

Adams, *Conquest of the Tropics: The Story of the Creative Enterprises Conducted by the United Fruit Company* (Garden City, New York, 1914), pp. 71–72.

23. Wilson, *Empire in Green and Gold*, p. 84.
24. *Ibid.*, pp. 99, 170–73.
25. Henry W. Macrosty, *The Trust Movement in British Industry: A Study of Business Organization* (London, 1907), p. 117.
26. This feature of British textile combinations is in sharp contrast with the U.S. experience, where combinations usually expanded into closely related fields using their established position as a stepping stone. See Ibid., p. 123; also, J. H. Clapham, *An Economic History of Modern Britain: Machines and National Rivalries, 1887–1934* (Cambridge, 1938), p. 230.
27. Macrosty, *The Trust Movement*, p. 24.
28. W. K. V. Gale, *The British Iron and Steel Industry: A Technical History* (1967), p. 110.
29. Burnham & Hoskins, *Iron and Steel in Britain: 1870–1930* (London, 1943), p. 237; G. C. Allen, *The Industrial Development of Birmingham and the Black Country: 1860–1927* (1966), pp. 152–55, 344–49.
30. D. L. Burn, *Economic History of Steel Making, 1867–1939: A Study in Competition* (Cambridge, 1940), p. 335.
31. Charles H. Wilson, *The History of Unilever: A Study in Economic Growth and Social Change* (1954), p. 20.
32. Tsusho Sangyo Sho, ed., *Shoko Seisakushi* [A History of Trade and Industrial Policies], vol. 5, p. 155.
33. See *Shoko Seisakushi*, vol.5, pt. 1, chap. 4.
34. This situation helped the rapid rise of large industrial firms in Japan, while the situation in the United Kingdom provided small-scale firms with the opportunities to survive.

COMMENTS

1

Yukio Yamashita
Chuo University

My impression of Professor Iwata's report and some problems I should like to present here are as follows.

I think Mr. Iwata's opinion concerning the relation between the price and nonprice competitions is very important, especially from the historian's point of view. In his report Mr. Iwata says that according to the popular view, "price competition (competitive production) was superseded by nonprice competition (competitive marketing) when oligopolistic business structure appeared, but this sort of view cannot be fully supported by historical facts. The historical facts tells us that nonprice competition, especially aggressive competition in marketing, was quite common in many of the U.S. industries far back in history before the oligopolistic structure had established itself, and it was this kind of nonprice competition that resulted in the rapid growth of oligopolistic structure."

I perfectly agree with him on this point. If the popular view insists that price competition existed only before the oligopolistic structure came into existence, and nonprice competition prevailed after that, this must be without doubt an oversimplified notion. However, I daresay that so-called nonprice competition should be interpreted differently in each period. Namely, nonprice competition under the oligopolistic structure makes its appearance as the so-called administered or managed price prevailed, where price competition becomes actually difficult. On the other hand, at the turn of the century, or even before that time, nonprice competition comes out nearly abreast with price competition. I think the main factor that divides the two types of competitions in this case is that concerning the kind and nature of the industry.

So it seems to me that whereas nonprice competition under oligopolistic structure shows itself as a limiting form of price competition, the nonprice competition at the latter part of the nineteenth century shows the intensity of business activities in general. In short, what I should like to say is that the popular view which was criticized repeatedly by Professor Iwata must be said to have some effectiveness with partial revision. This is my first point.

Secondly, I suppose Mr. Iwata has kept in mind that Professor Chandler's proposition, strategy effects structure, could be reversed in some cases: namely, structure effects strategy. He says that in case of the steel industry in the United Kingdom, the heterogeneous market structure limited the price competition and brought about vertical integration only as a form of competition or competitive strategy.

I am very much interested in this point. Naturally I know that these two patterns are interchangeable by circumstances. And yet it seems to me that this pattern of structure and strategy is showing some negativeness or limitation of entrepreneurship and business activities in general, and of course vice versa. I believe the key factor that divides the one from the other is the possibility of creating new markets for industry. Probably the nature of the market and some other factors, limiting or promoting such as Mr. Iwata states in his paper, will have influence upon producing the possibility, as mentioned above. If it is so, wouldn't it be possible that through these sorts of patterns, we can grasp the peculiarity of economic development of each country and classify the countries accordingly? This is the second.

Thirdly, in the case of Japan, we can see the same pattern of strategy and structure as in the United States in terms of aggressive entrepreneurship by large trading companies. However, the difference is that whereas in Japan the trading companies were taking the initiative in marketing, in the United States on the other hand, manufacturing companies themselves developed their own marketing organizations and carried out direct selling.

Such a difference as this is extremely important as it seems to reflect the different and distinctive situation, including market structure, in these two countries. I am keenly interested in the causes that brought about a situation like this. Hence my point is that when we try to use the set of patterns of strategy vs. structure as a tool for historical analysis, we have to be careful not to apply them automatically. With this remark borne in mind, marketing strategy and structural analysis will prove its effectiveness for the future.

2

Alfred D. Chandler, Jr.
Harvard University

In answer to the commentator, since *strategy and structure* has been used so much, it might be easier to title the paper "The Impact of the Marketing Policy of the Firm on the Organization of the Market," to get away from *strategy and structure*. Now with reference to the American experience, of the two types of firms that Professor Iwata pointed out, let's look at A for a minute. It seems to me that all the firms that were in A grew by creating a big market. They were either a brand-new process or a brand-new product. In doing this, they in a sense organized the market. I have listed three types in my paper. One was the new machines that required specialized services. There were farm machines, sewing machines, and business machines. Business machines were the typewriter, the cash register, and, a little later, the adding machine. These all required specialized marketing services. The innovators that created the modern firm weren't necessarily the inventors, but they were the firms that first built the marketing organizations: McCormick and two or three others, such as Deerlin. In sewing machines, really Singer. He had four competitors at first, but in time his was the most powerful organization. In typewriters there were only one or two firms. In cash registers it was only one firm, the National Cash Register. But they all did the same thing: they created a massive marketing organization. That in turn created the barrier to entry. The only way to get into the business was to have a comparable organization. And the reason this was so important was that you had to have the consumer services. You had to have the credit. As Professor Iwata said, there was a 10 % downpayment, which was a small downpayment on a big product. The repair and service was very important, and even the demonstration for selling.

Now the next, in type A, were the products that developed new processes for a large market. Some of them were relatively new; for instance, the cigarette was still quite new. The cigarette machine made possible tremendous production, which in turn led to Duke's entering the business on a large scale, where before there were only four or five people making cigarettes. Duke built a great marketing organization that dominated the industry. The other classic example is breakfast cereals. The development of the rolling machine in wheat, oats, cereal products, high continuous process machinery, meant that suddenly you could drown the United States in oats, and nobody ate oats, so they developed the breakfast cereal. Quaker Oats was the pioneer. Even today Quaker Oats is being sued by the government for dominating the industry. They dominated it from the very start. The others which were less new, but still new in the United States, were the canning processes. Heinz and Campbell were the very first to can foods, which is interesting because where the food processing was a *seasonal* operation, then the processing was dominated by the two big canning companies, American Can and Continental Can. Again it was the same thing; the marketing organization was the chief thing here. A very interesting example is Eastman Kodak and photography. He developed a continuous process film, but professional photographers wouldn't buy the film. So then he developed a camera which would use his film, and a great marketing organization which built on this industry. Now the others were Proctor and Gamble in soap, which in the United States I think was a little different from England. Soap tended to be a by-product of the farm. There was a continuous process, I understand, of manufacturing soap, and Proctor and Gamble was one of the first to realize you could cover the national market with Ivory Soap.

The third kind of firm dealt in products using refrigeration, which would be meat and beer.

I would say, then, that in a sense until the process or product was developed, there was no real market for this; but by developing the process or product and then creating a marketing organization, that led to oligopoly in these industries. Now the other industries went through the pattern that is more traditional for consolidation: price competition leading to consolidation, then cartelization. But then, as I stressed, in order to move further they too developed comparable, integrated organizations and began much more nonprice competition, a very long formation. But I think the factor that really counts is the historical development of when the process and product were first created, and the nature of the process and product, the newness. Where they were old, then the older theories still hold—whether it was in iron and steel, or even kerosene, but certainly in textiles, shoes, and so forth.

PART III

STRATEGY AND STRUCTURE IN WESTERN COUNTRIES

III–1

Organizational Innovation in the McCormick and International Harvester Companies

Kesaji Kobayashi
Ryukoku University

In the field of traditional economic history, the era of the first merger movement has been studied from the point of view of the formation of monopoly or finance capitalism, referring little, if at all, to the internal structure of such a capitalist enterprise. However, if we want to see the characteristic features of the recent growth of the American economy in relation to that of our economy, it is equally important for the historians to study aspects of the organizational changes which took place in this era.

Through the period from the latter part of the nineteenth century to the early part of the present century, many of the leading industrial firms of the United States came to be organized with a more or less similar form called "centralized, functionally departmentalized structure." According to Professor Chandler, this type of organization stemmed from two different business strategies. "By one strategy," he says, "a single company began to expand and integrate through creating its own marketing organization. By the other, a number of manufacturing companies which had joined together in a horizontal combination . . . consolidated their manufacturing activities and then quickly moved forward into marketing or backward into purchasing."[1]

This proposition would immediately lead us to the following consideration: when several companies, which had been managed through the departmentalized organization, merge into one company, would the former management structure work as effectively or would any remolding of the organization be necessitated? Concerning this point, the history of the International Harvester Company provides us an interesting illustration, because the constituent companies of this firm have already had a well-refined management organization to coordinate and control their huge vertically integrated business enterprise. Bearing this point in mind, this paper intends to throw some light upon the aspect of the organizational innovation in the formative era of the modern big business enterprise through a review of the earlier history of International Harvester Company together with one of its constituents, the McCormick Harvesting Machine Company.

1

The International Harvester Company was organized in 1902 in New Jersey through the merger of big five companies from among about twenty of the competing harvesting machine makers. The prime motive of this merger was the manufacturer's desire to eliminate the fierce competition, although that of the investment bankers aiming at the promoter's gain could not be overlooked.[2] The competition was so severe that it was called a "harvester war," yet the business was financially a profitable one. The success in the harvester business appears to have mainly come from the organizational as well as the technological innovation following the strategies to meet the market opportunities of the time.

The McCormick Harvesting Machine Company was one of the constituents of the International Harvester Company, but this firm was not only the biggest in terms of business volume but also the pioneer in terms of the new business strategy and structure in the agricultural implement industry. I would, therefore, like to take up the McCormick Company and analyze its business activities in relation to its management organization.

The McCormick Company was one of the earliest in the field of the harvesting machinery industry, established in Chicago in 1847 by Cyrus Hall McCormick, known as an inventor of the first mechanical reaper. Like the cases of other entrepreneurs who developed new products and commercialized them, the McCormicks could not use the existing marketing channels, and this situation led them to establish their own marketing facilities.[3] A series of economic developments, such as the influx of foreign immigrants, the creation of the independent farmer by the legislation, the improvement of transportation and communication, and the resulting agricultural development, gave impetus to the agricultural implement industry, and especially to the harvesting machinery industry which was expected to be a bottleneck breaker in wheat production. The McCormick Company grew with the expansion of American agriculture, beginning with less than a hundred workers in 1848; the number of the operatives exceeded 2,400 in 1898, and the output of the reaper increased from 1,500 to 190,000 in the same period.[4]

As the size of the enterprise became bigger, the job of management became more and more important for the McCormick Company; the problem of coordinating the flow of the products became most serious due to the seasonal character in the selling of harvesting machines. Although the refinement of the organizational structure was evolutional, the changes in top management after the death of the originator of the firm and the retirement of his brother, who was said to be a less active executive, seemed to be one of the turning points in this company. In fact, it was Cyrus McCormick II who adopted a newer type of harvesting machine as the main product line and expanded business so widely that organizational changes were needed. According to the statement made in 1902 immediately before the merger, the company had a centralized, functionally departmentalized organization. (See Table 1.) Among the departments, the Reaper Works was the kernel of the enterprise, but the sales business was so important that more than half of the eleven departments were related to sales activities.[5]

The products of the McCormick Company were sold through local agents spreading all over the country. The local agents were selected from country storekeepers and blacksmiths, and handled the McCormick reaper on a commission basis (20% for credit sale and 23% for cash sale), but they handled other makers' agricultural implements as well. It was, therefore, the strategy of the McCormicks to create a strong sales department with active sales forces to assist local agents. In addition to the service of the traveling salesman, whose duty it was to explore the market, that of the expert (mechanic) was

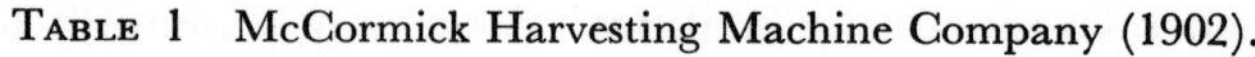

TABLE 1 McCormick Harvesting Machine Company (1902).

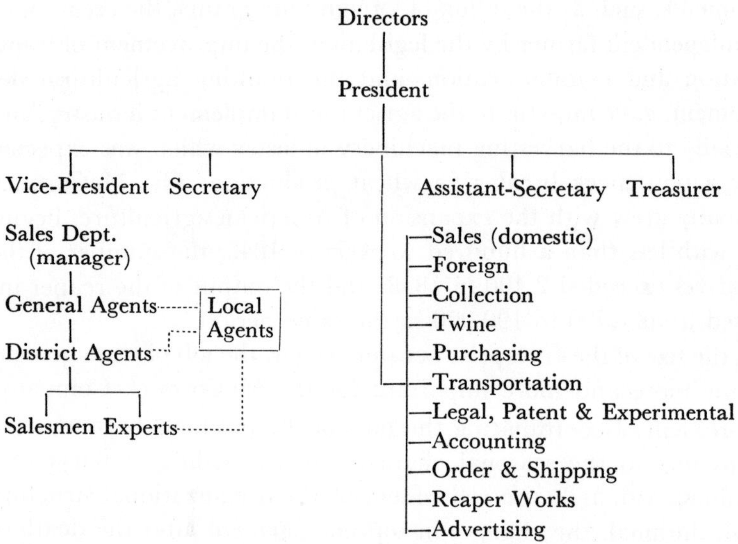

also very important for two reasons: firstly, the company sent the machine in "knock-down" to the company-owned local warehouse and delivered it through agents to the farmers who bought it. In most cases, however, neither local agents nor farmers could assemble the machine, so the service of the expert was indispensable. Secondly, any mechanical trouble had to be repaired as quickly as possible, and the broken parts had to be replaced with available ones. For these services the experts were again needed.[6]

The harvesting machine was expensive compared to other agricultural implements and most of the farmers could not buy it in cash. For this reason the McCormick Company developed the credit sale system, and a collection department was established for pursuing this system. The collection department had the same structure as the sales department, that is, with agents and servicemen, although their salary was a little higher than the salesmen because of their more difficult job.[7]

Other manufacturers of harvesting machines, including the constituents of the International Harvester Company, Deering, Champion, Plano, and Milwaukee, had similar management systems with an organization to coordinate or control various operating units. Among these firms, however, the Deering Company, which was the largest next only to the McCormicks, not only had the huge harvester plant but also had such facilities for the production of raw materials as iron ore and steel mills, and therefore, in terms of vertical integration, the Deering might be said to have been superior to the McCormicks.[8]

2

Immediately after the formation of the International Harvester Company, the basic strategy was carried out in three directions: (1) vertical integration, (2) diversification of products, and (3) enlargement of foreign business. Let us examine briefly each of these.

Vertical integration: In its report on the International Harvester Company, the Bureau of Corporations pointed out the main feature of the company as follows: "From the beginning an important feature in the organization of the International Harvester Co. was the inclusion with the implement factories of property in various natural resources, such as ore, coal and timber, and also plants for the manufacture of iron and steel."[9] When the merger was realized, properties of the constituent companies, such as McCormick's timber lands and twine farm, Deering's iron ore and steel plants, Plano's iron works, and so on, were concentrated into the hand of the newly established company. Adding together these facilities with factories and sales organizations, the International Harvester Company established itself as a huge vertically integrated corporation.

Diversification of products: Following the expansion of the harvester business through the acquisition of four competing companies, International Harvester went into the production of various farm implements such as manure spreaders, farm wagons, and tillage implements. Although these new additions resulted from the acquisition of noncompeting enterprises, the International Harvester developed by themselves such new products as gasoline engines, tractors, and cream separators. Adding these "new lines" to "old lines" the company now could put forward a "full-line" policy as the company's new strategy. In so doing, the company which manufactured only one item prior to the merger became a maker of as many as twenty-six items.[10] This strategy to diversify the products was clearly motivated by the desire to use the sales forces and facilities throughout the year.

Enlargement of foreign business: All the constituent companies of the International Harvester were eager to explore foreign markets as well as domestic markets, but the strategy for expansion was markedly changed after the formation of the new company. Prior to the merger, each company exported only finished products sold through foreign agents, and continued doing so even after the merger.[11] But from 1905 the company began to invest capital directly in foreign markets to establish subsidiary companies not only for selling products but also for manufacturing them using local resources. This strategy, which seems to be a forerunner of the multinational enterprise of the present day, was motivated by various factors: in some countries, the company had to take government regulations into consideration, and in other countries product differentiations forced the company to take this policy. The success of this pioneering strategy is indicated by the fact that in 1911 there were subsidiary companies in thirteen countries, manufacturing plants in eight countries, and the net sales from foreign business reached nearly 40% of the total net sales of the same year.[12]

3

The new strategies have naturally produced the need to renovate or modify management organization. In other words, without an effectively working organization, the implementation of the new strategy would have been difficult and resulted in the uneconomical use of business resources. The organizational remolding of the International Harvester took two steps: the first was the separation of the sales and the raw material procuring business from the production business, and the other was the intensification of centralization in management structure.

Separation of the sales and raw material procuring business: Immediately after formation, the International Harvester Company decided to make one of the constituents, the Milwaukee Harvester Company, a subsidiary by changing its name to the International

Harvester Company of America, and transferred to it all the facilities for domestic sales and foreign business. This procedure was clearly the result of consideration of the circumstances of the time. New Jersey was a rather generous state permitting the formation of monopolistic big enterprises, but the large majority of the states were generally unfriendly to big business, and in extreme cases, as in such states as Missouri, outside "trusts" could not get licensed for trade. It would then be reasonable for the International Harvester to have had built the sales department in the central office in order to coordinate and control its activities, enabling business to be freely carried out all over the country. However, the constituent companies were already dissolved in a legal sense, and therefore International Harvester had no license, and found one difficult to obtain. Under these circumstances, if International Harvester wanted to continue its business, the only possible way to do so would have been to have a subsidiary which did have a license in many states. Since this arrangement was devised as only a temporary expedient, the subdivision of the operating units was nothing but a legal one, and indeed all the executives of the American Company were the same as those of the parent company, and the profit of the former was arranged to be transferred automatically to the latter.[13] In the same way, the raw-material procuring business was transferred to the newly organized subsidiaries: the Wisconsin Steel Company for the production of iron and steel, and the Wisconsin Lumber Company for the lumber business.

Intensification of centralization: As a result of the separation of the above-mentioned businesses, there remained in the International Harvester Company only the manufacturing business, of which control by the central office was temporarily postponed. At the first meeting of the board of directors in August of 1902, it was decided that the business of each constituent company's factory should remain in the hands of its previous owner, so that the factories (which were now called "divisions") were supervised not by the central office but by the head of each division.[14] Eventually, the organization of International Harvester came to show a resemblance to GM's early organization. In short, it still remained at the stage of combination and not integration, although planning or allocation of business resources were subject to the decision of either the executive committee or finance committee in some respects.

The movement toward centralization took place at the end of the year of the formation of the company with the establishement of a dozen functional committees. But the urgent need to have more effective administrative organization led to the resolution of the board of directors as follows: "That we proceed to form an organization of the International Harvester Company for the years 1903 and 1904, with a view of centralizing the business, and particularly to effect savings through economy in the several departments of the company's business while at the same time extending and broadening the business as much and as far as possible."[15] Upon this resolution, there were established ten functional departments which were supervised by general managers reporting to the president. (See Table 2.) Nevertheless, as long as the factory business was carried out separately, this functional organization could not work effectively. In addition to this, the coordination of the functional departments was also difficult as indicated in the example of the proposal by the manufacturing committee to diminish the types of machine for the further

TABLE 2 International Harvester Company (1903).

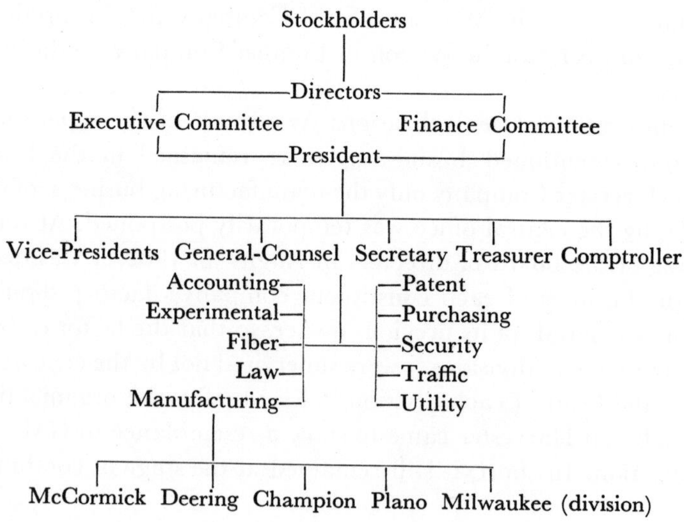

standardization of products being refused by the sales committee. At any rate, the realization of economies of scale through the merger was far from the reality.

The immediate result from such a loose structure was a heavy loss of business, and the company record showed the total decline both in the net earnings and the rate of profit. (See Table 3.) Further remolding of the organization was demanded. In January of 1904 the board of directors figured out how to intensify the control of the central office and decided that the president should have the "supreme power in the executive business." In addition to this resolution, the decision of 1902 as to the separate administration of the factories was finally abrogated. Referring to this organizational change, the Bureau of Corporations's Report pointed out as follows: "This appears to mark the beginning of an effective centralization of business, which for about one and a half years had been conducted as if the companies were simply an alliance of rivals, rather than a complete consolidation."[16]

TABLE 3 Net Earnings and Profit on Assets ($1,000 and %).

Year	Net Earnings	Profit (%)	Year	Net Earnings	Profit (%)
1903	797	0.73	1907	8,228	7.31
1904	5,682	5.34	1908	10,180	8.73
1905	7,511	7.01	1909	16,459	13.43
1906	7,407	6.74	1910	17,209	12.77

Source: Bureau of Corporations, *The International Harvester Company* (Washington, D.C., 1913), p. 238.

Swinging from centralized to decentralized and again to a centralized structure, the International Harvester Company thus firmly established its own vertically integrated and functionally departmentalized management organization. And here it should be noted that this organizational reformation was really instrumental in carrying out the company's new strategy. In fact, it was not until the readjustment of the organization was fairly under way that the new strategies began to show their effects in both domestic and foreign markets. This centralized organization was so suited to the strategy that it continued with only minor modifications until 1943 when the International Harvester adopted, by following the experience of

General Motors and some other companies, the multidivisional decentralized organization.[17]

4

I would like to finish this paper by mentioning briefly the relationship between business and society at the time. The control of industry by big businesses raised criticism from society. The Sherman Antitrust Law in 1890 was a reflection of the antibusiness feelings of the people based upon such traditional American ideals as the freedom of business, equal opportunity to all, and so forth. It was true that the legal restrictions on the trust were by no means perfect and, as Professor Chandler has pointed out, the effect of the legislation against the business activities of the big enterprises might have been far less significant than the forces of market.[18] Nevertheless, it is still necessary to take the social attitude of the time into consideration in order to study the history of business on a broad social background. When we look at the documents pertaining to the entrepreneurs who built the big enterprises, we are able to find as many examples showing how they feared criticism of the society as we are able to find evidence showing how they tried to cheat the legal restrictions.

The International Harvester Company tried to be a "good trust" by accepting a position of social responsibility. The company changed its labor-management relations from suppression to welfarism, the motive of which was considered to maintain the fame of the company as well as the enterprise per se, no matter how many maneuvers to avoid government prosecution might be involved in such behavior.[19] In this sense, we may say that in the United States, with the formation of the modern big enterprise came a new era in which the men in business began to take society into account as a factor restricting their business activities.

References

1. Alfred D. Chandler, Jr., *Strategy and Structure: Chapters in the History of the Industrial Enterprise* (Cambridge, Mass., 1962), p. 25.

2. Helen M. Kramer, "Harvesters and High Finance: Formation of the International Harvester Company," *Business History Review* 38, no. 3 (Autumn 1964), p. 291 and passim.
3. William T. Hutchinson, *Cyrus Hall McCormick: Seed-Time* (New York, 1930), pp. 350–76; Cyrus McCormick, *The Century of the Reaper* (Boston, 1931), pp. 96–99.
4. Pay Roll and Special Report, in the McCormick Collections, State Historical Society of Wisconsin.
5. Bureau of Corporations, *The International Harvester Company* (Washington, D.C., 1913), pp. 310–31.
6. *Ibid.*, p. 337.
7. Forrest Crissey, *Alexander Legg 1866–1933* (Chicago, 1936), pp. 62–70.
8. Bureau of Corporations, *Harvester Company*, p. 88.
9. *Ibid.*, pp. 267–68.
10. *Ibid.*, p. 152.
11. McCormick, *Reaper*, p. 133.
12. Bureau of Corporations, *Harvester Company*, pp. 165–66, 246.
13. *Ibid.*, p. 90.
14. *Ibid.*, p. 156.
15. *Ibid.*, p. 157.
16. *Ibid.*, p. 158.
17. Christian E. Jarchow, "Harvester's Divisional Organization: A Decade Expansion," paper read at the meeting of the Society for the Advancement of Management in 1953.
18. Chandler, *Strategy and Structures*, p. 384.
19. Robert Ozanne, *A Century of Labor-Management Relations at McCormick and International Harvester* (Madison, Wis., 1967), pp. 71–95.

COMMENTS

Alfred D. Chandler, Jr.
Harvard University

I really have very little to add to this excellent paper, excellent both in its data and analysis. All I can really do is to stress the importance of the subject. Mr. Stiegler was quite right. I said there were two groups in the creation of the large corporation in the United States. One was the firm that grew by building a marketing organization. The other group was the bringing together of the integrated horizontal combination out of a lot of single-function firms. There was indeed a third group, and this is the group that we have just heard described. That was the combination of vertically integrated firms.

I think it is in these very few combinations that we get an inside view of the beginnings of modern general management, as opposed to modern factory management, or even as opposed to the operations of railroads. There are very few examples of this. One is United States Steel, and it did not carry out the consolidation until 1927, as we talked about yesterday. There were a few others like Singer Sewing Machine, which, when they moved to take over another company, was so much bigger that it made little difference. They just incorporated the smaller company into their structure. The two most important companies, I think, that were bringing together many large, integrated firms with sophisticated organizations were General Electric and International Harvester. And before I go into just reviewing and bringing out certain points from the paper, I would like to say a little more about the formation of International Harvester.

The "harvester war" was in the nineties, and it was price competition. There was another kind of competition that began to worry the financial community, and this was the increasing of capacity in what someone like J. P. Morgan would consider an irrational way. My understanding from Garrity's book on Perkins was that the initial impetus for the formation of International Harvester came from a telephone call by Judd Gary, who had just become head of U.S. Steel. He was Morgan's man and head of Federal Steel, and it was, or was just about to be, U.S. Steel. But he was worried about the Deerings' building a new steel plant in part of their vertically integrated organization. He was worried about excess capacity in the steel industry. He phoned McCormick and said, "You should do something about this." He was a Morgan man, and in time the Morgan firm, through one of its partners, Bergen, was able to bring about the organization of International Harvester.

Now the important point in the whole development of modern management was that their constituent companies did remain separate, as you so well pointed out. They remained as separate operations. There was some attempt to coordinate things by having functional departments at the top and functional committees, but the committees didn't work. In the United States, this is what you almost always see: committees don't work. Somebody has to have some authority and responsibility. And the result, as you so well pointed out, was financial lack of success. The profit record went down. As for the response of the corporation, I suspect it was not the financial people but more the operating people, the people in performance, who said, "We ought to put this together under one roof." They brought the various plants into a manufacturing department, and then had their overall sales department, and their overall purchasing department. The final picture after three years at International Harvester was the creation of a classic, centralized, functionally departmentalized organization. And as you pointed out, only then could they move on their strategy of full-line and overseas extension. They had to in this sense develop a structure coming out of the traditional strategy, which was consolidating vertically integrated firms, putting them under one centralized operation, and then they began to move into a full-line strategy.

The full-line strategy, just to carry the story a little further, by World War I and more particularly in the 1920s, had moved rather quickly into a strategy of further diversification. In the 1920s the agricultural market fell off. International Harvester moved into making trucks and equipment for construction and building industries. This diversification in turn proceeded in 1943 to follow General Motors and set up a multidivisional form. But I would suggest for the record that you have a rare opportunity to see just what kinds of controls were adopted when administrative consolidation was finished, and I would think it would be extremely interesting to see what procedures were developed for the allocation of resources. In other words, were capital budgets developed?—capital budgets as to where to build new plants, particularly the overseas plants? What kinds of techniques were developed to allocate resources to carry out the basic strategy? And I don't know but I suspect (I know this is true in general) that from the techniques developed to carry out the strategy to run this great giant, most of the methods of modern management science came. This is not true, for instance, of U.S. Steel, but it is true of General Electric. I know that General Electric is, however, noted in its own right for things such as careful budgeting. But I suspect that the Harvester people were learning this themselves, and they may have been a model for the automobile industry and other firms.

This is all I have to say. It was a very, very good paper.

III–2

The Strategy and Structure of Cotton and Steel Enterprises in Britain, 1900–39*

Shin-ichi Yonekawa
Hitotsubashi University

Cotton and steel are examples of old established industries in Britain in this century. Until now it has been generally argued that their performance during this period has been rather poor, a point which I think cannot be disputed at least from a national perspective. However, when the analysis is made using materials concerning individual enterprises, their performances prove to have varied markedly from one other but, at the same time, to have demonstrated a common characteristic strategy on an industry-wide basis.

In the following study, attention is to be paid to tracing strategies and structures in several individual enterprises in some detail, and also to obtaining a general idea of the two industries' strategies and structures. Emphasis will be placed upon the period from the early 1900s to the late 1930s, partly because some work has already been done dealing with the period prior to the turn of the nineteenth century, but largely because I have access to original materials dated only after that time.[1]

In the cotton textile industry six companies were selected, all of which appear in a table listing the largest British industrial companies in 1905 compiled by Professor P. L. Payne.[2] (Courtaulds, however, is excluded.)[3] In the case of the iron and steel industry the selection of companies is rather arbitrary. Firms commonly called iron and steel companies carried out a broad range of mining and manufacturing activities, and the variations in their range of products were very remarkable. Seven such companies appear in Professor

Payne's table, three of which were chosen for this study along with two other well-known companies whose range of activities was not so wide.[4]

Organization of the Cotton Textile Industry[5]

The cotton textile industry was strongly export-oriented and at its peak on the eve of World War I more than 80% of its output was exported to overseas markets, capturing 65% of the international cotton trade. During the war when British cotton companies resigned themselves to some unfavorable conditions, the developing countries, especially Japan and India, moved to secure their home markets. As a result, their output continued to increase rapidly and grew competitive, largely because of the use of cheaper cotton and lower labor costs. The output of British cotton textiles decreased to such an extent that it amounted to less than half the prewar level by 1938 (see Table 1). Parallel with diminishing exports, markets for British cotton textiles also changed during this period, as indicated in Table 2.

However the important point is the remarkable difference in the rate of decrease between the four main kinds of exported cloth, as can be seen from Table 3. It was grey cloth that consistingly inflicted the most damage on British cotton trade throughout the period. On the other hand, exports of printed and bleached cloths, and especially of dyed cloth, remained relatively stable at a comparatively high level during the twenties, after the drastic decrease of 1920–21.

The British cotton industry was characterized by a high degree of specialization, which had gradually evolved in the course of the growing activity of the industry. In this respect it showed a striking contrast with the Japanese. Vertical integrations appeared only to a very limited extent. Usually there were six independent types of firms engaged in the industry: the cotton importers and brokers, the spinners, the yarn merchants and brokers, the weavers or manufacturers, the finishing trades, and the piece-goods merchants. Furthermore, the companies engaged in manufacturing or merchandis-

TABLE 1 Production and Exports of Cotton Textiles, 1912–38.

	Yarn (mn lb)		Piece Goods (mn sq. yd.)	
	Production	Exports	Production	Exports
1912	1,963	217	8,050	6,665
1924	1,395	163	6,046	4,445
1930	1,048	137	3,500	2,407
1937	1,375	159	4,288	1,922
1938	1,070	123	3,126	1,368

Source: G. C. Allen, *British Industries and Their Organization*, 1952, pp. 196, 223.

TABLE 2 British Exports of Cotton Piece Goods to Groups of Markets.

(mn sq. yd.)

	1909–13*	1929	1931	1933	1935	1936	1937	1938
Total	6,476	3,672	1,716	2,031	1,949	1,917	1,922	1,387
India	2,507	1,374	390	486	543	416	356	293
Dominions	382	340	258	384	389	405	450	390
Quota Colonies**	322	266	143	171	275	310	301	155
Twelve Trade Agreement countries***	599	308	229	306	274	267	278	229
All other countries	2,666	1,384	696	684	468	517	537	319

Source: R. Robson, *The Cotton Industry in Britain* (1957), p. 11.

* Million linear yards.

** The British Colonies in which quotas on imports of certain foreign textiles were imposed in 1934.

*** Norway, Sweden, Denmark, Finland, Latvia, Lithuania, Yugoslavia, Poland, Turkey, Argentina, Uruguay, Peru.

TABLE 3 British Exports of Cotton Piece Goods in Groups of Varieties.

(m. £)

Yearly Averaged	Grey Cloth	Bleached Cloth	Printed Cloth	Dyed Cloth
1910–13	2,164	1,889	1,259	1,081
1920–24	1,174	1,292	776	795
1925–29	1,151	1,355	622	779
1930–34	397	773	340	507
1935–38	299	551	378	466

Source: *Survey of Textile Industries* and *Statistical Abstract for U.K.*

ing were inclined to specialize in certain kinds of products, and in the case of marketing, merchants were separated into several groups according to their export areas.

Entrepreneurs in the cotton industry seem to have believed in "industrial individualism." They were actively opposed to state intervention until the thirties. Some federations were organized to push for their common interests in the twenties, but their efforts were never satisfactory. During the depressed years of the thirties, entrepreneurial attitudes came to favor state intervention, to the extent that it was considered desirable for the government to have some degree of control over working conditions, and to exercise a restraining influence over excess production.

J. and P. Coats and English Sewing Cotton[6]

J. and P. Coats originated in a small mill in Paisley near Glasgow in 1826 and, after absorbing four rival firms in 1895–96, grew to be one of the earliest and most successful world enterprises by the beginning of the twentieth century. Previous to a capital increase in 1919, a splendid dividend of 30–35% was paid during the prosperous years by controlling more than 80% of the market in cotton thread in Britain and by trading 80% of the group's products in foreign countries.[7] Considering the circumstances of its recent absorption of its former rivals, the management of the company was highly centralized, certainly in comparison with that of other associations to be considered below.

Two prominent aspects of management strategy during this successful period, overseas investment and control of marketing, should be noted. The overseas investment originated when the company secured works in Rhode Island soon after the beginning of the so-called Great Depression in the late nineteenth century.

As a consequence of acquiring thirteen mills in Russia and other countries in the following years, the company could state that "by far the larger part of the company's profit is now [1899] derived from the shares in foreign manufacturing companies."[8] Because the gap in costs of production tended to widen between Britian and other countries,this management policy was energetically pursued until the second half of the 1930s in spite of the loss of the Petrograd mill as a result of the Russian Revolution. In consequence of this policy, the company had more than fifty separate mills all over the world in 1930, and so "the position abroad is stronger than it has ever been."[9]

Unlike other cotton textile companies, J. and P. Coats had marketing power. "What the 'Combine' has done has been to destroy the business of the middlemen—All these smaller dealers and consumers can now buy direct from the Central Agency," which was its marketing subsidiary.[10] This, no doubt, was one source of the company's huge trading profits. On the other hand, the reason why it did not participate in organizing the spinning section is not difficult to understand. Since the fine cotton-spinning section was highly competitive at the end of the nineteenth century, it was reasonable for J. and P. Coats to have placed substantial contracts in competitive markets. When the Association emerged in 1898 to limit competition, Coats did not miss the opportunity of being connected with the association by means of acquiring 200,000 ordinary shares at the time of the amalgamation, and consequently the bulk of the company's orders went to this association.[11]

It may be difficult to describe the development of managerial organization using printed materials, but, as stated above, centralized management can, I believe, be inferred from the process of the company's growth. Even in the years following the absorption of rival firms the Coats family almost entirely controlled the board, which consisted of eighteen directors,[12] and at the same time held about 50% of the shares.[13]

The changing business situation in the cotton thread trade seems already to have been observed by the second half of the twenties. T. Glen-Coats, chairman of the company, said in 1928 that "household sewing . . . is becoming a lost art,"[14] and reference was made to the fact that the company was constantly on the lookout for new sources of business, and was bringing out new articles whenever possible. The results of this policy of diversification, however, were limited. The only newly developed field was in fancy products. The company, however, took a passive attitude towards artificial silk.

A year or so after J. O. M. Clark became the first chairman not connected with the Coats family, he adopted a policy of managerial decentralization. Too much detailed work had been concentrated in Glasgow. A separate operating company, United Thread Mills, was formed to unite all the mills in Paisley and England.[15] In consequence of this reform, J. and P. Coats came to be a pure holding company in 1931. Moreover, the influence of the Coats family seems to have diminished during the thirties.

The English Sewing Cotton Company began in a different way from J. and P. Coats, when fourteen firms were amalgamated as a defense measure immediately after the formation of the Coats group. But at the same time it should be noted that J. and P. Coats took up £200,000 of the ordinary shares so that the management of the company was, and continued to be, under the influence of J. and P. Coats.

The company was reorganized in 1902 as a result of overcapitalization and loss of management control. O. E. Philippi, director of J. and P. Coats, was appointed chairman of the reorganization committee.[16] Judging from the fact that the company could continue paying a dividend of no less than 10%, the management seems to have been successfully centralized into a small board, from which the old vendors were largely excluded. The company was also similar to J. and P. Coats in that the larger part of the company's profits depended upon its overseas subsidiaries, above all on the American Thread Company. The English Sewing Cotton Company actively participated in the formation of the latter, and made its control stronger by increasing its holdings of ordinary shares.[17]

Fine Cotton Spinners' and Doublers' Association

Originating in the merger of thirty-one firms in 1898, the Fine Cotton Spinners' and Doublers' Association came to be the only large company in the spinning section of the cotton industry. The original aims of the amalgamation were the following: cessation of unnecessary competition; centralization of office work of buying, selling, and distributing; and specialization of mills. The association seems to have been substantially successful in that the dividend expected in the prospectus—8.5%—continued to be realized until the world depression.

In the period following the prosperous years of 1910s, when new mills were being built and the price of cotton was rising, overproduction resulted in severe competition and price cutting. Then the management organized vertical combination by means of establishing a cotton plantation in the United States; this, however, was a difficult venture considering that it took a very long time to begin to earn profits.[18] The association did not intrude into the weaving section, perhaps because of the natural defensiveness of its managerial attitude.[19] It was thought wiser to intensify the restraint of competition in the spinning section. So the policy of buying up newcomers was continued during the twenties. In addition, the association seems to have given great consideration to its marketing policy from its early years. The commercial part of the association was regarded as being the most important. H. W. Lee, the most influential man during the period, took part in marketing activities before being appointed managing director. The method of advertisement during the twenties emphasized "personal visits to the principal users of yarn in every market of the world"[20]; mass advertisement by means of newspapers was avoided. The association began spinning materials other than cotton by degrees during the thirties. "Our efforts to make our name known to the public in connection with specialties are beginning to bear fruit."[21]

Thanks to long and well-reported annual meetings, it is possible to make the organizational development clear. The organization went through a process of evolution, not revolution. This organization building was influenced by, and in turn exerted an influence on, other similar associations mentioned below. The association had a large board with about twenty directors composed originally of vendors of associated firms, and, later on, of sons and relatives of former directors. A further step was taken after World War I when directors were promoted from among the departmental managers, that is, heads of departments.[22] Many of the directors seem, however, to have been promoted by reason of long experience in their mills.[23] Even after being promoted to directors, mill managers retained responsibility for a mill or group of mills, and usually were reelected for long periods of time.

It was emphasized at some annual meetings that the "*entente cordiale* between the executive and the board is perhaps somewhat unique."[24] It was the efficient executive board that successfully kept in check the tendency towards becoming a mere aggregation of individual firms. According to the annual meeting in 1923, "this Association is conducted almost entirely by the executive board,"[25] consisting of chairman, vice-chairman, managing directors, and two directors who were at the same time heads of departments. The following departments were set up in succeeding years: yarn, merchanting, statistical, research, and welfare, but it is difficult to date their formation with strict accuracy. Besides these sections, the association had some consultative committees. After 1933 when W. Howarth, the managing director, died, "an experiment" was tried. The exectives worked "as a committee, each member having equal voice in its deliberation"[26]; at the same the post of managing director remained vacant, a situation which reflected the concentrated managerial power of H. W. Lee, the influential chairman.

The Other Three Associations

Three other merger associations were formed one after another in 1898–1900, all in the finishing branches of the textile industry.

The Bradford Dyers' Association, dating from 1898, arose out of a merger of twenty-two firms and controlled 90% of the market share of the Bradford piece-dyeing trade, which finished, on commission, cloths supplied to them by merchants. At the same time, it was planned to keep each original firm independent by means of paying a bonus on the profit to the individual branches. A managerial policy of absorbing other firms included negotiations with the Bleachers' Association in order to transfer a dyeing section owned by the latter, and establishing a community of interest with the British Cotton and Wool Dyers' Association, the next largest dyeing combine. With the object of obtaining a cheap and steady supply of raw materials, the association held 50,000 shares in the Bradford Coal Merchants'

Association in 1899, and sent two directors to its board.[27] Following these measures, the next step in 1911–13 was to found mills overseas so as to avoid tariff barriers, although some old works in Alsace were sold to a large French company after the war.[28]

Despite the decline in exports of dyed cloth, these were not so drastic in the 1920s as in other branches (see Table 3), and the best trading results were achieved, in fact, in the first half of the twenties. This was probably because of the association's monopolistic position which originated in its large share of the market in the production of certain specialties, which was further supported by the Dyers' Federation. When other sections of the trade blamed it for the decline in exports of dyed cloth, the association in turn made accusations against the merchants engaged in the cotton piece-trade. It pointed out that it had made a considerable reduction in dyeing the price of pieces in the expectation of stimulating trade, but this hope had not been fulfilled, and the association had suffered considerable losses as a consequence. G. Douglas, chairman and managing director, talked openly in 1929 of "the advantages of the vertical combine, which aims at cutting out the cost of marketing at each stage and ensuring continuous full occupation."[29]

With the coming of the world depression profits were reduced to much less than half the predepression level, and during the 1930s they never recovered from their depressed condition. The evidence suggests that the world depression merely accelerated an already existing trend in the cotton industry, which had in truth originated in foreign competition, above all in competition with the Japanese. The policies of specialty development (which made a very small contribution to total earnings)[30] and of overseas investment could not, as supposed, check this trend.[31]

The organization of the association displayed some discernible changes. After the merger the board was composed of two managing directors and about twenty other directors, a rather loose organization from the point of view of efficient management. Nevertheless, departments for central buying, selling, and research were soon institutionalized, an the central office dealt with workman's compensation, insurance, banking, and patents.[32]

In the succeeding years the board's business for administrative purposes was divided into sections, in the operation of which the managing directors had the assistance of other directors. It worked very well. This system became so formalized by 1910 that those directors who had been assisting the managing directors were appointed to an executive committee which now acted under and assisted a single managing director, whose chief function was to supervise general policy making.[33] In the course of the following twenty years the company did not appear to carry out any reforms of any great importance, but in 1932 the board tried to strengthen its management function by means of adding four directors to oversee the central management of the business.[34]

The last firm of the three was the Bleachers' Association. This organization resulted from a merger of fifty-three bleaching firms in 1900, many of which were centered in Manchester. The association's business was the bleaching and finishing of cotton piece-goods, and did not include other textile cloths. The initial board was composed of forty-nine directors, almost all of whom continued to work at their mills as branch managers. Two joint managing directors were responsible for overall management policy. In addition to a lack of consistent policy, which resulted from the loose managerial organization, overcapitalization at the time of formation led to a reorganization in 1904. Management was concentrated in a small number of directors who made up the board of management.[35] Nevertheless, there was such undue caution against concentration that in order to prevent it "the association had, instead of concentrating its account at the head office, left the accounts of each works to be dealt with by each works, thus necessitating separate audits at each place."[36]

The principal policy from the amalgamation to World War I was merely buying up rival companies, while at the same time closing down several inefficient works. I cannot find any information about the policies for overseas investment and vertical integration. The war brought the Bleachers' Association handsome profits through the production of materials necessary to the manufacture of propulsive powder.

In the years following the war, the association attained the best trading profits because of its dominant market share and its consistent policy of consolidation. So the drastic postwar decline in exports of bleached cloth did not hit it so hard and it was not until the world depression that the profits suffered drastically, especially from the shrunken demand in foreign countries. The only effective policy adopted by the association in this adversity was one of more drastic consolidation: largely closing down old established works and taking over small firms, together with small organizational improvements. The association, however, seems to have thought that the future depended upon factors almost entirely beyond its control. Some minor technical improvements were put to practical use, and in connection with these an extensive campaign of advertising was tried, but it had little influence upon the trend of falling demand.[37] On the eve of World War II a new line, the production of chemical cotton, was initiated by the association in conjunction with the Hercules Powder Company of the United States.[38]

The Calico Printers' Association was the largest of the four associations mentioned above and represented "the highest development in British trade of the policy of amalgamation," but, at the same time, it was sometimes emphasized tht calico printing was an art, which seems to make this section of the cotton trade unique and to require special consideration with respect to its analysis.[39]

The association was originally formed in 1899 through the merger of fifty-nine firms engaged largely in calico printing, but it should be noted that some of the firms were merchant firms, and some also carried on spinning and weaving besides printing. It is well known that the association fell short of its initial expectations and a reorganization took place in 1902 in accordance with the "new scheme of management" drawn up by the Investigation Committee, two members each of which were sent from J. and P. Coats and the Bleachers' Association.

Exports of printed piece-goods reached their peak in the years prior to World War I, but the association seems to have maintained a satisfactory market share—55–45% of the whole trade in spite of its declining performance up to 1938.[40] Competition was keen even before the war because fashions exerted a considerable influence upon profit margin, economies of scale were comparatively small in this section, and the research and development advantageous to large firms was yet to come. Moreover, the efficiency expected from a policy of managerial concentration had not been achieved even a decade after the reorganization, to judge from the fact that the policy of handling all orders at the head office had proved to be a failure in 1913–14.[41]

The drastic fall and the continued decreasing trend in exports of printed cloth after 1920 would have been more damaging to the association without the price agreement which had followed the formation of the Federation of Calico Printers. But from 1928 onwards the price-fixing system was apt to break down as a result of diminishing sales so that the profit margin began to show a sudden decrease, and never recovered during the thirties.

Some measures, it seems, were taken to meet this situation. An immediate step was to intensify the policy of consolidation. Thus, only eleven mills were working in 1938, nineteen mills having been closed during the years following 1923. The competition within the association was eliminated to the extent that each of the mills had noncompeting specialties.[42] More notable was investment in developing countries. A vertical undertaking, including spinning, weaving, printing, bleaching, and dyeing, was set up in China in 1927, followed sometime later by similar ventures in Egypt and India.[43]

The most controversial question throughout the period considered was the method of marketing. Continual complaints seem to have been made to merchants, at whose mercy the calico printers were apt to be during the depressed years. It was also argued that mass production in the cotton industry was made possible only by vertical integration, including marketing, because otherwise there was no guarantee that the reduced margins of the printers had any effect in increasing trade. As a matter of fact, the more difficult it became for the merchant to secure business, the more he desired an exclusive product, which cost the association too much by increasing the number of designs.[44] As shown by the chairman's statement in 1937 that marketing was "the crux of the whole question," this problem remained unsolved throughout the thirties.[45]

Judging from the reports of annual meetings, there seem to have been no important changes in its managerial organization from 1902 to 1939. It was often said that the fundamental goal of reorganization was that the association should be "one concern consisting of a number of component parts, which would be controlled by a Central Authority."[46] In order to attain this goal three kinds of bodies with well-defined functions were formed. These were a board composed of six to eight directors, an executive with two to four directors, and seven advisory committees. On the other hand, the most interesting point is that the Investigation Committee failed to devise a suitable method to "prevent [branch managers'] indifference and lethargy gaining ground" so that it was forced to insist on "payment by results."[47] The new managerial structure devised by the committee seems to have been carried out with zeal because an enthusiasistic reformer, L. B. Lee, remained chairman of the association during 1908–37.

It is more difficult to trace the development of departmental organization in the printed materials section than in the case of the Fine Cotton Spinners' and Doublers' Association. Nevertheless, it would be safe to say that several departments were institutionalized during the period, since at least a traffic department certainly existed.

Organization of the Steel Industry

There have been a number of elaborate treatments of the progress of the British iron and steel industry,[48] but what is needed here is a mere outline of developments.[49]

It is well known that as the steel age matured, British supremacy in the iron and steel industry came to an end. In the boom years of 1871–73 over 6.5 m.t. of pig iron, about half the output of the world, was produced in Britian, and in 1880 the value of exports amounted to twice that of the combined exports of the United States, France, and Germany. Its comparative decline in world terms from then on was all the more astonishing. By the eve of World War I Britain had already come to be the largest importer and, furthermore, British imports of iron and steel rose from 1.8 m.t. to 3.3 m.t. on the yearly average up to the period prior to the world depression, while exports showed a decline from 4.6 m.t. to 3.9 m.t. One of the reasons was, of course, that those countries referred to above had a vast home market protected by tariff walls,[50] which made possible "dumping" in over-

TABLE 4 Output of Pig Iron according to Quality. (in thousands of tons)

Yearly Average	Hematite	Basic	Foundry & Forge	Blast Furnace Ferro-Alloys	Total
1900–04	3,660	965	3,750	264	8,639
1905–09	3,829	1,399	4,164	307	9,699
1910–14	3,540	2,019	3,635	300	9,495
1915–19	3,573	2,530	2,328	257	8,730
1920–24	2,026	1,960	1,818	200	6,060
1925–29	1,933	2,162	1,726	148	6,042
1930–34	1,228	2,052	1,336	78	4,729
1935–38	1,636	4,045	1,529	134	7,350

Source: Compiled from B. R. Mitchell and P. Deane, *Abstract of British Historical Statistics,* 1962, p. 134.

TABLE 5 Output of Steel Ingots and Castings by Process. (in thousands of tons)

Yearly	Open Hearth		Bessemer		Electric			
Averaged	Acid	Basic	Acid	Basic	Ingots	Castings	Other	Total
1900–04	2,736	445	1,195	579	—	—	—	4,955
1905–09	3,030	1,175	1,200	590	—	—	—	5,995
1910–14	3,401	2,097	971	558	—	—	—	7,026
1915–19	3,967	3,443	780	491	55	19	184	8,938
1920–24	2,247	4,166	382	174	34	23	41	7,067
1925–29	2,062	5,020	438	6	47	26	48	7,647
1930–34	1,483	4,923	195	—	43	28	61	6,733
1935–38	2,004	8,387	214	349	125	50	128	11,257

Source: Compiled from B. R. Mitchell and P. Deane, *Abstract of British Historical Statistics,* 1962, pp. 136–7.

TABLE 6 Exports and Imports of Iron and Steel. (in thousands of tons)

Yearly Average	Exports	Imports
1900–04	3,430	1,090
1905–09	4,502	1,164
1910–14	4,579	1,793
1915–19	2,540	658
1920–24	3,303	1,476
1925–29	3,911	3,317
1930–34	2,240	1,937
1935–38	2,293	1,503

Source: Compiled from B. R. Mitchell and P. Deane, *Abstract of British Historical Statistics,* 1962, pp. 142–3, 147–8.

seas markets. Moreover, together with the increasing use of scrap in steelmaking, the proportion of scrap suitable for steel furnaces rose more than 50% in the twenties and thereafter never declined. Consequently, a large excess capacity of pig iron remained.

This loss of world leadership by the British iron and steel industry was also linked with the construction of plants incorporating more modern technology on the continent of Europe. It was argued that British entrepreneurs generally were hesitant about adapting to technological advances in steel making. With the diffusion of the basic process at the turn of the century, Germany and Belgium became large steel-making countries by using their abundant phosphoric ores. The British steel industry did not follow the same course, but instead continued sticking largely to the acid open-hearth process, as one scholar argued, because of customers' prejudice against basic steel.

Generally speaking, the so-called iron and steel enterprise covered a broad range of activities. In the last quarter of the nineteenth century some companies had already adopted vertical combination to a considerable degree. But both their locations and their capital were not as concentrated as in the United States and Germany, and partly because of that, their scale in terms of capital, turnover, and marketing regions was much smaller than that of firms in those counties. A remarkable fact in contrast with these foreign companies, moreover, was that British companies had not held their control over the marketing process up to the war, although this situation appeared to have been partially improved through the formation of selling associations in the course of the twenties and through the formation of the British Steel Export Association in 1930. On the other hand, the British government, pressed by the association, took a step in 1932 towards the protection of the home steel industry by setting up a tariff of 35% and raising it to 50% in 1935. The remarkable recovery of production and improved trading results during the second half of the thirties, which are mentioned below, were largely due to this protection.

Guest, Keen and Nettlefolds

A considerable part of Britain's coal and iron output was exported in the last quarter of the nineteenth century. The price and the demand for both products were quite unstable, varying with economic fluctuations. This was the basic reason why the trend towards vertical integration was observed as early as the 1880s.

Guest, Keen and Nettlefolds was not only the most successful steel company during the period, but also one of those which had, at early stage, completed its vertical combination to the highest degree. It originally came into being in 1900 through a combination of the Dowlais Iron Company, Guest and Company, and the Patent Nut and Bolt Company. Likewise, Messrs. Nettlefolds was added to this combine two years later in order to limit competition, and, in consequence of this, trading results began to make steady progress. On the eve of the First World War the company, "famous for an exceptionally cautious and conservative financial policy," accumulated around £1.5 million in blue chip.[51]

The company entered upon a new stage of development after the war. By using its accumulated reserve, it acquired a controlling interest during the depressed twenties in a number of reputable companies, almost all of which were famous for producing specialties closely related to consumer demand.[52] The most excellent among these was John Lysaght and Company, the largest galvanized sheet makers in the world. These acquisitions derived from a policy that aimed at "being self-contained in all available directions."[53] Only small additions were made to its own properties between 1919 and the mid-twenties, but investment in subsidiaries increased to more than twice the prewar level during the period. It tended to be a holding company, proud of its astonishingly stable trading results, and it was said that the secret of its success was largely that each of the subsidiaries occupied a leading position in its own sphere.[54] The trading results during the twenties were splendid in comparison with other iron and steel companies in Britain, but with the advent of the depression in 1929 the decreasing demand for the company's specialties and fierce competition made it impossible in 1931 to continue the long-sustained dividend. Nevertheless, payment of dividends was suspended only for a short period and with the coming of protective tariffs the profits tended to increase rapidly.

The company had been keeping its eye on overseas investments since the late twenties, a policy which resulted in the building of several mills especially in the empire. The policy of overseas investment might be considered one response to the new business situation[55]; another was organizational improvement.

It would be quite impossible to describe the organizational development with precision from the scanty records. The company's board was composed of a small number of directors. Given its composition, the board was doubtless under the strong influence of the Keens, who had been among the original founders of Patent Nut and Bolt Company. On the amalgamation with Nettlefolds, four members of its staff were added to the board. With the expansion policy of the 1920s the problem of coordination appears to have been of prime importance. Besides pursuing overall policy, the executive committee decided that in order to maintain the efficiency of day-to-day management, it should divide into two regional committees — one dealing with the business of works in the Midlands, and the other with the business of the South Wales section of the company.[56]

With the coming of the depression, a timely organizational improvement was instituted: both the coal and steel sections were separated and amalgamated with the same sections of other companies on the basis of the Welsh region. Thus, through the issue of a mortgage debenture, Welsh Associated Collieries and the British Iron and Steel Company came into being in 1930, Guest, Keen and Nettlefolds holding 25% and 50% of each company and "transferring to reserve the capital profits arising from the two rationalization schemes."[57]

Dorman, Long and Company

The development of this company is well known from H. W. Macrosty's description.[58] To sum up, it dated from 1876 and specialized in making bars and angles for shipbuilding. But it was in constructional work that it made its name known throughout Britian.

Up to the end of 1890 the company's range of products was so limited that it was merely a steel-making company, and so a policy of both backwards and forwards combination was essential for the stability of profits. The first step towards backwards combination was taken when it went into partnership with Bell Brothers in an experiment in the manufacture of steel from Cleveland ores by the open-hearth process. The success of this experiment resulted in the company holding 50% of the ordinary shares of Bell Brothers at the time of its conversion to a public company. Possessing coal and iron mines in Cleveland, the latter company had the capacity for producing more than 300,000 t. at the turn of the century, and was looking for stable outlets. A new capital issue made it possible for the company to turn its hand to increase its production of finished steel for shipbuilding and other purposes. Dorman strengthened this cooperation in 1902 by increasing its shareholding. Likewise, the company acquired the ordinary shares of the North-Eastern Steel Company, which manufactured rails, in order to develop a wider range of products.

Much still remained to be done before this policy of balanced growth could be completed. Short of pig iron, the company bought up an old established iron-making company adjacent to its works in the 1910s.[59] At the same time, it launched into the making of black and galvanized sheets based on a policy of providing more advanced products, considering that only one-fourth of the steel ingots consumed by its own works was for manufacturing girders, plates, sheets, wire, etc.

Actively responding to the government's demand during the war, the company adopted a positive policy of expansion, under which a new steel plant with the greatest motive power in the world was built. Thus, the company took pride in having the largest iron and steel making capacity in Britain right after the end of the war.[60] A. J. Dorman, chairman of the company, had an optimistic view of the future, in remarkable contrast to A. Keen, who was always taking a pessimistic one.[61] In retrospect, this difference was crucial. With the advent of the postwar depression, cheap scrap and semifinished materials imported from European countries made the company's sections involved in extracting raw materials and making pig iron a burden instead of an asset. This was an entirely unexpected situation. Burdened with the increased capital of wartime the company's profits were so reduced that no dividend was paid from 1922 to the end of the thirties.

The immediate response to the depression was an organizational improvement in 1923. The amalgamation of allied companies was felt to be urgently necessary. Four large companies including Bell Brothers and Company became operating parts of the group, and effective consolidation and coordination were realized.[62] Moreover, a further minor improvement was to build up closer connections between each department, which included changing the location of the headquarters. The next response was overseas investment. Confronting rising tariff walls, the chairman of the company said in 1928, "In an increasing degree we have had to recognize that these markets have become valuable for the purposes of investment rather than as means of absorbing a portion of the output of this country."[63] In 1929 amalgamation with another famous large steel company of the North-East, Bolckow, Vaughan and Company was brought about, together with other organizational changes.

A prominent increase in trading activity reversed the declining trend in profits in 1934, but this was only achieved as the result of protective tariffs. At the end of the thirties the company's policy of pushing into the more advanced stages of the industry was yet to come.

From the beginning of this century A. J. Dorman had been a driving force behind the company, remaining both as chairman and managing director until 1923. With the organizational improvement of 1923, A. Dorman, son of A. J. Dorman succeeded his father as managing director. The amalgamation in 1929 added five new directors to the board. An additional vice-chairman and managing director were added along with three ordinary directors; one of the managing directors worked in London. Moreover, "as in the past, the majority of the board are taking an active part in the daily management of the company," and so the executive management was placed "in the hands of a management committee composed of the principal officers of the company, who are responsible to the board."[64] Besides some general managers responsible for specific works, I found a commercial manager, and departments such as the bridge and research departments though their headquarters were separately located. These appointments might be regarded as indicating a kind of decentralization policy.

John Brown and Company

The rise and development of the steel industry before World War II had, generally speaking, something to do with the munitions industry. This was the case with John Brown and Company, but probably not to such a great an extent as with Armstrong and Whitworth and Company.

The company dated from the middle of the nineteenth century. Introducing Bessemer converters in its early days, it became the largest steel-rail maker in Britain. Moreover, by means of buying coal mines in 1870 with the capacity shortly afterwards of producing 1 m.t. yearly, and a shipbuilding company on Clydebank near Glasgow in 1899, the company engaged in a wide range of activities, from extracting coal to making finished products of high quality, and probably including an iron-making section.[65] In 1907 the company reinforced its shipbuilding section by obtaining an interest in Harland and Wolff.[66] Thus, having steel, shipbuilding, and ordinance works respectively in Sheffield, Clydebank and Belfast, and Coventry, its network of trading activities spread all over Britain—a rare case at that time. But, at the same time, the rumor that "the gentlemen concerned vied with one another as to their importance and the size of emoluments"[67] suggested some lack of cooperation, though I can not add anything further from the present evidence.

The trading results in the course of the postwar years were, as predicted, poor. The already declining profit margin received a fatal blow with the advent of a coal strike in 1926, and a dividend paid every year with difficulty during the first half of the twenties ceased from 1926, the first time this had happened in more than fifty years since the company's corporation.

Having depended upon the government for many of its selling contracts in the past, the company did not find it easy to respond rapidly to changing market conditions. With the advent of capital reorganization in 1930, the steel-making sections of the companies in Sheffield were amalgamated, and, as a result, Thomas Firth and John Brown came into being, 90% of whose shares were held by the company.[68]

But, even in the darkest days, it never abandoned its research work, and by the time of the emergence of Messrs. Thomas Firth and John Brown, the finished product sections of the group had been strengthened to the extent that they included tool steel, motor steel, aircraft steel, and stainless and Staybrite steel sheets.[69] This operating company showed increasing activity from 1933 on. Moreover, as a result of a consolidation project, in conjunction with the English Steel Corporation, Firth-Vickers Stainless Steels was formed in 1935 and both companies' sheet sections were transfered to this company, which drew its supplies of ingots from the two parent companies. Thus, Lord Aberconway, chairman from 1912, could say that notwithstanding its popular description as an armament firm "the improvement of the company's business during the year 1935 was independent of any orders placed under the new armament programme."[70] This positive policy of diversification was illustrated by the fact that in 1938 it had 50% interest in Westland Aircraft in conjunction with Associated Electrical Industries.[71]

Pease and Partners and Pearson, Knowles and Company

Pease and Partners, founded by the Pease family and their Quaker associates, seems to have been a unique and quite interesting firm in some ways. It was a typical family business, whose board was, except for one or two members, entirely composed of the Peases until World War I. They had a unique management philosophy. A. Pease said in 1920 that "the question of efficiency in management rests far more on personnel than it does on the system, however good it may be."[72] From this point of view he considered the company "too big" in 1917; he therefore thought further amalgamation undesirable, and did not try to add a steel section. Moreover, since its emergence, the company had emphasized the importance of the labor question, and this seems to have gained firm roots in its management policy.[73]

The company's first venture was in the rich coal and iron mines of Durham and South Yorkshire, and its coal was best for coke making. At the end of the nineteenth century, it had turned its hand to iron making through obtaining a controlling interest in the Skinningrove Iron Company as an outlet for its mineral supply, and it pursued this policy actively during the early 1910s.[74] The profits in the 1910s were fairly satisfactory and after the war it increased its capacity in coal production by adding some subsidiaries.

Notwithstanding increasing difficulties in the coal and iron trade after that time, the company mistook them for cyclical fluctuations. A serious error in its policy was the continued production of pig iron from Cleveland ore. Production was not stopped until the company's profit margin was reduced to a loss in 1925, although it had already been aware of the trading loss of this section in the early 1910s. One response to the depression was further consolidation through absorbing subsidiaries step by step into its operating units.[75] Although it was clearly impossible to go against the tide, it tried nevertheless to do all in its power to stem the onrushing tide of the depression. Burdened with a bank debit exceeding £ 1 million, the company's capital was reduced to half its previous size in 1933, and at the time of this capital reorganization, the managerial influence of the Peases seems to have disappeared with the family's retirement from the board.

Entering the second half of the thirties, the increasing demand for coal reflected the renewed activity of the industry and the company made rapid improvements in its trading profits, but the iron-making section was still far from satisfactory. This imbalance in both the coal and iron sections was such that the company's annual coal production amounted to over 3 m.t. while the pig iron produced at the rather backward works amounted to less than 200,000 tons per year.[76] The fact is that the company's policy of vertical integration was not as consistent as that of the larger iron and steel companies.

Despite distrust in the managerial system, it seems to have been an iron and steel company with a well institutionalized, departmentalized organization. For instance, the annual report for the year 1911 told us that the iron-making section of Pease and Partners accompanied by Wilson, Pease and Company formed an "ironworks department" after May 10.[77] Such departments as a foundry department and a coal mines department certainly came into being. Besides the small board composed of four or five directors there was a small head office staff as well.

With regard to the extent of vertical combination Pearson and Knowles and Company stood midway between Guest, Keen and Nettlefold and Pease and Partners, and differed markedly from Pease and Partners in that the founder's family had lost its influence by the beginning of this century.[78]

Founded in 1874, the company was engaged in mining coal and making steel, and at the outset of this century began to carry out an aggressive policy of seeking steady outlets for its products. It had an interest in Rylands Brothers, a large wire-rod maker, and its activity covered so wide a field, including railway wheels, axles, iron and steel plant, and wire rods, that "every department was very seldom bad at once."[79] The company's next policy of importance was backward combination which resulted in a large interest in pig iron. The Partington Steel and Iron Company was founded in 1911 in order to end dependence upon imported iron.[80] Almost all of the ordinary shares were held by the company. It was lucky enough to meet the large demand during the war without the need for imported iron from Germany, with the result that it fully enjoyed the boom. It was in 1920 when the boom was still considered durable that Armstrong and Whitworth and Company Launched a takeover bid for the company's ordinary shares, which ended in success.[81] Even if, as *The Times* said, the company considered it preferable to undertake considerable capital expenditures to meet its requirements, this policy cannot be understood without observing the composition of the board of directors. It seems that there were no members of the founders' families except the Blecklys. But this self-contained combination was ill-fated because immediately after its emergence, the munitions boom fell off and the depression in this industry continued year by year, reducing Pearson and Knowles' dividend on ordinary shares to nil in 1924. The Partington steel and iron plant was completely closed by 1926,[82] and it was this company that was, from that time onwards, the source of trouble for Armstrong, Whitworth and Company.

With the reorganization of the Armstrong group in 1929, Pearson and Knowles, as well as contending with the reduction of its capital, had to make its own way. After long and exhaustive consideration,[83] both the Pearson and Knowles group and Wigan Coal and Iron, two large Lancashire coal, iron, and steel companies, were merged in 1930. Each of the coal and steel sections in both companies were amalgamated respectively into one operating company, and the former two companies became holding firms. Thus, as a consequence of this merger the Lancashire Steel Corporation, controlled by Securities Management Trust, came into being. A modernized works, with coke ovens, blast furnaces, open hearths, and rolling mills, was constructed at Irlam near Manchester.[84] Moreover Lancashire and Corby Steel Manufacturing Company, a company in which the corporation and Messrs. Stewarts and Lloyds were jointly interested, was formed for the production of cold rolled strips.[85] Increasing improvement in the corporation's trading profits was shown after 1934.

Some Preliminary Conclusions

I would like to emphasize that the fact-finding I was able to do using printed records of annual meetings never covered all the pertinent points which I desired for compiling my research data, and so my conclusions may be somewhat premature.

Firstly, it is important to appreciate the cotton and steel companies' relative size in the second half of the period studied in this paper. Table 8 shows the largest companies in 1929 in Britain, ranked according to their issued capital. When I compare my list with the other list already mentioned, several points attract my attention. Both the top and bottom companies in my list had increased their capital fourfold during the first quarter of this century. It is possible to find the above-mentioned cotton companies, except the English Sewing Cotton Company, in my list, but these companies, with the exception of J. and P. Coats, rank comparatively low among the listed companies. Textile companies which previously ranked low all disappear from this list. As for the iron and steel companies, they seem to maintain their order, but some companies among the high-

TABLE 7 The Largest British Industrial Companies, 1905.

Rank	Name of Firm	Industrial Group	Year of Registration	Capital in 1905 (to nearest £1,000)
1.	Imperial Tobacco	Tobacco	1901	17,545
2.	Watney, Combe, Reid	Brewing	1898	14,950
3.	J. & P. Coats	Textiles	1890	11,181
4.	United Alkali	Chemicals	1890	8,490
5.	Calico Printers' Ass.	Textiles	1899	8,227
6.	Vickers, Sons & Maxim	Steel, shipbuilding, armaments	1897	7,440
7.	Fine Cotton Spinners' Ass.	Textiles	1898	7,290
8.	Associated Portland Cement	Cement	1900	7,061
9.	Bleachers' Association	Textiles	1900	6,820
10.	Arthur Guinness	Brewing	1886	6,000
11.	Sir W. G. Armstrong	Steel, shipbuilding, armaments	1897	5,316
12.	Samuel Allsopp & Sons	Brewing	1887	5,095
13.	Whitbread	Brewing	1889	4,767
14.	Bass, Ratcliff & Cretton	Brewing	1880	4,640
15.	Guest, Keen & Nettlefolds	Iron, steel, coal	1900	4,536
16.	Dunlop Pneumatic Tyre	Rubber tyres	1896	4,396
17.	Bradford Dyers' Ass.	Textiles	1898	4,310
18.	Barclay, Perkins	Brewing	1896	4,270
19.	Bolckow, Vaughan	Iron, steel, coal	1864	4,246
20.	Cannon Brewery	Brewing	1895	4,200
21.	Wall Paper Mfg.	Wallpaper	1899	4,141
22.	Charrington	Brewing	1897	4,025
23.	Lever Brothers	Soap	1894	4,000
24.	Ind, Coope	Brewing	1886	3,698
25.	Truman, Hanbury, Buxton	Brewing	1889	3,515
26.	Mann, Crossman & Paulin	Brewing	1901	3,250
27.	English Sewing Cotton	Textiles	1897	3,101
28.	Peter Walker & Son	Brewing	1890	3,000
29.	John Brown	Iron, steel, shipbuilding	1864	2,947
30.	United Collieries	Coal	1898	2,843
31.	Linen Thread	Textiles	1898	2,726
32.	Cammell, Laird	Iron, steel, shipbuilding	1903	2,623
33.	Maple	Furniture	1891	2,620
34.	Salt Union	Chemicals	1888	2,600
35.	Courage	Brewing	1888	2,500

Table 7 (cont'd)

Rank	Name of Firm	Industrial Group	Year of Registration	Capital in 1905 (to nearest £ 1,000)
36.	Bovril	Meat extracts	1897	2,500
37.	William Beardmore	Steel, armaments	1902	2,500
38.	Huntley & Palmers	Biscuits	1898	2,400
39.	Hoare	Brewing	1894	2,354
40.	Brunner Mond	Chemicals	1881	2,299
41.	Waring and Gillow	Furniture	1897	2,205
42.	Wigan Coal & Iron	Coal, Iron	1865	2,193
43.	City of London Brewery	Brewing	1891	2,127
44.	British Cotton & Wool Dyers' Ass.	Textiles	1900	2,070
45.	Distillers' Company	Distilling	1877	2,049
46.	Threlfalls	Brewing	1888	1,997
47.	Wilson's Brewery	Brewing	1894	1,992
48.	Yorks Wool Combers' Ass.	Textiles	1899	1,966
49.	Reckitt & Sons	Starch, Blacklead, blue	1878	1,950
50.	Lister	Textiles (silk)	1889	1,950
51.	J. & J. Colman	Mustard	1896	1,916
52.	Dorman Long	Iron, steel	1889	1,910

Source: P. L. Payne, "The Emergence of the Large-Scale Company in Great Britain, 1870–1914," *Ec. H. R.*, 2nd series 20, pp. 539–40.

TABLE 8 The Largest British Industrial Companies, 1929.

Rank	Name of Firm	Industrial Group	Year of Registration	Capital in 1905 (to nearest £ 1,000)
1.	Imperial Chemical	Chemicals	1926	65,746
2.	Lever Brothers	Soap, margarine,	1894	56,628
3.	Imperial Tobacco	Tobacco	1901	42,810
4.	Courtaulds	Textiles	1913	32,000
5.	British-American Tobacco	Tobacco	1902	28,040
6.	"Shell" Transport	Oil	1897	26,988
7.	Anglo-Persian	Oil	1909	23,925
8.	Coats (J. & P.)	Textiles	1884	20,250
9.	Destillers	Brewing	1877	12,771
10.	Guest, Keen & Nettlefolds	Steel	1900	12,590
11.	Vickers	Steel, shipbuilding, etc.	1867	12,469
12.	Dunlop Rubber	Rubber	1896	12,184

Table 8 (cont'd)

Rank	Name of Firm	Industrial Group	Year of Registration	Capital in 1905 (to nearest £ 1,000)
13.	Harland and Wolff	Shipbuilding	1885	10,340
14.	Armstrong (Sir W. G.)	Steel, shipbuilding, etc.	1896	10,013
15.	British Tobacco	Tobacco	1927	9,619
16.	Guinness (Arthur)	Brewing	1886	9,500
17.	United Steel Companies	Steel	1918	9,324
18.	Amalgamated Anthracite	Coal	1923	8,673
19.	Candles	Illuminants	1922	8,500
20.	British Celanese	Textiles	1918	8,461
21.	Fine Cotton Spinners	Textiles	1898	8,350
22.	Watney, Combe, Reid	Brewing	1898	8,056
23.	Dorman, Long	Steel	1889	8,018
24.	Amalgamated Cotton Mills	Textiles	1918	7,250
25.	British Oil and Cake Mills	Vegetable Oil	1899	7,152
26.	British Match	Match	1927	6,709
27.	Ocean Coal & Wilsons	Coal	1908	6,598
28.	Lautaro Nitrate	Chemicals	1889	6,560
29.	United River Plate	Telephone	1886	6,280
30.	Bleachers' Ass.	Textiles	1900	6,266
31.	Thomas (Richard)	Steel, tinplate	1884	5,911
32.	General Electric	Electurical manufacture	1900	5,854
33.	Amalgamated Press	Newspaper	1926	5,700
34.	Stewarts & Lloyds	Iron and steel tube	1890	5,514
35.	Tanganyika Concessions	Mines	1899	5,500
36.	Bolckow, Vaughan	Steel	1864	5,497
37.	Portland Cement	Cement	1900	5,285
38.	Calico Printers' Ass.	Textiles	1899	5,027
39.	Consolidated Gold Fields	Mines	1892	5,000
40.	Mond Nickel	Mines	1914	5,000
41.	Jurgens	Margarine	1914	5,000
42.	Morris Motors	Automobiles	1926	5,000
43.	British Dyestuffs	Chemicals	1919	4,776
44.	Niger Company	Vegetable Oil	1882	4,750
45.	Associated Electrical	Electurical manufacture	1899	4,732
46.	De Beers	Mines	1888	4,726
47.	Bradford Dyers' Ass.	Textiles	1898	4,670
48.	Babcock and Wilcox	Heavy Engineering	1900	4,579
49.	Brown (John)	Iron, steel, shipbuilding	1864	4,500
50.	Jute Industries	Textiles	1920	4,500
51.	Cammell, Laird	Iron, steel, shipbuilding	1903	4,459

Source: Compiled from the Industrial Sections of Stock Exchange Official Intelligence, 1929.

ranking ones in this list were destined to reorganize their capital within a few years, and some previously listed companies dropped off and new companies appeared in their place. Also, several famous new companies founded after 1905 are listed. Many of them emerged from amalgamations; for example, I. C. I., British Match Corporation, United Steel Company, Amalgamated Cotton Mills, and Amalgamated Press. It should be noted that companies belonging to the so-called new industries rank quite low with the exception of I. C. I., Shell Transport, and Anglo-Persian Oil. General Electric, Morris Motors, and Associated Electrical Company rank respectively 36th, 46th, and 49th.

Generally speaking, a company making a line of products can increase its profits through increasing sales volume or increasing unit profits. The increased sales volume has to be directed to the home or overseas markets. If the home market does not extend in parallel with the increase of production, which held true for the cotton industry during this period, increased volume can only be achieved by means of increased exports. However, if foreign countries establish tariff barriers in order to restrict imports, or production costs are comparatively lower in foreign countries, a company is inclined to build its plants overseas.

On the other hand, increased profit margin per product is achieved by means of technological or organizational innovation. And organizational innovation or improvement is classified according to internal and interfirm reorganization. In the case of both industries in Britain, technological innovation appears to have played a minor role during the period. So organizational innovation was of great importance.

Finally, a company with one line of products generally does not stick to its original manufacturing field. Experience suggests a life cycle of a product, and a company producing traditional goods, and facing an increasingly stagnant market situation, can venture into the manufacturing of new products through research and development or by means of introducing new know-how. This is a risk-bearing venture, but it is sometimes the quickest way to success, as Courtaulds's story tells us. Courtaulds, dissatisfied with traditional crepe production, ventured into the artificial silk goods' line with splendid success.

Since the cotton companies were burdened with a saturated home market, they essentially became export-oriented, when they stuck to established lines of products. As a logical development from this, one would have thought that when facing both increasing production costs at home and tariff barriers abroad, they would have tended to invest overseas and build plants there. However, this happened only rarely.

On the other hand, having little room for epoch-making technological innovations in manufacturing established ranges of products, cotton textile companies were driven to organizational innovation or improvement. But organizational change worthy of being called organizational innovation does not result from a mere temporary combination among companies, or an amalgamation of many companies largely with the object of maintaining or raising product prices, but from consolidation, that is, reorganization that results in lowering unit costs. From this point of view, judging from the study already mentioned, the merger movement of the British cotton industry remained incomplete in many respects. This situation prevailed to a considerable extent, up to World War II.

J. and P. Coats and, to a lesser degree, the English Sewing Company were surprising exceptions in the spheres of overseas investment and centralized integrated management; the latter was controlled by the former, with whom it shared a common selling subsidiary. This marked contrast between J. and P. Coats and the other four associations can be easily understood from the way they emerged, as has already been outlined. The main problem in this context seems to be the question why such an energetic firm as the original Coats did not appear in the spinning and weaving sections of the British cotton industry during the second half of the nineteenth century. With the limited opportunity for technological innovation, and the conditions of free competition, which existed in Britian at that time, one would have expected British entrepreneurs to have tried to seek refuge in monopolistic or oligopolistic combinations. Why did this not turn out to be the case in Britain?

Many plausible arguments have been suggested. The great importance of rapid adaptability to changing fashions and the comparative unimportance of scale in the cotton industry may have made it easy for many newcomers to enter these sections successfully during the rapid and continuous expansion of the industry's overseas markets. It was also natural that when newcomers were engaged in some manufacturing process they entrusted export sales of their goods to established merchants specializing in the trade of the particular cotton piece-goods which they manufactured. Moreover, they were requested to produce specialties in this quite competitive trade and "specialization, for whatever cause, tends to become increasingly irreversible."[86]

On the other hand, it was common for well-established entrepreneurs to stop ploughing back their yearly profits and, instead, to withdraw large amounts of money for speculation on the London Stock Exchange, or for the purchase of estates. It is not difficult to understand that in the light of the rather aristocratic social climate prevailing, there was little incentive for them to maintain their entrepreneurial activities as energetically as they had previously done. Anyhow, once such an industrial organization became established it remained unchanged, and it was extremely difficult to transform it and to realize a vertical combination or integration even if the trade situation worsened. Many directors were promoted from the position of mill manager and so their business horizon was rather narrow.

Likewise, why didn't the four Associations launch into overseas investment on a large scale when they were losing their competitive power? It would appear that the lack of vertical combination was a serious handicap, because generally it would have been difficult to succeed in the management of works engaging in merely one manufacturing process in a different business climate. British entrepreneurs could not expect to have such personal connections with merchants in foreign countries, as in Britain. But at the same time, it would have been difficult for them to be engaged in all processes of manufacturing and marketing only in foreign countries. Only the Calico Printers' Association could do so in China, because it had all sections of the industry in that country.

So much for the cotton industry. As observed in this paper, it would not be easy to discuss the so-called iron and steel industry together, but, on the other hand, when they are separated there are disadvantages also. There were some common features between British cotton and steel industries in this period: traditional establishment, export-orientation, and minor technological innovations. But the iron and steel industry had some different features: its earlier and rapid loss of competitive power, the emergence of high protective tariffs in Britain, its connection with the munitions industry.

On looking over this study three kinds of policy were found: vertical combination with the object of securing raw materials and products' outlets, consolidation, and overseas investment. As for the vertical combination, the key to its success or failure seems to have lain in the section and the entrepreneur's playing a leading part in the process of combination. For instance, Guest, Keen and Nettlefolds Company was superior in its diversity of high-grade finished goods, and its success was due to its first chairman, A. Keen, who was a former chairman of Patent Nut and Bolt, a company engaging in the production of high-grade specialties. The comparative importance of the steel-fabricating section was instrumental in achieving its managerial success, so that every iron and steel company did its best to seek its own special products. But when the diversification of finished products made steady progress through self-contained vertical combination, each company controlled by an iron-making company seems to have remained only a subsidiary, and the original iron-making companies tended to become holding companies, as in the case of Guest, Keen and Nettlefolds. On the other hand, when this diversification was attained to such a limited extent that the weight of the iron section was still high, amalgamation and consolidation resulted from the effects of the depression, as in the case of Dorman, Long and Company.

As repeatedly mentioned, it is quite hard to trace the development of the internal organization of the above-mentioned companies. So the following statement is only my personal impression. Professor D. C. Coleman has told us that Courtaulds's management structure did not correspond closely to its strategy. Even in the thirties it remained loosely institutionalized. In the case of Coats and English

Sewing Cotton, their management was centralized, but one cannot say to what extent they were institutionalized. The managerial aim of the four associations which had emerged through the amalgamation of a number of small or medium firms was management centralization. Each of them was, to a greater or lesser degree, on the road towards centralized management. But most director–mill managers tended to be spokesmen for their own mills, so that despite the emergence of institutionalized departments, it would appear that centralized and departmentalized managerial organization was, on the whole, only partly successful. Fear of overcentralization persisted in Courtaulds and these associations.

In the case of the iron and steel industry, it is more difficult to trace the development of management organization from the reports of annual meetings. My impression is that there were two forms of organizational structure according to their range of activities. One was Dorman Long Company which was in the process of setting up centralized and departmentalized administrative organization through the transformation of subsidiary companies into operating units. On the other hand, in the case of Guest, Keen and Nettlefolds, the administrative problem arose from making diversified products from steel. Here the organizational trend was towards decentralization with the result that the company became a holding company. This was also the case with John Brown, Armstrong, Vickers, etc. Generally speaking the British steel industry carried out this process of regional and horizontal amalgamation in the iron and steel-making section during the depressed years. This resulted in horizontal integration in the iron and steel sections. Thus, such operating companies as British Iron and Steel, Lancashire Steel, Thomas Firth and John Brown came into being. As for internal organization, departmentalized managements seem to have been on the path to institutionalization, but it is difficult to trace the process with accuracy, or to distinguish whether or not such departments were being set up to secure a clear-cut line and authority system, although Dr. C. Erickson's pioneering work suggests the possibility of further research to me.[87]

Lastly, Pease and Partners was unique in that this firm appears to have become conscious of the organizational disorder which would have resulted from its rapid growth from a family business.

I am afraid I mentioned the darker side of British enterprise. But this derived, I think, largely from my selection of industries. I hope Professor C. Wilson, who has published masterly works displaying wide and comprehensive research and keen discernment in connection with the other, that is, the bright phases of the British economy, will surely amend my premature understanding of the British economy in this century.

Appendix 1 Dividends of Cotton Companies.

	JPC	ESC	FCSDA	BDA	BA	CPA
1900–1	20 (%)	3 3/4(%)	9(%)		nil (%)	
1901				7(%)		nil (%)
1901–2	20	nil	8		3(7)	nil(8)
1902				7		
1902–3	20	nil	8		3	2 1/2
1903				7		
1903–4	20	nil	8		nil	2 1/2
1904				7		
1904–5	20	nil	4		2	2 1/2
1905				7		
1905–6	25	8	6		4	4
1906				7		
1906–7	30	8	10		4	6 1/4
1907				7		
1907–8	30	8	12		3	nil
1908				5		
1908–9	35	8	8		nil	nil
1909				5		
1909–10	35	10	8		4 1/2	2 1/2
1910				5		
1910–11	35	10	8		4 1/2	3 3/4
1911				6		
1911–12	35	10	8		5	3 3/4
1912				6		
1912–13	35	12 1/2	28		6	3 3/4
1913				7		
1913–14	30	13	8		6	nil
1914				5		
1914–15	30	13	8		3	nil
1915				10		
1915–16	30	18	8		6	2 1/2
1916				15		
1916–17	30	20	10		7 1/2	5
1917				17 1/2		
1917–18	30	20	10		7 1/2	5
1918				17 1/2		
1918–19	40	25(2)	12(4)		10	5
1919				22 1/2		
1919–20	17 1/2	15	20		20	10
1920				20		

Appendix 1 (cont'd)

	JPC	ESC	FCSDA	BDA	BA	CPA
1920–21	17 1/2	15	10		10	5
1921				10		
1921–22	17 1/2	15	8		12 1/2	7 1/2
1922				35		
1922–23	17 1/2	20	12 1/2		20	12 1/2
1923				25		
1923–24	17 1/2	20	14		20	10
1924				25		
1924–25	17 1/2	20	15(5)		20	15
1925				15(6)		
1925–26	17 1/2	20	12		14 3/8	7 1/2
1926	8 3/4(1)			10		
1926–27		15	10		7 1/2	7 1/2
1927	17 1/2			10		
1927–28		15	15		10	7 1/2
1928	20			11 1/4		
1928–29		15	9		10	5
1929	17 1/2			8 1/3		
1929–30		12 1/2	6		6 2/3	nil
1930	15			4 1/6		
1930–31		10	nil		nil	nil
1931	10			nil		
1931–32		10	nil		nil	nil
1932	12 1/2	7 1/2(3)		nil		
1932–33			nil		nil	nil
1933	13 3/4	10		nil		
1933–34			nil		nil	nil
1934	13 3/4	10		nil		
1934–35			nil		nil	nil
1935	10	10		nil		
1935–36			nil		nil	nil
1936	10	10		nil		
1936–37			nil		nil	nil
1937	10	10		nil		
1937–38			nil		nil	nil
1938	10	10		nil		

(1) 6 months
(2) +100% capitalized bonus
(3) 9 months
(4) +20% capitalized bonus
(5) +20% capitalized bonus
(6) +60% capitalized bonus
(7) 9 months
(8) 6 months

Appendix 2 Dividends of Iron and Steel Companies.

	GKN	DL	JB	PK	PP
1900–1	10(%)	8 1/2(%)	20(%)	12 1/2(%)	17 1/2(%)
1901–2	10	6	15	6	8
1902–3	10	4	10	4	8
1903–4	10	nil	8 1/3	3	3
1904–5	10	nil	8 1/3	4	5
1905–6	10	5	10	5	8
1906–7	15	7 1/2	10	10	10
1907–8	15	6 1/2	10	11 1/4	12 1/2
1908–9	15	4	7 1/2	4 1/2	8
1909–10	15	5	7 1/2	3 1/4	10
1910–11	15	6	7 1/2	4	8
1911–12	15	7 1/2	7 1/2	5	4
1912–13	15	8 1/2	7 1/2	8	12
1913–14	15	7 1/2	10	5	12
1914–15	15	13	12 1/2	7 1/2	10
1915–16	15	14	12 1/2	15	15
1916–17	15	8	12 1/2	15	17 1/2
1917–18	15	14	12 1/2	15	17 1/2(3)
1918–19	15(1)	12	12 1/2	15	12 1/2
1919–20	15	10	12 1/2	10	18
1920–21	10	5	10	10	14
1921–22	10	nil	5	5	5
1922–23	10	nil	5	5	6
1923–24	10	nil	5	nil	8
1924–25	10	nil	5	nil	1 1/2
1925–26	10	nil	nil	nil	nil
1926–27	10	nil	nil	nil	nil
1927–28	10	nil	nil	nil	nil
1928–29	10	nil	nil	nil	nil
1929–30	10	nil	nil	nil(2)	nil
1930				nil	
1930–31	nil	nil	nil		nil
1931				nil	
1931–32	nil	nil	nil		nil
1932				nil	
1932–33	nil	nil	nil		nil
1933				nil	
1933–34	nil	nil	nil		nil
1934				nil	

Appendix 2 (cont'd)

	GKN	DL	JB	PK	PP
1934–35	nil	nil	nil		nil
1935				nil	
1935–36	5	6	16 2/3		nil
1936				nil	
1936-37	6	10	15		5
1937				nil	
1937–38	7 1/2	10	17 1/2		10

(1) +300% capitalized bonus
(2) 6 months
(3) +20% capitalized bonus

References

* The topic of this Conference, I understand, has stemmed from Professor Chandler's well-known book, which I have not mentioned in this paper, but bore in my mind while writing it. I am much indebted to Dr. C. Erickson, who read my typescript after the Conference and gave me her advice.

1. The printed records I use in this study are, in the main, *The Times* and *The Statist.*
2. P. L. Payne, "The Emergence of the Large-Scale Company in Great Britain, 1870–1914, *Ec. H. R.*, 2nd ser. 20, pp. 539–40.
3. Courtaulds is excluded not only because it has no connection with cotton, but also because Professor D. C. Coleman has published excellent books concerning the history of Courtaulds; I refer to this company in the conclusion of this paper.
4. Among all of the largest fifty-two companies listed in the table, there were nine iron and steel companies. Of these companies, Vickers, Armstrong, and William Bearmore are excluded because they had too close a connection with the munitions industry to be used in this study. The development of Blockow was quite similiar to that of Dorman, and Dorman amalgamated with it in 1929, as mentioned below. Likewise, Cammell's history resembles John Brown's. Pearson and Wigan Coal were also amalgamated, as I state below.
5. As for this subject, many scholars have considered it. The statement which follows is a mere rough outline of what is related to my study. I am above all indebted to the well-known *Survey of Textile Industries*

(1928) and G. C. Allen's *British Industries and Their Organization* (1933). The postwar works are as follows: S. Pollard, *The Development of the British Economy, 1914–1950*, 1962; D. H. Aldcroft, ed., *The Development of British Industry and Foreign Competition, 1975–1914*, 1968; D. H. Aldcroft, *Inter-war Economy, 1913–1939*, 1970: B. W. E. Alford, *Depression and Recovery? British Economic Growth, 1918–1939*, 1972.

6. In this study, to a great extent, I owe my description of the period prior to 1906 to H. W. Macrosty's *The Trust Movement in British Industry*.
7. *The Times*, August 27, 1920.
8. Macrosty, *Trust Movement*, p. 128.
9. Annual meeting for 1929–30 (*The Statist*, 14 June 1930, p. 1157).
10. Macrosty, *Trust Movement*, pp. 128–29.
11. *The Times*, 1 December 1911.
12. This conclusion is derived from my compilation of *The Stock Exchange Official Intelligence*, 1900–37.
13. *The Times*, 7 November and 12 December 1913.
14. Annual meeting for 1926–27 (*The Statist*, 11 June 1927, p. 1131).
15. Annual meeting for 1930–31 (*The Statist*, 13 June 1931, p. 1061).
16. Macrosty, *Trust Movement*, p. 135.
17. *The Times*, 10 July 1913. The company had the whole of the American Thread Company's ordinary shares by 1913.
18. Annual meeting for 1910–11 (*The Statist*, 27 May 1911, p. 682).
19. This seems to be quite a debatable question, and so I will give it further consideration below.
20. Annual meeting for 1928–29 (*The Statist*, 1 June 1929, p. 1084).
21. Annual meeting for 1936–37 (*The Statist*, 5 June 1937, p. 906).
22. The chairman talked about this subject in some detail at the annual meeting in 1921 (*The Statist*, 28 May 1921, p. 1029).
23. There was usually enthusiastic support for a director who was promoted from among the mill managers at annual meetings.
24. Annual meetings for 1911–12, and 1913–14 (*The Statist*, 1 June 1912, p. 653; 30 May 1914, p. 722).
25. Annual meeting for 1922–23 (*The Statist*, 2 June 1923, p. 1018).
26. Annual meeting for 1932–33 (*The Statist*, 3 June 1933, p. 934).
27. Macrosty, *Trust Movement*, p. 158.
28. Annual meetings for 1910 and 1919 (*The Statist*, 4 March 1911, p. 462; 28 February 1920, p. 429).
29. Annual meeting for 1929 (*The Times*, 1 March 1929).
30. Rigmel, a shrinkage-proof product, was developed. Annual meeting for 1933 (*The Times*, 1 March 1934).

31. A works was erected in Egypt in 1937. Annual meeting for 1937 (*The Times*, 1 March 1938).
32. Macrosty, *Trust Movement*, p. 159.
33. Annual meeting for 1908 (*The Statist*, 29 May 1909, p. 1141).
34. Annual meeting for 1931 (*The Times*, 1 March 1932).
35. Macrosty, *Trust Movement*, p. 143.
36. Annual meeting for 1908–9 (*The Statist*, 29 May 1909, p. 1141).
37. The process of Sanforizing against shrinkage was developed in 1934 and another process was produced in 1937 under the name of Bleapel, a product resistant to spots and stains. (*The Statist*, June 1936, p. 1,099; 2 July 1938, p. 29).
38. Annual meeting for 1937–38 (*The Statist*, 2 June 1938, p. 29).
39. This applies to all finishing sections to some extent, but above all to the printing section.
40. P. L. Cook, "Calico Printing Industry" in *Effects of Mergers*, ed. P. L. Cook. (1958), pp. 179–80.
41. Cook, "Calico Printing," pp. 173–74. But the chairman said in 1913 that much greater efficiency had resulted from the centralizing of warehouses and administration, and this explained the increasing profits, but this policy seems to have met so strong a reaction that disorganization resulted from it and it made the payment of dividends impossible in 1914 (*The Times*, 1913).
42. Cook, "Calico Printing," pp. 190–91.
43. Annual meeting for 1933–34 (*The Times*, 20 September 1934).
44. Annual meetings for 1925–26, 1927–28, 1928–29, 1933–34 (*The Times*, 17 September 1925; 16 September 1926; 15 September 1927; 21 September 1928; 20 September 1929; 20 September 1934).
45. Annual meeting, for 1936–37 (*The Times*, 16 September 1937).
46. Macrosty, *Trust Movement*, p. 150; Cook, "Calico Printing," p. 163.
47. Cook, "Calico Printing," pp. 164–65.
48. L. D. Burn, *The Economic History of Steel Making, 1867–1939*, 1940; T. H. Burham and G. O. Hoskins, *Iron and Steel in Britain, 1870–1930*, 1943. The most recently published book is D. N. McCloskey's *Economic Maturity and Entrepreneurial Decline, British Iron and Steel, 1870–1913*, 1973.
49. I am greatly indebted to G. C. Allen's *British Industries and Their Organization*.
50. This is especially emphasized by P. Temin. Cf. P. Temin, "The Relative Decline of the British Steel Industry, 1880–1913" in *Industrialization in Two Systems*, ed. H. Rosovsky, 1966.
51. *The Statist*, 19 August 1911, p. 525; *The Statist*, 12 August 1914, p. 475.

52. Annual meeting for 1919–20 (*The Times*, 27 August 1920).
53. *Ibid.*
54. *The Statist*, 25 June 1927, p. 1210.
55. Annual meeting for 1928–29 (*The Statist,* 29 June 1929, p. 1291).
56. Annual meeting for 1919–20 (*The Times*, 27 August 1920). Apart from this, committee meetings composed of directors and managers for specific purposes seem to have been opened at various works. Cf. annual meeting for 1922–23 (*The Times*, 29 June 1923).
57. Annual meeting for 1929–30 (*The Times*, 26 June 1930).
58. Macrosty, *Trust Movement*, pp. 127–31.
59. It was impossible to raise ₤400,000 for building a new modernized mill, of which the chairman complained, and so, instead, the company had took on interest in Sir H. Samuelson and Co. Cf. annual meeting for 1910–11 (*The Statist*, 9 December 1911, p. 723).
60. It had an yearly output capacity of 1,250,000 t. of pig iron and 1,000,000 t. of steel. Annual meeting for 1919–20 (*The Statist*, 3 April 1920, p. 652).
61. *The Statist*, 21 August 1915, p. 314; annual meeting for 1917–18 (*The Statist*, December 21, 1918, p. 1160).
62. Annual meeting for 1922–23 (*The Statist*, 29 December 1923, p. 1097).
63. Annual meeting for 1927–28 (*The Statist*, 22 December 1928, p. 1156).
64. Annual meetings for 1928–29, 1930–31 (*The Statist*, 21 December 1929, p. 1085, *The Times*, 18 December 1930).
65. Moreover, in 1915 the company had a controlling interest in Cornforth Hematite Iron Co. in order to secure the supply of Hematite pig iron. Cf. Lord Aberconway, *The Basic Industries of Great Britain* (1927), p. 66
66. Annual meeting for 1907–8 (*The Times*, 2 July 1908).
67. *The Times*, 2 June 1913.
68. Annual meeting for 1930–31 (*The Statist*, 4 July 1931, p. 36).
69. Annual meeting for 1932–33 (*The Times*, 30 June 1933).
70. Annual meeting for 1935–36 (*The Times*, 27 June 1936).
71. Annual meeting for 1938–39 (*The Times*, 1 July 1939).
72. Annual meeting for 1919–20 (*The Statist*, 12 June 1920, p. 1114). Incidentally, the Peases were a famous Quaker family.
73. So the chairman said at the annual meeting in 1918 that we should not only consider the question of making money, but that the business should be carried on with due regard to the welfare of both officials and

workmen connected with the firm. (*The Statist*, 22 June 1918, p. 1094). Likewise, this firm was unique for its long and detailed annual meetings.

74. Annual meeting for 1911–12 (*The Statist*, 15 June 1912, p. 779); Annual meeting for 1924–25 (*The Times*, 27 May 1924).
75. Annual meeting for 1923–24 (*The Times*, 29 May 1924).
76. Annual meeting for 1937–38 (*The Times*, 15 June 1938).
77. Annual meeting for 1911–12 (*The Statist*, 15 June 1912, p. 778).
78. Only one of the Pearsons was included in the board by 1900.
79. Annual meeting for 1908–9 (*The Statist*, 2 October 1909, p. 764).
80. *The Statist*, 7 October 1911, p. 29.
81. *The Times*, 28 January 1920.
82. *The Times*, 22 May 1930.
83. *The Times*, 1 April 1933.
84. *The Times*, 18 March 1937.
85. *Ibid.*
86. P. L. Payne, "The Emergence of the Large-Scale Company," p. 525.
87. C. Erickson, *British Industrialists, Steel and Hosiery, 1850–1905* (1959), chap. 8.

COMMENTS

Charles Wilson
Cambridge University

I wish I knew as much about Japanese cotton or steel as Professor Yonekawa knows about the English, but I am afraid I know very much less about *English* cotton or steel than he does. I have very little to say in detail about his paper, which seems to me to be a very just and learned assessment of the subject. May I begin by some very general remarks about the British economy, which forms the framework of the two industries which he writes about.

Cotton, the original nursery of the industrial revolution, localized a very large labor market and to some extent it started here. I think it emerges through this paper, but perhaps it could have a little more emphasis, that the United Kingdom was not only an industrial producer, and the problems of particularly its industries arise to a considerable extent not merely from age but from the fact, as I said this morning, that the United Kingdom was also the entrepôt for a large, world commercial organization of importing and exporting. The United Kingdom was also an economy and a society in a late, as it seemed then, stage of development, a society where consumers were already formulating new needs and demands. The point I am trying to make is that in the period of which Professor Yonekawa is writing, there is very little attraction to anybody in the prestige demands of an industry like steel, or copper, at any rate down to about 1912. There were, on the other hand, a great many interests amongst the middle classes in the city of London, amongst the merchants and business people, to say nothing of the consumers of Britain. There were all these interests which were concerned to maintain the free flow of goods in and out of the British market. That is to say, the cards were very heavily stacked against the demands which came up from time to time from producers for protective tariff assistance.

Now this economy of course was also facing growing and changing external problems—the emergence of foreign competition, especially in the two industries to which this paper is devoted. Textiles were one of the first industries to go under, so to speak, to the new rivals, and iron and steel were also running in the same battle. I don't want to spend these comments defending the performance of these industries. I would only like to say that it seems to me that in all business, success is relative, and only a failure is absolute. But while there is adaptation, as Professor Yonekawa has shown, one way of adapting this economy to its situation was to let some sections of industry fade away. And I think that the spinning industry, particularly, and such industries as pig iron, or certain generalized species of iron and steel production, are places where it was probably a rational decision just to let them disappear. This is to say, makers of more finished, advanced, and perhaps more profitable products who were nearer to the market were amongst these interests who were anxious to have the right to import raw materials or semifinished components for their manufactures. This position of the producer in the free-trade entrepôt, I think, is basic to understanding the difficulties with which the cotton and steel industries were faced.

Just look at cotton. Here you have an industry which is in a sense a very remarkable historical growth, working in what had previous to the Industrial Revolution been one of the more remote and backward regions of England, importing its raw materials over thousands of miles by sea, and still in this late nineteenth/twentieth-century period making a great deal of material of a semifinished kind. As the paper points out, it was this kind of semifinished goods, the grey cottons, which were the first victims of the new competition, and the reason is quite obvious. It seems to me you have here an industrial situation which is very like that of the English cloth industry in about 1600, when the English were still manufacturing and exporting a cloth which was in fact a semifinished job. It was not a fully finished job, it was undyed. They called it "in the white," by which I suspect they meant "in the dirty sort of grey," rather like the grey cloth. I once worked out the costs of production and the margins of profit and markup on English cloths in 1600, and it works out that about 60% of the manufacturing costs of a finished piece of cloth were incurred in England. The remaining 40% represented the cost of dyeing the cloth (about 5%), and the Dutch merchants' profit. That is to say, this was a total industry which was, like cotton, still concerned with a semifinished job, and where the control of the market and profit margins were largely the concern of the seventeenth-century Dutch. Now I am not suggesting that this is a perfect parallel, but I think a great deal of the Lancashire industry in the conditions of the time is comparable to the English cloth industry of 1600.

The problem which nobody has solved wholly was how to organize for the new competitive world in which these manufacturers of Lancashire and Scotland found themselves. There were many ways, as the paper suggests, in which this could be done. What I am interested in personally, because of my studies dealing with multinationalist enterprises, is why one answer, which seems to be an obvious answer in retrospect, was not more often adopted. Professor Yonekawa has pointed out in his paper that of all these cotton manufacturers we have been talking about, there was really only one: there was only J. and P. Coats, and they were Scotch, run by a German manager. I think this is in a sense a very important remark: there was only one who really decided on, or seems to have seen the possibility of, going overseas. That was, I believe, partly because the Coats were outside the sort of miasma that seems to me to overcome a large part of the Lancashire industries.

Coats quite evidently had a few very good entrepreneurs. I know nothing about the industry in detail, so I am only guessing, but when I think of J. and P. Coats, I think of cotton mills, which were in themselves a kind of symbol. And the fact that when you looked in your mother's or your grandmother's sewing basket, you found dozens of reels of Coats's thread is an indication that, at any rate, Coats were in touch immediately with the retail market. That is to say, they were commercially minded. I think the trouble with a lot of the spinners, and I should suggest that the same thing is true in considerable sections of the iron and steel industry, is that the people who were running the industry were just not commercially minded. They were pursuing very limited horizons, as you made the point about the managers promoted from mill hands. They were simply carrying out a repetitive business, and I think their horizons were really so limited that this does explain why they reacted in such a tired way to the problem. I think this highly divisive, specialized character of this old established industry with a lot of old plant, situated in dismal industrial towns, is also the explanation of why there is such a shortage of entrepreneurial talent. This is also connected with multinationals. But I think that it is the shortage of entrepreneurial talent that explains in turn why the multinational situation, which apparently served Coats's pretty well, was so little adopted by other manufacturers.

Now to look at iron and steel. I would like to just take note first of all of the comment in the summary which has been distributed and say how very much I agree with it, particularly with the statement that the form of the iron and steel industry seems to change drastically after the mid-thirties. We began then to protect with tariffs and to end the entrepôt function. I had to look a few years ago at the workings of Dorman and Long, and I came to know fairly well the man who had become chairman of the company. Dorman and Long were completely bankrupt around 1929, and the shareholders put in as chairman and general manager an accountant called Ellis Hunter. Ellis Hunter was a very remarkable man who not only put Dorman and Long back on their feet by carrying out a drastic program of reorganization and integration. He also became the chairman, almost permanent chairman, of the Iron and Steel Federation, which was formed in order to carry through the program under the government tariff of 1930 and 1932, and the organization of the industry for rearmament purposes. But, with the exception of one or two firms, like the reorganized Dorman and Long under Ellis Hunter and like Guest, King, and Metofo who drew attention several times, again I think the industry as a whole carries the mark of an old industry carrying a lot of dead capital, out-of-date machinery, and to a large extent manufacturing semifinished products like many industries connected with mining, which is migratory. The face of England is covered with the remnants of defunct mining industries, ranging from the more or less picturesque, worked-out tin mines of Baumol to the disgusting slag heaps of the Midlands. The mining industry, and the steel industry that went with it, were again in the process of migrating in this period. The new industries on the northeast coast, and the new industries of Lincolnshire that were set up to work the low-grade ores of that part of England and the Midlands, were distinctly different and more progressive than the older industries of the Midlands in the west. And I think Guest, King and Metofo; Dorman and Long; and later on, Stuart and Lloyd, were alike in this respect, that, like J. and P. Coats, they were all nearer to the market, they were forward integrated, particularly in the case of Dorman and Long, into bridges, construction work, shipbuilding, and so on.

As regards the use of new technology, I agree that its adoption on fundamental matters in the iron and steel industry was small. I think it is worth remembering that, as with the controversy about retaining the mills as against bringing in spinning, so with the controversy about the adoption of the open hearth process, and so on. There was in England a tempting abundance of cheap acid ores, and of course there was an abundance of scrap from overseas. So that it could be argued that the United Kingdom had less need to develop the Gilcress-Thomas process, which was in fact inaugurated and tested out in Alcobourne at Middlesborough, which later became part of the Dorman and Long complex.

Now again, you have a small number of works which, faced by the problem of foreign competition and overseas tariffs, adopt a partial solution through overseas development, as pointed out in the paper that we have just had circulated to us. As in the cotton industry and as in many other industries, I am again impressed and depressed by the failure of the iron and steel industry in England to throw up any kind of reasonable proportion of industrial leaders—entrepreneurs. You have all sorts of reasons why it was difficult down to 1930. Your own figures show that just the quinquennium before the tariff was put on, imports of iron and steel into England were running at 85% of the value or volume of exports. That is a situation in which it is not very encouraging for new men to go into an industry; they are more likely to come out of it. I think, as in cotton and in other industries, we lacked this thing that we were talking about this morning. We lacked any kind of systematic organization on any meaningful scale to harness brains—scientific brains, technological brains particularly

—to the problems of industry. I think that here is a perfectly simple thing: old industries, poor prospects, unprotected, and therefore not attracting the sort of people they most needed.

Throughout the discussion of these two industries this point keeps occurring to me: when we talk about the lack of entrepreneurs, it isn't simply that they were old industries; it was the fact that the very structure of the industries meant that a great many of the people in those industries were a long way from the market, that is to say, a long way from anybody that handled other people or other investors for the market. Since they were remote from the general market, they were therefore unlikely to produce entrepreneurs with market sense, the sense of market opportunities. And yet I think this is what both cotton and steel now needed if they were to adapt themselves to this new world of international competition. This kind of leadership was nevertheless what both industries were shortest of. Professor Yonekawa has pointed out that too many of the people even at the top of the industry, the top and middle management and even higher, were promoted mill managers in cotton. The same thing was true in the steel industry. You could go even quite recently through a British iron and steel works and meet nothing but technical steel men. Probably very good, but to me seemingly deficient in market sense. This is true even when you find, as you do in the history of the Dorman and Long complex, an unusual individual in a firm such as, for example, Bell. Now the last member of the Bell family to sit on the board was Sir Lobian Bell, who was an extremely distinguished scientist, a Fellow of the Royal Society and a Fellow of the Chemical Society. Unfortunately, this does not, I am afraid, contradict the argument that the industry was just short of the right men. Lobian Bell was a charming old gentleman deeply interested in all the most academic problems of metallurgy, but he was completely remote from even the problems of his own business. I think it is true that in the end they had to fire him from his board position as chairman because his real role was as a professor of metallurgy doing fundamental research, not running the business.

Those are some random reflections on what, if I may say again, was the professor's illuminating paper.

III–3

The Multinational in Historical Perspective

Charles Wilson
Cambridge University

1

A number of British (and European) enterprises which now possess the full status called multinational have multinational histories dating back at least a century. Such a case history (Unilever) is attached as an appendix to this paper. The history of the "multinational" does not, however, simply begin with the 1870s, though the years of the so-called Great Depression saw economic institutions passing through a phase of change which was important for the initiation of novel and characteristic forms of business organization foreshadowing some of the features of our own day.

More remote in time but still of prime relevance to an understanding of the modern multinational are certain mechanisms of international investment, certain psychological propensities in the minds of investors, without which capital export in any form could not have taken place. This paper will briefly examine the development of such institutions and attitudes and the manner in which they evolve over time into the modern multinational.

The Preindustrial Era: The Background to Multinational Enterprise

It is worthwhile recalling (what modern economists sometimes forget) that the history of the concept and practice of international investments goes back many centuries. In the Middle Ages, Italian bankers like the Bardi and Peruzzi were operating in England on behalf of the Papacy, gathering that part of the English wool crop which was due to Rome as ecclesiastical taxation, transferring it overseas and receiving their share of the cash accruing from its sale.

Such operations involved the Italian bankers and merchants in a wide range of other operations which may be seen in full spate by the sixteenth century. Antwerp and Bruges in the Low Countries, as well as London and Amsterdam, became centers of their activities, which included increasingly the all-important but highly risky business of financing governments. All the governments of the new "modern states" became steadily aware of the growing gap between their income and expenditure as their costs of war and luxury grew, especially in the inflation of the second half of the sixteenth century. It was a prime part of the business of the Italian "nations" (i.e., colonies) in Bruges and Antwerp to collect deposits from clients and lend them to the Holy Roman Emperor or the king of Spain in an early form of deficit financing. Even more important were the operations of the South German merchant/bankers like the Fuggers.

The security on which such advances and loans were based was (a) taxes due to the princes and (b) deposits of mineral wealth in their territories.

The German bankers in particular were active in the mineral field, for they not only held the imperial mines and deposits in large areas of Germany as collateral but undertook the actual mining operations. Another German bank, the Hochstetters, were similarly active in England; the seventeenth-century operations of the Dutch bankers, Trips and de Geers, in Sweden represented a similar service to Gustavus Adolphus.

I do not want to draw too much of a parallel here, but these Italian and German bankers' operations were (1) international and (2) multinational (in the sense that they involved mercantile, financial, and even industrial enterprises in countries other than that of the parent company). Offices of the parent companies in Florence or Siena or Nuremberg, etc., were to be found in many other cities of Europe. To this extent they exhibit, in a partial form characteristic of the times, a multinational element. This in turn demonstrates that in a period when the international component of economic activity was still very limited, there were entrepreneurs with the propensity to engage in international enterprise and the necessary techniques to do so.

One must, however, note that the number of such enterprises and participants in them was strictly limited. If we move on to the next phase in which the propensity to lend internationally is extended, we see that the operations are on an altogether wider scale. I refer to the investment by the Dutch in the English national debt in the eighteenth century. I have shown in my study *Anglo-Dutch Commerce and Finance in the 18th century* (1940) how the high reputation of the English funds combined with high rates of interest (twice as high as could be got in the Dutch Republic) attracted the savings of Dutch investors into England down to the American War of Independence and the French Revolution. The invested capital of institutions such as churches, synagogues, orphanages, municipalities, etc., and of thousands of individuals were channeled from Holland to England on a large scale for three-quarters of a century and may be found in Government Annuities, and the stocks and bonds of the Bank of England, the East India Company, the South Sea Company, the Royal Africa Company, the Sun and London Assurance Companies, etc.

Such international investment, which was switched into U.S. and French investment from the 1780s onwards, forms an institutional and psychological link with the next great phase of overseas lending, that of Britain after 1815. And this in turn takes us into the age of industrialization.

The Age of Industrialization and British Capital Export, 1815–1914

It will be convenient to abandon chronology for a start and show the extent and analysis of British overseas investment in 1914. It was in four broad categories, thus:

			(£000,000)
1.	Loans to Governments:		
	Dominion and colonial	675.5	
	Foreign	297.0	
	Total		= 972.5
2.	Loans to Municipal governments overseas:		152.5
3.	Railways:		
	Dominions and colonies	306.4	
	British India	140.8	
	U.S.A.	616.6	

Elsewhere (esp. Europe)	467.2	
Total		1531.0
4. Industrial and Other Transport etc.		
Mines	272.8	
Investment Companies	244.2	
Iron, Coal and Steel	35.2	
General Commercial: industrial	155.3	
Banks	72.9	
Electricity	27.3	
Telegraph etc.	43.7	
Tramways	77.8	
Gas and Water	29.2	
Canals and Docks	7.1	
Oil	40.6	
Rubber	41.0	
Tea and Coffee Plantations	22.4	
Nitrate	11.7	
Breweries	18.0	
Miscellaneous	8.1	
Total		1138.3
	Final total	3763.3

(from H. Feis, *England the World's Banker* (1930), p.27)

The table makes it apparent that a vast change has overtaken the nature of nineteenth- and twentieth-century investment when compared with that of previous centuries. Then the emphasis had been on lending to governments. This still accounts for (very roughly), let us say, one-third of the British total export of capital by 1914. But two-thirds were now directly related to industrial investment, including railways.

It is not my purpose at this point to enter upon the much debated problems of the merits and demerits of foreign investment, except to say that in Britain the controversy began to rage about the turn of the century and it has raged, on and off, ever since. My main points are these:

1. Down to 1900, the major flow of capital was into railways, most of it in the form of bond, or debenture or preferred, fixed-in-

terest investment of some kind. Such investment flowed not only to lands in some way under British control but to areas under entirely independent political control—the United States, Mexico, Latin America, and European countries like France, Belgium, Italy, and Germany.

2. The management of the capital and the railway itself, often built with British materials, equipment, and labor, remained frequently under British control. Often two boards of directors existed, one in London mainly concerned with financial management, the other where the railway ran and concerned with its immediate management.

3. Similar arrangements were in operation for the growing mining and other properties—gold and diamonds in Africa, copper in Africa and South America, tin in Malaya and Bolivia, rubber plantations in Malaya, coffee and tea in India, Africa, and Latin America, oil drillings in Persia, Turkey, Russia, Rumania, Indonesia, Mexico, etc. In the case of mining companies, the multinational element was becoming stronger as ownership was increasingly shared with French, Belgian, and American entrepreneurs.

4. Such industrial investments grew more slowly between 1870 and 1900: but meanwhile a new type of industry, more closely related to new consumer needs, was growing up. Comparatively small as yet, it was to be very important as the twentieth century went on, and it grew fast after 1900 in the shape of jute mills, cotton factories, engineering works in India, iron and steel and paper mills in Canada, tobacco companies and department stores in Latin America, soap factories and breweries in Europe. European demand, better communications, and other factors helped to explain the growing success of such enterprises. In one very important respect, however, the new development illustrates "multinational" investment in its final phase, with a multiplicity of enterprises operating in countries other than that of the parent company, and feeling compelled so to operate because of the tariffs arising against the British product after 1870.

5. Such tariffs were a characteristic feature of the newly industrializing nations like the United States, Germany, and France. A major part of their aim, as of tariffs before and since, was to induce a process of import substitution. Much multinational development,

in consumer goods output especially, was a necessary response to their policies of economic nationalism.

Let us now look back and examine the element of multinationalism in earlier nineteenth-century British capital export programs. Along with state loans in the old eighteenth-century tradition to Greece, Spain, and Latin America, after 1815 joint-stock enterprises were floated in London for overseas industrial development—canals in Suez and Nicaragua, copper mines in Colombia, and other South American ventures. Some were offshoots of other companies operating similar (and in some cases dissimilar) enterprises in Britain. One firm with widespread interests in Bogota and Caracas, which even maintained a newspaper in London called *The American Monitor* to encourage British investors' enthusiasm for South American affairs, was also deeply concerned in the Stockton and Darlington Railway, founded three years earlier (1821) and the first public steam railway in Britain. Their engineer, who surveyed for a Caracas railway, was the great Robert Stephenson, inventor of the famous Rocket.

Most of these companies were short-lived. Only the Anglo-American, Real del Monte, and Imperial Brazilian survived 1850. The collapse was one of those quoted by critics of capital export around 1900 and after to demonstrate the absurd risks of such wild adventures. Yet (as Leland Jenks observed in his brilliant, ebullient if often obscure study, *The Migration of British Capital,* 1927) it is not clear whether the charges are all just. In particular, it does not follow logically that if capital had been withheld from such overseas ventures, it would have been put into housing, or rebuilding old cities, or developing industry at home. In a trenchant paragraph Jenks summarized his doubts. "It may be questioned whether anticipations less dazzling would have aroused any comparable financial effort. Credit capital is not a fund, supplied by streams of calculable volume, exerting continuous pressure of the hydraulic type in search of the weakest outlet. It does not accumulate in proportion to disuse; it does not exist for all purposes alike. In some degree the hopes entertained with respect to South America created the resources with which it was sought to realize them."[1]

These words could be applied to many other projects and areas in the century that followed, right into our own day.

After the first excitement of the 1820s, a long period of disenchantment with foreign industrial ventures followed. But domestic industrial and transport development (which reached its peak in the Great Exhibition of 1851) demanded more raw materials for Britain and more surplus capital with which to finance Britain's needs in overseas territories. Such was the context which produced the next great phase of international enterprise between 1852 and 1866. It was dominated by great contractors like William Jackson, Thomas Brassey, and Morton Peto. Brassey, an enlightened entrepreneur, had a vast army of 80,000 engineers and navvies, a locomotive and carriage works at Rouen, France, and at one time railways and docks under construction in five continents. In a business life of thirty-five years he constructed 8,000 miles of railway in almost every European country.

British and Anglo-Belgian companies pioneered the spread of the rail system from Britain to North France and Belgium (after her separation from Holland in 1831). The first connections from the French Channel ports to Paris were developed by the London and Southampton Railway Company, which operated its own railway on the English side of the Channel. The Paris-Rouen Railway was the first exercise in British foreign rail construction, using British capital and technology. Other groups of established railway entrepreneurs in Britain helped to follow on with the Orleans and Ouest, Nord, and Paris-Lyons in France, and the Dutch Rhenish railway in Holland. From here the mania spread. London companies built and owned a railway in Tuscany (Italy), from Florence to Pistoia, and another from Cologne to Dusseldorf in West Germany. The early Belgian network was almost entirely British-owned, though it used iron from the works of Cockerill, the English ironmaster who had developed the great Belgian plant and locomotive works at Seraing.

From France and Belgium, the infective railway spread ineluctably to Italy, Russia, Canada, India, and Latin Africa. English companies, barred from importing machine-made tables into France, set up their own factories in North France making either the textiles or the machines which made the new textiles. It was a story to be repeated on a much huger scale in the 1900s and 1950s.

In 1866 a major crisis put an end to the railway mania, as the 1825 crisis had done to South American mining projects. Yet from the

1860s a new phase directed towards, especially, Africa and other colonial areas was to repeat the whole story over again. Before we pass to this new phase with its novel situations, let us note the characteristics of the phases so far reviewed:

1. A substantial expertise in the technique of organizing and administering the business of direct capital export. Some of the legal instruments by which this was done were applicable only to state loans (like the methods developed in Anglo-Dutch finance in the eighteenth century) but some were useful in overseas industrial investment.

2. The entrepreneurs had managed (only too successfully it might be thought) to stimulate enthusiasm amongst British investors, who included all classes, from peers of the realm to working men, for overseas enterprise.

3. It is difficult to know how correctly one may apply the term *multinational* to the enterprises described above. It seems justifiable, however, in the case of the rail and mining enterprises set up by British capitalists overseas. Many were operated by groups of British entrepreneurs carrying on similar developments in several different countries. Sometimes the legal identity of the companies was precise (as in the case of the British rail companies operating the Paris-Rouen-Havre railway in France). At other times, the composition of the boards was more shifting but the same names appear on several different boards and technical experts are a common factor. In many cases the contractors like Brassey or Morton Peto retained a substantial interest in the railways they built. Relations in this period, it must be confessed, were more shifting than in a later age when legal requirements kept the business corporation a more concrete and identifiable entity than it used to be. Subject to this proviso, the element of multinationalism is certainly present.

4. It owed its existence not least to the existence of the basic propensity to extend investment from the earlier types of investment limited by kinship or locality or even national boundaries, until it was on a truly world scale. Just as this extension was itself the product of technological innovation, the dominance of the technological factors in this type of economic progress brought multinational forms of business into being because technology and the technologist were the

necessary link between the advanced area (Britain in the case of railways and mining technology) and the virgin territory. Hence Scottish, Cornish, and Welsh engineers were prominent figures in this type of development.

5. Finally (and this is worth bearing in mind in any consideration of modern multilaterals and public opinion), most of those long-distance enterprises met with strong hostility from various sections of opinion. The Dutch investment in Britain was the object of long-continued criticism. So was British investment in French railways in the 1850s (there was a sustained compaign by the London newspaper *The Morning Post* in 1843–44 directed against all types of foreign railway promotion).[2] These were conservative and presumed patriot voices; but later the hostility became transferred to radical and socialist publicists, whose criticisms rested on the alleged robbing of English workmen of their means of livelihood. Britain's industries and social progress itself were being starved of capital by foreigners. Such criticisms, mélanges of progressivism and conservatism, are precisely like those still brought against modern multinationals. The intensity with which they are argued seems to depend entirely on circumstances. But a position of economic dependence always leads to resentment, however beneficial the economic consequences may be, and xenophobia remains universal—and classless. It is against this background of political psychology that the economic merits and drawbacks of multinationals must always be considered.

The New Phase: Tariffs, Imperialism and Postimperialism

The multinational in many ways most characteristic of the years of so-called Great Depression might be considered a product of that era. For the "depression" was principally a depression of heavy or basic industries and it grew out of the very success of the investment enterprises of the previous century. That period had seen the opening up of the new lands of the Americas and Australasia, Asia, and even some of Africa, by rail and the linking of continents by new fleets of shipping. The harvests were reaped in the seventies as the new sources of grain, meat, and raw materials poured out their product on the world markets. Falling prices hit worst the capital goods industries which had created these new means of production and transport;

they benefited most the classes with money or employment and through their increased purchasing power brought into existence a whole range of new light industries—newspapers, magazines, publishing, pharmaceutical products, cigarettes, tobacco, ready-made clothing, sewing machines, soap, margarine, toys, entertainment industries, chain stores, etc.

Their products had two characteristics. First, many of them were immediately vulnerable to the tariffs which were, as has been said already, a feature of economic-nationalist policies in this age of combined depression and attempted growth. Second, they were capable of being adapted easily to production and consumption in almost any country and fitted together easily with new concepts of advertising growing up as an important feature of the newspaper and publishing industry, itself one of the new "communication" aspects of the new consumer boom, especially of the eighties and nineties, with their emphasis on popular literacy and elementary education amongst the industrial working classes.

To read the correspondence of William Lever or his Dutch partners, joint founders of the world oils and fats multinational called (since 1929) Unilever, leaves one in no doubt that when these firms decided to develop factories all over Western Europe, the United States, and later in Canada, Australia, New Zealand, etc., from the 1880s onwards, their first reason for doing so was to get over the tariff wall. When the time comes (wrote Lever in 1900) that the amount of a tariff exceeds the costs of a local factory, we will put down a local plant. On another occasion he writes quite specifically that in a free-trade world there would be no need for him to manufacture soap anywhere but in Britain. Similar arguments were used by Dutch margarine makers compelled to put down factories in Germany to supply their great German market, supplied earlier—before Bismarck's tariff—from their Dutch factories. Such arguments resulted in a world business with more than 600 businesses by 1950. Courtaulds, the great British textile makers who pioneered the manufacture of rayon, the earliest man-made fabric, followed the same line. In 1910 they bought and developed a factory in the United States to supply their growing market there. The Swiss manufacturers of concentrated preserved tinned milk (today known as Nestlé though the combine embodies several other businesses) likewise built or purchased a world network of plants which today includes more than 200 businesses.

It is not easy to detach the element of compulsion due to tariff pressure (or so they regarded it) from the voluntary element of convenience which led increasingly towards multinational solutions in such businesses. Certainly, once the entrepreneur had decided, perhaps reluctantly, to put down a local plant in another country, he often realized the advantages that it brought him. Local manufacture in close contact with local consumers gave the maker a clearer sense of what local tastes demanded. Advertising was easier: conditions, including the characteristics of local labor laws and of local religions or political customs and opinions, were more easily understood.

This type of multinational development was undertaken by the producer of goods with a view to maintaining markets in the first place: if his threatened exports from country X to country Y were not to disappear, a factory must be put down in country Y. The resulting development might be welcomed or feared—welcomed by governments (who thus achieved the import substitution they aimed at); welcomed especially by governments concerned with economic development and the provision of more employment; distrusted and feared where competition was already sharp or employment high.

Meanwhile, multinational activity increased also in the older lines of mining and mineral development as demand for minerals old and new increased. South African diamonds and gold, copper in the Congo, oil in the East, Middle East, and America represented economic targets very different from markets for textiles or soap. They might be necessities or luxuries: whichever they were, they were something the entrepreneurs of Europe—of Britain particularly—did not have in their own native soil. They called for the intrepid qualities of the explorer, the foresight of the entrepreneur, the scientific and technological skill of the geologist and the mining engineer. They also demanded large aggregates of capital. If the hallmark of the "consumer" multinationals of around 1900 was salesmanship, high finance and technology were the mark of companies like Shell (British and Dutch), Nobel (Anglo-Swedish), Rothschilds (British/International), and De Beers (British/South African).

Together, the corporations representative of these two different types of multinationalism did much to shape the character of the British and European economies by 1914. The interwar years (1918–39) and the postwar period, from 1945 to our own day, brought much more development in volume, and of course much in the way of new technology, new business organizations, better communications. The world shrank faster than ever before. Yet in retrospect it looks as if the 1870s marked a definite turning point in the development of world industry. If the representative entrepreneurs of that age, founders of the companies from which Unilever, Imperial Chemical Industries, Shell, Courtaulds, etc., are today composed, could come down to view the multinational giants of our day, they would doubtless be astonished, excited, and perhaps even alarmed by what they saw; but I do not think they would have any difficulty in identifying them as unmistakably their own progeny.

2

It is a common feature of topical comment on the multinational (1) that it is highly critical and (2) that its criticisms stem from the argument that it is:

(1) too large to be acceptable;
(2) unaccountable to any authority;
(3) therefore open to devices for tax avoidance, unfair labor practices, and other transgressions;
(4) somehow culpable because it is largely American in ethos and ownership;
(5) subject only to the law of "growth for growth's sake";
(6) uniform in its characteristics.

The aim of my paper is not to dismiss all these arguments and criticisms out of hand: only to demonstrate that, historically speaking, they misrepresent the origins and purpose of the multinational. History may be irrelevant or outdated: we should at least be aware of its existence and its implications.

Let me begin with argument (4). Topical evidence (not wholly reliable but the best we can collect) suggests that two-thirds of the world's multinationals at present are owned and based in the United States. To combine this with argument (1), many multinationals are large or very large, and getting larger, conjuring up a vision (or nightmare) of a world economy dominated by large, American-owned multinationals.

I do not doubt the current truth of the evidence, and futurology is beyond me or the scope of this paper. What I wish to emphasize is that the multinational was not American in origin or inspiration. If it has become so in recent years this is a phenomenon of the post-Second-World-War quarter-century and may not be permanent.

Far from being American in origin, the multinational was specifically (a) European and (b) associated particularly with the smaller, rather than the larger, national economies of Europe. Miss Mira Wilkins's study of U.S. multinational investment has shown that while U.S. direct investment in industrial enterprise outside the United States down to 1914 was substantial, it was mostly in highly specific mining and transport enterprises on the very geographical fringe of the United States—Canada, Central America, Mexico, etc. The notable exceptions to this were Singer's sewing machines and harvesting machinery—examples, we may think, comparable to the natural expansion of a successful domestic product selling itself abroad by a process of natural success at home.

More typical of multinational developments—and I repeat that these came from small, as yet unprotected market/production areas—were such European Companies as Nestlé (Switzerland), Jurgens/van den Bergh (Netherlands), Solvay (Belgium), Lever Brothers (Britain), Nobel (Sweden/Britain), Brunner-Mond (Britain), and Courtauld (Britain).

You will observe that all these were manufacturing companies and all shared certain characteristics and problems during the period (broadly 1871–1929) of "multinational" expansion and development. First, all benefited to a greater or lesser extent from the fall in prices which afflicted "basic" industry and agriculture between 1870 and 1896, for the falling prices of essential foods and raw materials left more spending power available to consumers and thereby benefited consumer goods and the industries that produced them. Thus the so-called Great Depression proves on examination to have been a Golden Age for those perceptive entrepreneurs who seized upon the growing profitability of consumer goods production. Preserved milk, chocolate, cocoa, soap, margarine, glass, tobacco, confectionery, chemical-pharmaceuticals, etc., were some of the products in demand.

From the 1870s, however, producers of such articles who wanted to enlarge their relatively small domestic markets and engage in world trade found themselves facing new difficulties. France, Germany, the United States were followed by many other countries as they raised their tariff walls against imports. The correspondence of the great European entrepreneurs of the period (especially British, Dutch, Belgian, Swiss) shows clearly how they were compelled (or felt themselves compelled) to turn from export trade based on their home factories to a multiplicity of factories established abroad in countries (previously good export markets) in order to maintain (let alone expand) their business. Thus Nestlé, Levers, the Dutch margarine makers, Courtaulds, etc., all felt compelled to set up German, French, British, and American factories between 1871 and1914.

About the same time, a quite different set of motives drove other entrepreneurs overseas to found industries which could never have been founded at home. This second group did not go in search of markets (which existed plentifully at home) but in search of raw materials or commodities which did not exist (in terms of contemporary technology) in Europe: they did, however, exist in Southeast Europe, the Middle East, and the Orient itself in great abundance. These consisted of mineral deposits, either in solid form as mineral wealth—precious metals or stones, copper, tin, lead, etc.—or in the form of crude oil. A remarkable example of the way in which the later great oil companies developed is provided by the history of Shell. The founding family were the Samuels, a small London merchant business trading in the East which exchanged oil for Japanese fishermen's lamps against bric-a-brac which included pearl shell: hence the later name which came to cover the Anglo-Dutch combine of 1900. This formed an important early rival to the companies beginning to exploit the Black Sea deposits, and the great U.S. companies like Standard Oil.

To Shell and Royal Dutch were later added Rio Tinto (a British

Company beginning in Britain and Spain and now a world multinational), Burma Oil, the South African gold and diamond companies, the Belgian Congo copper and other mining enterprises, the Malayan tin and rubber companies, the African oil-bearing seed traders, etc.

As regards argument (6), I will only suggest briefly that in capital structure, labor relations and many other respects, there were very important differences between the first group of multinationals, highly orientated to the mass consumer market, and the second group, which was more exclusively concerned with technical problems of mining and refining technology and sold through limited market channels.

To summarize: in historical and economic origins the multinationals of Europe were highly varied in activities, technology, economic motivation and ethos. But they came to a large extent from small nations and they were, one and all, a response to the challenges of that economic nationalism which characterized the world of the late nineteenth and the twentieth century and which is still the dominant policy-molding feature of our own world. Without the device of the local company, or the *congeries* of such companies which we call the multinational, it is difficult to see how the international exchange of goods and services in certain types of business could have expanded as it has. (It should be noted that a limit to the operation of economic nationalism is always set in those highly innovative enterprises [e.g., aircraft manufacture] where the sources of technology are often kept carefully guarded secrets for decades or more. Such highly technological industries usually maintain themselves on a basis of export for long periods. It is the simpler but nevertheless often socially beneficial industries which tend to develop along multinational lines.)

Since 1945 the pattern of multinationalism has changed radically. The United States, formerly concerned principally with the exploration of its own highly protected market, has followed the multinational patterns established by small European predecessors. The effects of this on the reputation of multinationals has (I fear) on the whole been adverse, in spite of the high technological and marketing efficiency of U.S. business. The reasons seem to me to be as follows:

1. The often latent but ever present antipathy in the United States itself to large-scale industrial and commercial capitalism springs from the fact that for a long time American capitalism enjoyed vast preferential benefits—a protected market and large supplies of immigrant skill. This was to a limited extent compensated by the operation of antitrust institutions intended to check its economic and political power—but the check was only a limited one, and in the most highly capitalistic nation in the world anticapitalist sentiment was more virulent than anywhere except in the socialist countries of Eastern Europe.

2. As U.S. industry, for various reasons, began to follow the multinational pattern of development, these anticapitalist sentiments also followed it on its world circumnavigation: all the more because the U.S. multinational tended to be centralized in its government—that is, controlled from a U.S. headquarters according to a cultural ethos recognizably American. (The European multinational had often tended to grow by a centripetal process converging inwards towards a single center as businesses merged yet retained something of their national, local characteristics: the U.S. multinational on the other hand often developed by a centrifugal process outwards from a vast U.S. market but remained centered in New York, Chicago, Wilmington, or Minneapolis, etc. It should be said that the best U.S. multinationals are aware of the political and social consequences involved and have done much hard thinking to offset the results.)

3. Rightly or wrongly, business in the United States is frequently associated with attempts at interference in politics—more frequently than in smaller and older states. Again, some of these political anxieties have "rubbed off" on the multinational offspring of U.S. industry.

To conclude: history suggests strongly that the multinational has a legitimate, functional economic purpose. The criticisms and accusations of recent years may or may not have some basis in fact: but so long as economic nationalism remains a dominant feature of our economic society, the multinational will have a positive function to fulfill. In spite of attempts to propose "international control in the interests of the international community" in a recent report by the U.N. Economic Department, the multinational is more likely to be efficiently accountable to the various national governments under whose sovereignties it operates than to any international body. And international intervention would be naturally resented by the national governments whose laws and regulations have brought the multinational into existence.

Meanwhile, in an admittedly uneasy relationship, the national-multinational partnership has been responsible for an unprecedented degree of import-substitution industrial development in less industrialized countries, and for a vast transfer of capital and technological, economic, and commercial skill. It is difficult to see how such results could have been achieved in any other way.

3

Amongst the multinationals which are based and owned in Europe, Unilever is certainly a leader. It dates from 1929, when nearly three decades of alternating association and fricton in the business world of oils and fats found their climax in a grand final merger. It brought together two established multinational concerns: the Dutch Marganne-Unie, representing the classic makers of edible fats and other foods, and the British firm of Lever Brothers, principally famous as soap and detergent makers. Their union was crystallized in a treaty of September 2, 1929, which retained a dual Anglo-Dutch structure under the names Unilever N.V. and Unilever Limited, though for all practical purposes the two organizations were one. The directing boards, that is to say, were identical. An "inner cabinet" of the boards called the Special Committee was entrusted with wide powers over the whole organization, and financial equality was ensured by an "equalization agreement" which provided that Limited and N.V. shareholders received equal dividends and equal distribution should the concern ever be liquidated. Finally, associated with the Dutch and English concerns in those interwar years was the great oil and fats concern of Schicht, with interests widely spread over the Succession States of the old Austrian emperor and centered in Czechoslovakia at Aussig.

Forty years later, after much rationalization, acquisition, and growth (especially in continental Europe), Unilever was operating more than 500 businesses in more than sixty countries. Their total turnover was £2,326 million a year, or three times its volume in 1948. The original products of the parent companies—margarine and edible fats in the Netherlands, soap in various forms in Britain—had been developed and diversified. The growing application of scientific technology had enabled both manufacturers to use an increasing range of raw materials in their processes. To animal fats were added first oil-bearing seeds and fruit from Africa and the South Seas, then the new chemicals for "nonsoapy" detergents. Research into raw-material uses and marketing links had suggested logical expansion into other related fields—canned, preserved, and frozen foods, industrial chemicals necessary to a score of other industrial users, etc.

Thus a giant and highly diversified multinational, manufacturing, selling, advertising, and researching in many countries, had evolved from what had originally been three relatively modest manufacturing centers—Port Sunlight in Cheshire (1888), the Oss factories of Jurgens and Van den Berghs in North Brabant (1871–72) and the Aussig factory of Schichts (1882). (All had antecedents but the dates given represent the effective starting dates of industrial expansion.) How and why had three become 500? If we can answer this question we may help to disperse some of the fog which has gathered round the problem of the multinational, its rationale and function in the modern world.

First, it is worth noting that all those starting dates fall within the period classically known as the Great Depression (1873–96). Prices of basic industrial goods and foods fell as the effects of railway and shipping investment over the previous decades made themselves felt. But the misfortune of the coal, iron and steel, and cereal farming industries was the good fortune of the workers who could keep their jobs. Living costs fell. More consumers were able to afford a little extra expenditure on needs and luxuries, and this in turn encouraged enterprising opportunists to launch into new industries. Which is precisely what the ancestors of Unilever did.

Within an astonishingly short space of years William Lever, son of a Lancashire wholesale grocer, had established a dominating position in the British soap market, previously neatly shared out by agreement between half a dozen old established makers. His weapons were aggressive advertising and a new type of free-lathering soap he called Sunlight. Important for the future (and for our particular enquiry) was that before he completed his conquest of the British market, he was building up a considerable export trade in soap to British Empire countries as well as to continental Europe. For the margarine makers of Oss, export was from the start their main objective. It was among the millions of still poorly paid workers of the rapidly growing industrial cities of Germany and (slightly less so) of Britain that Jurgens and Van den Berghs looked for their turnover and profits. Their home markets, Scandinavia, Belgium, and North France, were not ignored, but they were peripheral to the great German and British potential.

But now came the first serious challenge to the new expansion. Faced with a crisis of low prices, foreign—especially British—competition, and motivated by natural ambitions to cultivate home industries, one country after another raised their protective tariff walls in the eighties and nineties. Continuous attention to tariffs from 1883 took the United States into the twentieth century as a rapidly protected market. Bismarck's tariff of 1887 was designed to protect German agricultural and food interests and encourage local industry. Other states, including France, followed suit, until Britain and the Netherlands alone remained free-trader nations. The threat posed by tariffs, actual and potential, was immediately evident to manufacturers who relied to a greater or lesser extent on exports.

The answer soon emerged: to jump over the tariff wall and establish factories in local national markets hitherto supplied by export. William Lever, the most articulate of our entrepreneurs, put the matter in a nutshell in a speech to his shareholders in 1902. If all the world remained on a free-trade basis, he declared, and the only extra cost to be considered in an export business was the freight charge, there would have never been any need to manufacture his soaps anywhere but in Britain. The erection of a works in another country entirely depended on the amount of the tariff. When that rose to a point where it was more economical to pay a separate management and labor force and provide capital for a factory, a local company was the obvious and logical answer to the tariff problem. And undoubtedly tariffs were the main reason for the Lever factories which were built or acquired throughout the world during the 1890s and the early twentieth century—at Boston in the United States, Olten in Switzerland, Mannheim in Germany, Brussels in Belgium, Lille in France, Vlaavdingen in Holland, Sydney in Australia, to say nothing of a chain of factories stretching across Canada.

Jurgens and Van den Berghs were equally swift to reach the same conclusion. In 1888—just a year after Bismarck's raised tariff—came Jurgen's first German factory at Goch and Van den Bergh's factory at Cleves a little further north, both just inside Germany over the Dutch border and easily manageable from Holland. These were followed by other factories to supply the vast German market and by entry into the oil-milling industry, which in its turn supplied raw materials to the margarine factories. Apart from establishing factories in Belgium, an advanced case of early industrialization with a large urban working-class market, the Dutch manufacturers were otherwise slower than Lever to venture into direct foreign investment. That was to come in the 1920s and onwards.

They were, however, like Lever, acutely conscious of their need to secure raw material supplies. New technologies of fat hardening (hydrogenation) and refining were widening the range of raw materials suitable for both soap and edible fat industries. While Lever therefore was exploring the jungles of West Africa (eventually establishing himself in the Belgian Congo) in search of palm and other vegetable oils, Jurgens were in the Cameroons (but very briefly and inconspicuously). They were on the other hand to be prominent in the whale oil business, and in the French and German oil-milling business at Marseilles, Hamburg, and Bremen. And both Dutch and British entrepreneurs were jointly involved in 1912 and 1913 in attempts to develop the fat hardening and refining processes. One result of these maneuvers was Lever's stake in the Norwegian fat-hardening industry.

In the following decades the complexity of these economic relationships steadily drew the enterprises described ever more closely together—reluctantly, for it must be said that there was no love lost between any of them. Agreements were made, over technical exchanges, markets, prices, profits, etc., only to be abandoned or become the object of protracted and sometimes bitter litigation. The "multinational" evolution nevertheless continued, and the 1920s and 1930s saw the Dutch manufacturers putting down or acquiring factories in France and Scandinavia. Tariffs were still one of the motivating forces. But experience showed that the local factory, in the first instance accepted reluctantly and under duress, had unquestionable benefits for the manufacturer. It enabled him to assess better local preferences. Sunlight soap, for example, was never a success in the United States. A disinfectant soap, Lifebuoy, and the new soap flakes *Lux* which were introduced by Lever in the nineties, had their biggest triumph there. Local managements could test and probe such market peculiarities in a way no distant headquarters could.

The Dutch makers were even more conscious of the risks they ran from the tangle of legal regulations prescribing the color, content, and shape of margarine as governments responded to local farmers' lobbies in the agrarian countries. Only local knowledge and management could handle satisfactorily the ensuing legal complications. Besides, tastes in margarine, as in butter, varied from country to country. The English, for example, liked a salted margarine, a taste not shared by most continental consumers. Local market preferences were everywhere best understood and handled by local managements who could adopt advertising, manufacture, and formulae accordingly.

This trend to multinational organization was naturally and strongly reinforced by the expansion of the Unilever food companies in the postwar years. Few problems show up local or national differences of taste in such sharp relief as the gastronomic. No British factory could make a convincing replica of any of the hundred varieties of sausages commonly consumed in Germany or Italy. It is doubtful whether a German sausage factory would even wish to try and make an English sausage. The English do not like *petits pois*. The French abominate the large minted pea so dear to the English. A scent business which long held a good share of the perfumery trade in Mediterranean and Latin American markets never made much of a mark in Britain. Such, at random, are a few examples of market situations which have inevitably directed Unilever into multinational paths.

Then there is the managerial and human aspect. From the beginning, all the parent firms made a practice of using local managers to some extent who were themselves nationals of the country concerned.

The war years, leaving local companies severed from London and Rotterdam headquarters, strengthened their sense of independence. So did the granting of political independence to former colonial territories in Africa and the East. The following years saw training and appointment turn into a principle—sometimes known as the "-ization" principle. Nationals were to be used to the optimum extent, and optimum frequently meant maximum. Yet the opportunities for cross-fertilization of ideas and the diffusion of new technology were clearly too precious to be missed. Every Unilever organization will therefore be found today to contain a mixture of races and nationalities drawn from those many countries in which Unilever enterprises are located. Thus had multinational management come to match multinational manufacture and multinational markets.

Some readers may be disappointed to find this account of Unilever Multinational remote from the lurid melodrama often conjured up by writers about multinationals. The truth is that multinational evolution has always represented for the Unilever companies a set of functional solutions to practical problems which may be summarized as tariffs, tastes, and political realities. Out of these has emerged something like a commonwealth of businesses which has constantly to reassess its internal balance between central control and local independence. To strike this balance correctly is one of the most delicate and important tasks of the multilateral.

Looking back over a century of history we can see that multinationalism was a functional necessity for the development of the industries which Unilever comprises. Without this form of business development it is indeed impossible to see how the oils, fats, and foods industries could have grown as they have done throughout the politically and economically fragmented markets of the world. In that case the world would have been economically and socially a poorer place.

References

1. Leland Jenks, *The Migration of British Capital* (1927), pp. 60–61.
2. *Ibid.*, p. 146.

Remarks of Professor Charles Wilson Pertaining to His Paper

Gentlemen, we are, I believe, running rather late, and this gives me a good excuse not to read you the whole of my paper. In that paper I attempted to write an introduction to the origins and the problems of the multinational in a quite general way; then to say something about the development of the multinationals which seemed to me to be more recognizably like the multinationals of 1974, and indeed in cases to be their ancestors; and finally, to give you a case study of the multinational about which I know most, which is Unilever. I am afraid it has become altogether too evident many times in this conference that this is the one I do know most about, and I apologize if I have used the evidence too frequently. As a matter of fact, I must confess that I wrote the end of this paper at the beginning, so that if it has a merit for an audience of Japanese scholars, it is perhaps appropriate that I began at the end and went steadily on until I came back to the beginning.

Now, as regards the first part of the paper, I will only say that this, I think, is only related to the problem of the multinational today in a quite general way, but it does seem to me to be important, before we begin to take the multinational for granted, to find out a little about the process by which men began to think it possible to lend money to make investments over very long distances. Much investment is, naturally, local, and therefore what I wanted to elucidate in this first section were some of the ways in which people in the fairly remote past, from the sixteenth century onwards, evolved methods and systems for investing quite a lot of money in places that were a long way from their homes. And I therefore quoted the Italians, who had investments in the Netherlands; and then on a much larger scale, the Dutch, who evolved many of the legal instruments by which international investment is still negotiated, and who put a great deal of money into British government debt in the eighteenth century.

That led me into the next phase and a shift away from government investment in foreign government debt, to the nineteenth century and the move into railways, mines, and various other commercial ventures where we do find something that I think can justifiably be called multinational. I think Professor Kinukasa has agreed that that comes within the possible definition of a multinational. As far as I know, nobody has investigated the nineteenth-century international railway system in Europe as a multinational system, though Miss Wilkins, in her admirable book about American overseas investment, has pointed to American railway investment in the countries in South America and indeed in North America as one of the ways in which early American multinationalism developed. I am not going to say any more about this introductory section, but I shall be very glad to try and discuss it if that is desired. But I think it does bring out the fact that before 1870 a number of industrial developments had taken place which involved, in this case, entrepreneurs in Britain creating businesses in other countries. And here the prime factor was the availability of capital, and willingness to export that capital, and the willingness and the ability to export also the skilled labor and to find the management with which these railways and mines and allied enterprises could be carried on. Well, that as I say, is the introduction.

I think the modern problem really begins in the section titled "The New Phase." I think it began with all those related economic changes of the 1870s: the coming of tariffs in Germany, in France, in Scandinavia, in the British colonies or the dominions (because let us not forget that the Australians put up tariffs against the British, for example), in America, and so on. Connected with this was the coming of the so-called Great Depression, usually dated from 1873 to 1896. In reality it was a depression primarily of basic industries, but in turn stimulating, first of all, a rise in real incomes on the part of the middle and working classes, and, through that, creating opportunities for entrepreneurs who saw the markets for consumer goods such as pharmaceuticals, tobacco, ready-made clothes, newspapers, magazines, and, last and not least may I say, soap. One historian of late Victorian England, G. M. Young, has said that this period was one in which it was characteristic that light industries were overtaking the old basic industries. I think this is very true, and they overtook them not only domestically, but they also became a typical representative of the new kind of multinational. That is to say, these industries joined the older multinationals, if you can call them that—like railways and mining—as industries in search of their future.

Now what were the problems they faced? They faced first of all, except in Great Britain, tariffs almost everywhere. The tariff was partly, in Europe and in America, a response to the depression. It was also partly an instrument of import substitution. In many countries it was part of a conscious policy for industrialization, as it still is in many places. This was the trigger which turned many of these countries away from the export trade, which they were building up, toward the multinational solution. This is the conventional explanation, or one of them, of the multinational company: that a company that had previously done a valuable export business in Germany or the United States or wherever it was, found that the tariff was becoming too high and decided to move into that country and put down a factory. Now as we saw by this curious accidental discovery, which I made just as Professor Kobayashi was reading his paper, there were other reasons too. Usually those justifications for the multinational company did not emerge until after the tariff had provoked the entrepreneur, the British entrepreneur in this case, to put down a local plant. But once he had put it down, all kinds of reasons began to emerge why this had been,on the whole, a good decision. Mind you, it was very often the case that anybody engaging in a multinational project had to face several years, in some cases many years, of investment before the project showed a profit. But what was the alternative? If we are to believe what a number of these entrepreneurs said, this was not just a voluntary move on the part of the entrepreneurs. It was the recognition of the fact that if they did not do this, their export trade would have disappeared, the domestic market was not large enough to allow further expansion, and a valuable opportunity for business growth would have been lost. This, as I see it, is the way they argued. Whether they were correct or not is open to discussion, but this is what they said.

May I say at this point that in suggesting that the multinational of this period is more characteristic of, or perhaps more important to, the small European countries than it was to America, I am not in any way passing any kind of judgment on that great country. It is merely that it seems to me that for many years, as Miss Wilkins's book shows, the American overseas investments in industrial enterprise that developed on a multinational basis, aside from mining and railroads particularly on the fringes of the United States, were things like harvesting machines and a relatively small group of rather complicated mechanical devices of one sort or another. I think that the American entrepreneur had plenty to keep him busy in his enormous domestic market, where he had on the one hand all the troubles that were going to beset him with criticisms (antitrust actions and the like), but on the other hand the great comfort of a nice protective tariff. So whereas, as we've seen with International Harvester, the American multinational operation was very important for the future and is to be found here and there in some important sectors, it doesn't seem to me that it was so vital to the American economic development as it was to the development of the smaller countries. I apologize for making this point at such length to an audience of scholars, but I make it because there has been so much written in recent years in which the multinational is often the target of political criticism, and because the multinational today is often an American company. I think it is worthwhile making the point not that Europeans invented the multinational, but simply that the multinational method was perhaps more important to these countries, where an entrepreneur very soon found that his domestic market was too small to contain his ambitions or even to absorb his capacity.

Now in the second part of the paper, which begins on page 276, I have enlarged on some of the firms such as Nestlé in Switzerland; the Dutch margarine makers; *Solvay*, the Belgian chemical firm; Lever Brothers; Nobel, the explosives firm of Sweden; and in Britain, Brunner-Mond, one of the founding companies of Imperial Chemical Industries; Courtauld, and so on, who all, in one way or another, found it convenient, and even necessary I think, to follow the multinational method of evolution. Now I have suggested, and this is a debatable point, that those in this group that are manufacturing industries, particularly the consumer manufacturers, are perhaps to be differentiated from the other group which I deal with on page 278, firms such as Shell, Royal Dutch, Rio Tinto, who were also engaged in multinational development. The reason I make this point is because it seems to me there are, broadly speaking, two reasons why a firm decides to go overseas and turn itself into a multinational combine with manufacturing or mining enterprises and drilling enterprises in a number of different countries. The manufacturer goes there because for reasons such as tariffs, labor costs, the convenience of the consumer, the convenience of the entrepreneur in following the consumers' tastes, local religious conventions, or finding out accurately how to obey the law of a country which is a particular market, there is great advantage in conducting local operations. By the way, there is a very important point, for example, in margarine, where countries had different legal regulations about what a margarine manufacturer must do. Most of this legislation was the result of pressure from local agricultural interests who saw margarine as a competitor to butter. But all these things create a very complicated set of problems for the entrepreneur, and therefore quite apart from the tariff there are many other reasons why manufacturers found it convenient to go multinational.

But their reasons are different from those of the mining or the oil company. They go abroad simply because the thing that they are looking for—oil—doesn't exist at home. At any rate, that was the case with the British and Dutch oil and mining entrepreneurs. They were looking for the deposits of materials which simply didn't exist in Britain. The American case, of course, is different here. But even America was looking for oil outside her own borders, though again usually in countries adjacent to the United States. There wasn't the enormous geographical distance separating the parent headquarters from the operating company that there was in Britain or in Holland.

I will now come to the third part of the paper. I am not going to read this paper, but with your permission I would just like to sketch as briefly as I can some of the major points in the evolution of Unilever as a multinational company. And I think it might be helpful if I did it in a rather different order from the order in which I have written it, so as to fill in some of the narrative and factual detail which I was not able to do in the paper. So I am going to talk at the board, sketching in as I go a few of the major points in the history of the development of this company, which is either the first or the second multinational of major importance to the British economy.

I will start off in a village called Oss. Oss is a small and extremely unattractive village in Holland but near the Belgian border and not very far from the German border. This is important for the subsequent multinational development of the two firms which emerged in the 1870s as the original, and still the largest, makers of margarine. One was a Jewish family called Van den Berghs, originally emigrants from Germany, and the other was a Catholic, Brabant family called Jurgens. They were both butter merchants who would sell Dutch butter for, in the Jurgens case, I think, nearly a century before 1870, both to the British market and to the German market. So they were already in edible fats, and they were already doing an international business.

What really changed their future was the emergence of an invention in 1870 to 1871 by a French gentleman called Mr. Merjes Moriet. Merjes Moriet entered himself for a prize offered by Napoleon the Emperor, Napoleon the Third, for any kind of process which would enable him to reduce the food bill for the French army. And Merjes Moriet produced—I can only call it a substance, which, because it had a pearly coloring to it, was called margarine, *margar* meaning pearl. Now this invention was not fully developed, and it took both of these firms and a number of Danish and other firms in Holland a long time before it was turned into a really edible product. But nevertheless they were selling it from 1870 on, from Oss. Later on when the trade became big enough, they moved to Rotterdam.

Now the basic materials of margarine were in the early stages animal fats, and they relied on animal fats from the stockyards of Chicago imported into Rotterdam for this purpose. Their markets for margarine were the same as they had been for butter. They sold some of it at home. They sold some of it in Britain, though not so much because British standards of living were sufficiently high that even the working classes ate butter, and cheaper and cheaper butter was going to come in from Australia and New Zealand. So the British market came second to the huge German market, where the industrialization of Germany was proceeding rapidly by the 1870s, and where large cities were developing based on a population very often immigrant from east to west into the Rhineland, and so on. So this German market was the one that was to be the most important market for the Dutch margarine manufacturers.

The troubles began for these Dutch firms, as we see for so many industries, in the 1870s with the imposition of Bismarck's tariff to protect German agriculture and industry, which made it more difficult and less profitable to export margarine into Germany. So that was the first multinational move, and you can take it that both these firms tended to act at about the same time, and each did exactly the same thing. These two village rivals were to fight continuously from 1871 right down to 1927, through 1906, 1914, 1918, 1922, 1927. We shall see Jurgens and Van den Berghs engaged in a sort of classic conflict, occasionally coming to an agreement about prices or profits or advertising budgets, only to find themselves cursing each other and breaking it all up a year or so later. Lawyers made hundreds of thousands, if not millions, of guilders out of these interminable lawsuits. The Van den Berghs, as I say, were Jewish; the Jurgens were fervent Catholics, so there was a good amount of fuel for a row. But not only the result of the tariff problem, but also the problem of the perishability of the product made this a perfect setting for multinational activity. And it wasn't very long before Rotterdam became the center of a whole complex of businesses, both of Van den Berghs and of Jurgens. Wherever Jurgens went, Van den Berghs went; and wherever Van den Berghs went, Jurgens followed. And so they went to Scandinavia; they went to Belgium, just over the border; they went to Germany; they went to north France, the industrial area of France; they of course operated at home in the Netherlands. Unlike the International Harvester Company, they did not put down a factory in England until the war of 1914 made it necessary. In the United Kingdom they continued to send their produce from Rotterdam, and this does suggest that here the tariff was an important issue.

Let me just sketch out some of the characteristics of this Dutch group. To get back to our old problem of integration, they were rather uninterested in backward integration. There was one point where Anton Jurgens, who was an aggressive entrepreneur, got himself mixed up in the Arctic and Antarctic whaling business, but it was a pretty disastrous experiment which was not repeated. There was also a brief period when Jurgens took an interest in the Cameroons in West Africa, with an idea of getting oil seeds from there. But that again was a small affair and very short-lived. What they were interested in was forward integration, and from a quite early stage, at any rate from about 1900, both these firms began to acquire shops—grocers' shops, dairy shops, sometimes chains of them—in London and in the other large industrial cities, including those of Scotland. The justification for these shops rested on the need to convey the product from the factory to the shop and then to the customer in the shortest possible time, in the best possible condition to keep the flavor and the quality from getting any worse than it was anyway. So they carried out this exercise in the British market, and to some extent in Germany, in the Netherlands, and in the other countries.

It was executed with all the assistance of the modern apparatus of marketing and salesmanship. Brands were invented with curious and exotic names. They were advertised in many, many different ways. One of our papers on the Japanese grocery firm Morinaga mentioned the interesting devices by which shops sold their confectionery. Some similar tactics were employed by one of the most famous groups of shops which Jurgens/Van den Berghs bought up in the United Kingdom. Thomas Lipton was an entrepreneur of a very florid kind. I don't know whether he was responsible for it or whether the Dutch did it, but one of their devices, for example, was having an occasional elephant pass through the streets with advertising material, or having tumbling clowns perform, rather like Morinaga. Another one was to have at the entrance to the shop a distorting mirror in which the customer saw himself or herself reflected as looking something like this, you see. . . . This was yourself as you saw yourself when you went into the shop. (Laughter) And when you had purchased Mr. Lipton's admirable foods, you came out this way (more laughter), and there was a kind of happy glow about you. I had better rub that off the board, otherwise I don't know whether I shall lose your subsidy.

Now at the same time that all this was going on, there was a development going on at Port Sunlight in Cheshire, next door to Lancashire, where W. H. Lever, a grocer's son, set up in 1886 a factory to make a soap which he had accidentally discovered was selling very well to the local ladies. He made it first of all on contract to a subcontractor, and one day he was in a grocer's shop when he heard an old woman come into the shop and say, "I want some of that stinking soap that I had a month ago," but they said they didn't have any. The stinking soap was the type of soap which later became famous as Sunlight Soap, and which continued to have exactly the same formula for about forty years without change. It was in fact not only a packed soap, as somebody mentioned earlier on, but it was also a different formula of soap. The soaps being marketed by this group of respectable old gentlemen, who, as we have heard, managed most of the English soap trade at the time, were what were called filled soaps, and the proportion of actual pure soap in the bar was very small. A woman had to work very hard to create a lather and to get enough washing power out of the soap. Sunlight was a more or less pure soap, which contained quite a lot of fats made out of tropical oil seeds, and it lathered very easily. And Lever was able to claim, when he realized that the old lady was thinking in the same way as a lot of other ladies, old and young, that here was a soap which made their work easier. At any rate that is what he continued to claim for the rest of his life. And with that soap he built at Port Sunlight a remarkable model village full of very good houses for the workers, a thoroughly hygienic and pleasant village to live in, one of the early experiments in enlightened entrepreneurship, which is still an interesting kind of period piece. He designed it all himself; he was a keen architect. Every house, and this was in the late 1880s, was equipped with an indoor lavatory and bathroom, which was a social revolution in the Lancashire area, where most people didn't have either.

We can watch his plans developing from the 1880s, from his diaries, which recalled his travels not only around England, but also to Scandinavia and Germany in Europe, and all round the British Commonwealth at the time. By 1906, a rather crucial year, he too had branched out with factories in, again, Scandinavia, Germany, France, Switzerland, Belgium, the United States, South Africa, Canada (where he either built or bought a chain of factories that stretched from one coast right across to the other), New Zealand, and

Australia. His diary of his visit to New Zealand—I think it is New Zealand—incidentally, records a very interesting interview that he had with an old gentleman who was a retired cannibal. It records a discussion about the merits of the taste of human flesh, which, the old gentleman explained to Mr. Lever, was very nice: it tasted like roast pork, only more tender.

The interesting point, I think, is that while this battle to control the English market was going on between 1885 and 1906, he had already spread his companies over all these areas both in Europe and in the British Commonwealth. That is to say, long before he had in fact conquered the British market for himself, which he did to a very large extent by 1914, he had already gone overseas, and the reasons why he did it are very clearly set out. He was a most brilliant letter writer, the most articulate entrepreneur I think in our English history, and he has written many letters in which he explains why he was putting down factories here and there and everywhere. This was partly in response to criticisms, very topical criticisms, made at the time, not only at Lever but in other industries that were going overseas. His critics, particularly the labor interests, said, "You're robbing English workmen of their work by going and putting a factory in France." And he said, "No. I'm not doing that. I have no alternative. We are exporting, it is true, to France. But the French tariff (or the German tariff or whatever it was) has now reached the point where it will pay us better to have a factory inside France itself, and indeed if we don't do this, our trade will disappear altogether. So I'm justified in putting the factory down in France (or wherever) to make soap there." In one letter that I discovered, he does make a classic comment, stating categorically, "If all the world were free trade, I could make all my soap in England and export it. But the whole world is not free trade, and it is the tariff which compels me to (in modern language you would have said) go multinational."

He was not only putting down soap factories here, in Europe and the Empire, but he was also engaged in our old occupation of integration. And from 1902 onwards, we find him in the Pacific Islands, in the Solomons, in a small venture with a cotton mill; in the Mississippi Valley somewhere; but above all in the Belgian Congo, where in 1910 he himself with his experts reconnoitered the Congo jungles. He had to go to the Congo because all attempts to persuade the British Colonial Office to let him go into British West Africa failed because the British were committed to not alienating one single foot of native land. So he had a frightful row with the British Colonial Office, whom he never forgave. He thought their action was stupid; and perhaps it was. But he went off to the Belgian Congo and made, as though he were a sovereign prince, a treaty with the Belgian government, and set himself up with a vast area of about seven enormous plantations, which, under the treaty, he had to equip with hospitals, schools, roads, and everything. Another kind of multinationalism, those Congo villages, together with the model village at Port Sunlight, were the two things I think that meant the most to Lever in his life. They were his children, his mind's children. And the Congo certainly never turned in a single penny of net profit until 1926. But at any rate this is the first part of the exercise in backward integration. It was completed only in 1920 by the acquisition, under very dramatic and disastrous circumstances, of the great United Africa Company, which was a combination of the old Royal Niger Company and a number of other companies which the Niger Company had acquired. Lever, still worried (but I think increasingly megalomaniac) about the growth of his business, continued to be anxious about his raw materials, or professed to be. His colleagues tried to persuade him that his arguments were illogical. They said, "If you get all these enterprises, you will never produce more than a small fraction of the materials you need for your factories." He tried to argue that the price depended not on total volume but on the old Manchester merchants' calculation that if the supply was 5% above the demand, the price went down, you didn't know where to, and vice versa. He was a merchant genius at defending his own decisions. But he was a man of great courage and tremendous imagination, nobody could doubt that.

Well, in the meantime, while backward integration was going on, he had been carrying on attempts to rationalize the English domestic market. He managed finally to drive most of the other manufacturers out of business, or at any rate to persuade them to come to him and offer to sell their businesses. They didn't like Lever; they regarded him as not quite a gentleman because advertising in the soap trade was not a gentlemanly thing to do at that stage. But Lever was not bothered by such considerations. In 1894 he turned the company into a public company. He had only one brother, who retained a few shares, but the brother was a sick man and I think in the end even his small number of shares came to Lever. So that right down to the day of his death, he remained the sole ordinary shareholder. And when he wanted money that he couldn't find out of his own pocket, he went to the public, but only for fixed interest, preference shares which carried no voting rights whatever. So he remained in fact the dictator of the business right down to his death.

I must say that I think towards the end of his life, for example, when he bought the United Africa Company, his mind had begun to soften. He bought the United Africa Company for £8 million without even looking at the accounts, and it was only a week or two later, when he had to look round to find the £8 million, that he discovered that £6 million of it were tied up in stocks of oil seeds which the United Africa Company had been hoarding in the hope of a price rise. In fact, the bottom fell out of the market two days after Lever had signed the agreement to buy, and he found himself having to find £8 million for a company whose real value was probably by this time about a million pounds. This had one providential result: the only way he could get the money was to go on his knees to the banks. Lever did not like banks; he'd always hated them. Banks are nowadays in England regarded as respectable, but much earlier England had shared a tradition that still tends to go on, I think, in the United States, by which people don't trust bankers nearly as much as we do in England nowadays. But anyway, he had to go to the banks, and the banks as a condition of lending him the money, insisted (there's no documentation of this, I only know it from personal information) that the bank put in a watchman to keep an eye on what he was doing—a remarkable man called Francis Darcy Cooper. And it was Darcy Cooper who set himself, from 1921–22 onwards, to try and bring some sort of order into this straggling empire that was beginning to look pretty chaotic.

Now a point about this Lever Brothers: it had integrated, as we see, backwards. It never integrated forward. Lever never had any belief in trying to go into the retail end of it. He was of course a tremendous advertiser, a great salesman, full of all sorts of ingenious plans and plots of advertising, but he never took any interest in anything strictly outside the advertising and, incidentally, the distribution. He organized his own distribution system. But he did not go forward into shop companies as these Dutch people did. So that in the 1920s, the business of rationalizing went forward. In the process of acquiring all these companies in England, he had acquired scores if not hundreds of brands, and they were still in existence in 1930 when Darcy Cooper, who succeeded Lever as chairman when he died in 1926, took charge. He then was succeeded in turn by Jeffrey Hayworth, Lord Hayworth, who was chairman when I first knew Lever Brothers in 1947. They set to work to cut down the number of brands, to rationalize all these companies. This is an acute case, I think, of what we have seen in a number of these instances of horizontal integration, that although the companies had been acquired, very little had been done to justify the acquisitions. The companies went on much as they did before. Now in one paper, one of the authors mentioned the curious fact that two companies under the same zaibatsu were competing with each other. Well, I was struck by this because the whole theory of Lever's acquisition of companies was that the business of all these companies horizontally was to compete with each other. This was his theory, that competition between these different soap companies kept them efficient.

The third company—very briefly, because it is much less well documented—was the firm of Schicht. The Schichts were Czech, a family of German origin who had developed a large and extremely efficient oils-and-fats business at Aussig in the German part of Czechoslovakia in the days of the Hapsburgs, the last days of the old Austrian empire. The Schicht brothers became associated by a series of agreements with, particularly, Van den Berghs and, to a lesser extent, with Jurgens. They were a very large, as I say, and efficient company, which the ending of the Austrian empire in 1918 left as merely a collection of individual companies still with their biggest business in Czechoslovakia. All those businesses of course have now gone with the Russian influence, the communization of those countries, but the Austrian business of Unilever, which is now very prosperous and very profitable, has developed out of the remnants of the old Schicht empire.

Those are the three main constituents which began to come together round about 1910 or 1911. What brought all these firms together in the end was raw materials. All these firms, whether they were making soap or margarine or cooking fat, tended to draw on the same pool of edible oils, and as the technology progressed, it became possible, and is today possible, to use almost any kind of edible oil for any purpose. A key development in this was the invention of the fat-hardening process, or hydrogenation process, in about 1910. The possibility of hardening fats was the first occasion when Van den Berghs, Jurgens, Lever, and Schicht all came together to see whether they could not evolve some system of control and exploitation of the hydrogenation process. The development of hydrogenation was followed by technical improvements in the milling of the seed, the treatment of coconut fats, the refining of the oil, the deodorizing and neutralization which is necessary to ensure that no off-flavors, as they're called, get into the particular margarine or the cooking fat. So all these technical developments created a kind of club. It wasn't always a very friendly club; it was more like a battlefield, I think, on many occasions. But at any rate all these technical developments meant that there was more and more personal knowledge created between the members of these three great organizations, which amongst them controlled by this time a large part of the oils and fats industries of the world. In 1927 Jurgens and Van den Berghs finally buried the hatchet and formed a permanent union, the Marganne-Unie, in Dutch, in conjunction with the Schichts. This formation of the margarine union in 1927 was followed in 1929 by the formation of Unilever itself, which comprised Schichts, Levers, Jurgens, Van den Berghs, and one or two other smaller, parent companies who got a member on the board. The discussions began in 1928 as an attempt to find out whether all these people could keep out of each other's way. They weren't devoted to trying to create a union; it was an attempt to provide a friendly divorce, and not a happy marriage.

But in the end they found that the central processes which they all shared were right in the middle of the industry of each of them: oil mills, hydrogenation, refining, all these that I have described as the essential nucleus of processes. The Dutch had an enormous group of oil mills in Germany, another lot in the south of France; England had three huge oil mills; Schicht had their oil mills and refineries. They could not agree who was to have which. So in the end Unilever emerged as the decision which really divided them least—that was the way they saw it. What emerged, and what still exists today, is the system of two identical boards of directors, one in London, controlling Unilever, Limited; one in Rotterdam, controlling Unilever N.V. N.V. really controls the old European operations, both soap and margarine, and Unilever controls the operations of the former British and Commonwealth countries—that's a very rough kind of approximation. The organization which they controlled until only five years ago was a system of national and regional group managements, to which the operating companies were themselves responsible. That is to say, we are watching a set of companies all over the world united by a process which is, one might say, almost unavoidably and partly accidentally coming together but retaining very strong national and regional roots. It was not a divisional or product organization at all. And the national and regional organizations had a very large measure of independence. They had to budget annually, but they had a good deal of autonomy. So the problem was, and still is, how to reconcile the temptations to conservatism, parochialism, that were involved in these local roots, together with the kind of necessary ingredient of brutality necessary if you are going to innovate and change and keep up with the times. That is still the problem.

That is to say, there is a contrast in my mind between the way this European multinational has developed, by a process which I would call centripetal, and the very distinctly different method of the great rivals of this group, the Proctor and Gamble firm in the United States, which has expanded centrifugally by moving outwards from its vast domestic market, equipped, I may say, with a much greater measure of technology, particularly during the war and afterwards for a time, than Unilever could ever muster, at one time at any rate. The Unilever method is an attempt to bring together a vast group of once independent companies spread all over the world. They developed in two different ways, and I think the centripetal method, which is described here, and the centrifugal method, which is represented by Proctor and Gamble, mean that they are organized and controlled in two very different ways.

Just one last point. The traditional method of government that had emerged originally was national and regional organization. That was altered five years ago into something much more like the Du Pont or the Imperial Chemical Industries' product division. Unilever is now organized into product divisions, but they are linked by a polite process which is known by the name of coordination: there are coordinators. This really means that they are trying to get the best of both worlds, or at any rate effect the transition from this kind of organization to divisional or product organization. This became necessary in order really to compete with Proctor and Gamble: this is the plain truth of it. And what has emerged is something that is almost a product division organization, but nevertheless because of the historical evolution of this business, it has to still pay a considerable amount of respect to the local forces which are represented and managed by the old method of national and regional divisions. That organization controlled or consisted of I think over 600 businesses by 1949. It is still well over 500. There has been an increasing measure of diversification as various marketing and technological considerations have suggested that they should go into frozen foods, indeed into foods of all kinds, so that detergents, margarine and edible fats, foods, and of course chemicals and so on have emerged from the large technological laboratory developments.

There is only one thing more I want to say, and that is that I suppose having made myself familiar with this business, I am acutely conscious, as I think everybody in that business is, of the enormous value of the international exchange that is thus made possible, particularly the exchange on commercial, marketing, production, and technological problems; and especially of the value of the presence in the organization of this American business, now represented by that splendid building in New York, still one of the achievements of New York's skyscraper architecture, and of course the great technical resources of Germany, and particularly of Holland. But you find even a small country like Austria suddenly making a very remarkable contribution to oil refining, which resulted in enormous savings on production costs. So it is, I think, a fact that while every multinational creates problems of many kinds and they are not to be underestimated, an organization like this has itself, curiously, ensured that tariffs have resulted in import substitution, and it has brought a great deal of industrial knowledge, technology, to countries which were initially backward, even to Africa. And at the same time the multinational still ensures that forward movement, whether on the technical side or on the marketing side, does get spread right through the organization so that sooner or later everybody in this firm can benefit from the discovery made in one of its parts.

COMMENTS

1

Yōsuke Kinugasa
Yokohama Municipal University

It is a pleasure and honor that I have here an opportunity to comment on Professor Wilson's paper. Let me first briefly give my background. I am in the area of international management and marketing, and currently engaged in various projects related to the growth strategies and administrative organization of the multinational corporation. Therefore, I am not a historian in the strict sense. As a result, my comment is only from the specific angles of my general field.

The essential points of Professor Wilson's paper consist of three parts. In the first part, Professor Wilson examined the historical background of British and European multinational corporations with specific reference to their entrepreneurial activities. In the second part, Professor Wilson stressed that the origin and inspiration of the multinational corporation existed in Britain and Europe instead of in the United States. The third part deals with Unilever. It appears that the first and third parts can be grouped together as opposed to the second.

I would first like to comment on the first and third parts. Professor Wilson classified the background period into three eras. He emphasized that premultinational tendencies already existed in the Italian and German bankers and merchants in the preindustrial era, particularly in their propensity to go international and the techniques to do so. In the next industrialization era, reference was made to some international railroad investment which required international activities similar to those of today's multinational corporations, such as international transfer of management resources and two separate boards of directors, one in the home country and one in the host country. Another factor in this period, as pointed out in the paper, is that the nature of the Great Depression heightened production of consumer goods in Britain, which resulted in the promotion of the export of such goods. These goods, however, easily became the targets of import tariffs on the part of the importing countries. This compelled the exporters to start producing in the importing countries. This is considered by the author of the paper to be the advent of the multinational corporation. Problems related to this are dealt with in the third era of tariffs and imperialism. Also the example is Unilever in the third part.

My own feeling has been that we must study historical developments of multinational corporations to understand multinational corporations properly. This is exactly what Professor Wilson is doing in this paper. I do think that this approach is commendable and that Professor Wilson's paper makes a significant contribution to filling the gaps in existing knowledge. Also, his paper is a significant achievement that fills in the blank period prior to the one dealt with by the recent work of Mira Wilkins.

For instance, the railroad story he relates is an interesting case. Though it is not entirely clear to me what definition Professor Wilson has for the multinational corporation, the railroad case can certainly be considered to be a forerunner of the multinational corporation to the extent the following criteria are satisfied. It appears that the case satisfies the structural conditions of the multinational corporation well, while I wonder how the case meets criteria of performance yardsticks and managerial outlook. For instance, what proportion of sales or profit originated in their foreign activities, and what kind of managerial outlook did the management of the company possess? I would be very much interested in knowing how aggressive or passive the management was in considering foreign alternatives for investment. If the case should satisfy some criteria while no sign of attributes satisfying others can be seen, then the case can be considered to be a forerunner only in a partial sense.

Let me move on to the second part. Professor Wilson has achieved a good success in convincing the audience that the multinational originated in Europe and Britain rather than in the United States.

This was in the period when Britain (and some parts of Europe) were more advanced than the United States. At present the United States is recognized as the most advanced, and U.S.-based multinationals are spreading down the stream in that sense. In other words, the direction of the current switched at some point in history for the British company from down-the-stream expansion to up-the-stream expansion. Professor Wilson's paper stimulated my interest in the impact of the change of current upon the multinationals. My interest would particularly be in connection with possible extension of the product cycle model for international trade and investment developed by Raymond Vernon.

In general, the paper was very instructive and inspiring, particularly to the present thinking of myself and others on the future of Japanese multinational corporations in regard to the transformation from passive international investors reacting to tariff barriers into aggressive multinationals based upon a global outlook.

2

Shin-ichi Yonekawa
Hitotsubashi University

I am very happy to have the honor of commenting on Professor Wilson's paper. He is more a political and economic historian than a business historian in the narrow sense, and it is his historical insight based on his long research in the international economic history of Europe, especially the Anglo-Dutch relationship, that makes his paper on this subject most brilliant.

As a historian studying the history of the United Kingdom, I would like to comment on his paper in its entirety, but his profound and extensive knowledge of European history is such that it is quite beyond my powers to cover the whole period that he examined.

It might seem superfluous to sum up his paper, but it appears to me that he emphasized the following points:

(1) Proper understanding of multinationals should be based on historical backgrounds.
(2) When considered historically and logically, the emergence of multinationals resulted from economic necessity, and in this sense the emergence of multinationals is understandable.
(3) It is not commonly known, but we can find forerunners of the present multinationals in small European countries after the Great Depression.

Professor Wilson expertly examined the evolutionary process from the original multinationals to the modern multinationals, which he does not define explicitly, but whose characteristics seem to be a going concern with production activities not only at home, but also in foreign countries in the form of direct overseas investment.

Surely his paper is an excellent British counterpart of Dr. Wilkins's book, because her book is only an American approach to multinationals, as is obvious from its subtitle, and thus it is with good reason that Professor Wilson emphasized the European origin of modern multinationals.

While Professor Wilson has approached this subject in a chronological way, I would like to mention some differing aspects of American and European multinationals, of which he is, I am sure, aware, though he does not mention them.

If we examine so-called multinationals in terms of shareholders and top management, we find all American multinationals are controlled by American shareholders and have American top management. Professor Wilson's points are connected with this fact. But in contrast to their American counterparts, the capital and top management of typical European multinationals are shared internationally by people from many countries. As for shareholders' diffusion, this is closely connected with a company's legal position. A typical European multinational was not a single entity. The forerunner is the Royal Dutch-Shell Group of Companies (1907). This is a remarkably European phenomenon. Since the Second World War there have been several transnational amalgamations between European countries such as Agfa-Gevaert and Dunlop-Pirelli. In this respect, European firms are more multinational in the true sense than American companies.

I wish to lay stress on the considerable degree of European multinationalism, rather than on its origin.

SUMMARY OF CONCLUDING DISCUSSION

Keiichiro Nakagawa

1. Two Concepts of the Growth of Firms

The first major topic of the concluding discussion was the concept of growth of the firm, i.e. growth by subdivision versus growth by addition, presented by Professor Chandler, to facilitate the comparative study of strategy and structure of large-scale managerial multi-unit enterprises in many countries. His primary objective in coining these concepts was to emphasize that the growth of large-scale enterprises was not simply the result of the market mechanism, but was rather a result of organizational growth. He maintained that in the United States since the middle of the nineteenth century the large-scale enterprise developed through process integration, functional integration, and product diversification. Thus, in the United States the large-scale enterprise seems to have developed mainly through growth by addition. But in Japanese business history we can find many cases of growth by subdivision, such as can be seen in Nakagawa's paper. For example, the Mitsubishi Electric Manufacturing Company was separated from the Mitsubishi Shipbuilding Yard; the Hitachi Electric Manufacturing Company had originally been an electrical repair shop in the Hitachi Copper Mine; and the Toyo Raw Cotton Trading Company was an offshoot of the Mitsui Trading Company. This type of growth by subdivision can be found not only in the earlier stages of Japan's industrialization, but also in its later phases in the twentieth century. Then the discussion turned to the question of how we can understand these developments using of the concepts Professor Chandler presented.

After a discussion, we reached the conclusion that this pattern of growth in Japanese business should still be called "growth by addition" because in these Japanese cases, new lines of businesses were legally spun off but still remained within and were controlled by the same respective zaibatsu groups. Therefore, if we consider a zaibatsu group a single firm, then we can apply without reservation Professor Chandler's concept of growth by addition to the development of big business in the course of Japan's industrialization. On the other hand, Professor Wilson argued that in English business history such growth by addition was rather rare, and the concept of growth by subdivision can be applied more effectively to British industrialization. In this connection he emphasized that the entrepot nature of the British economy should be considered the main reason for such a pattern of growth. As England was a center of European and worldwide trade, there developed in England by the middle of the nineteenth century many specialized merchants and commodity exchanges. Therefore, English manufacturing firms needed to expand their activities neither forward into marketing nor backward into purchasing. Further, the existence of such specialized merchants or exchanges in Britain precluded the necessity for process integration which was taken for granted in the United States by the mid-nineteenth century. Professor Wilson seemed to accept the concept of growth by addition for explaining the British firm, and the concept of growth by subdivision more willingly for purposes of explaining the British national economy.

As a general conclusion on this topic, we can explain the developments in the three countries as follows. The English model seems to tend toward subdivision and integration via the market. In the American experience there were both growth by addition and growth by subdivision, but in any case new units were integrated with the existing units institutionally via management or administration. In Japan there were many cases of growth by subdivision; however, a new unit was not really spun off but usually remained in the same zaibatsu group, being integrated by finance and family control rather than through management or administration.

2. Multinational Enterprises

The second major topic of the concluding discussion was the multinational enterprise. Professor Wilson emphasized in his paper that the basic problem of the multinational enterprise is not that of holding or financial control, but is rather the problem of management resources and the problem of management decentralization or centralization. Hence, we can discuss the multinational enterprise using the two concepts of the growth of the firm presented by Professor Chandler. For Professor Chandler, multinational enterprise seems to be the final stage of the development of large-scale managerial multi-unit enterprise. He stressed that American multinational enterprises simply expanded their extensive domestic marketing organizations into overseas markets and, as a result, the American multinational enterprises were usually highly centralized. But according to Professor Wilson, European multinational enterprises emerged for controlling overseas sources of oil and other raw materials. In their marketing activities to overcome the tariff barrier, European multinational enterprises usually rushed to build independent firms in foreign countries. Therefore, European multinational enterprises generally turned out to be much more decentralized than the American ones. Another cause for the development of English multinational enterprise, Professor Wilson pointed out, was the transfer of technology to the backward or developing economies, as there were many technologies which other countries wished to borrow from England. The technological element in the multinational enterprise seemed to be important but was left mostly to be discussed later.

3. Problems of Finance

In this first meeting of the Business History Conference, we discussed the strategy and structure of big business mainly in relation to markets or marketing. But once we consider another element in business strategy, that is, the problem of finance, the horizons of business history studies suddenly become much broader. In this connection, Professor Chandler explained the difference between large-scale managerial multi-unit enterprises, investment bankers, and conglomerates in the United States. Around 1900, Morgan and other investment bankers in Wall Street started to reorganize some of the competitive American industries and established their firm financial control over such newly merged firms. However, the investment bankers usually did not establish any extensive organization for controlling industrial enterprises, but simply tried to supervise, with very limited staffs, the financial situations of the industrial enterprises under their control.

Now the conglomerates of the 1960s are very different. They are not investment banks of the Morgan type but probably more like the Japanese zaibatsu, and compared to the investment banks, they oversee investments much more systematically. The top office of a conglomerate still has a crew of executives who spend all their time supervising the divisions. They have a big financial staff, much bigger than Morgan had. The profits for the conglomerate, like the zaibatsu, are not in the buying and selling of securities at all, but in the profits of the different units in the conglomerate. Professor Wilson emphasized the need for future studies on the relations between financial control and industrial management. He stated that in England financial control had not been supported by effective professional industrial management, and when many competitive firms in an industry merged to form a single enterprise, the board of directors of the new enterprise was composed of too many major shareholders—that is, the owners of the constituent companies—who were unable to agree on a decisive management policy. This fact was discussed as the main reason for the poor performance of the British merger movement.

Financial control and industrial management relations also seem to have been very different among the three countries. In the Japanese zaibatsu, both the basic financial control and industrial management were delegated by the zaibatsu family members to nonfamily professional managers, and these professional managers decided the zaibatsu business policy in accordance with the ideology of the unity of the zaibatsu family enterprise. The concept of the Japanese family (*ie*), more than just kinship relations, implies a sense of corporate relations, and it worked quite effectively in maintaining the unity of zaibatsu enterprises through the course of Japan's rapid industrialization. But the influence of such a traditional Japanese concept on big business policy will be discussed in the second meeting of this Fuji conference.